THE BLACK AMERICAN SHORT STORY IN THE 20TH CENTURY

A Collection of Critical Essays

Edited by Peter Bruck

B. R. Grüner Publishing Co., Amsterdam
1977

© by B.R. Grüner Publishing Co.
ISBN 90 6032 085 9
Printed in The Netherlands

3-19

THE BLACK AMERICAN SHORT STORY IN THE
20TH CENTURY

CONTENTS

PREFACE

This volume is a collection of essays on black short stories written between 1889 and 1965. Indirectly I hope it manages to say something about the black short story as a genre and the development of the racial situation in America as well. It should be stressed from the outset that the primary aim is to try to introduce the reader to this long neglected genre of black fiction. In contrast to the black novel, the short story has hardly been given extensive criticism, let alone serious attention. The numerous anthologies published in the late 1960's and early 1970's are the case in point. Seeing that the editors hardly ever bothered to introduce the stories they anthologized, it comes as no surprise that viable criteria of classification and standards of evaluation are still very much in the dark. Since a sound framework for the interpretation of black short fiction is as much a *desideratum* today as it ever was, the individual essays of this collection aim at presenting new points of critical orientation in the hope of reviving and fostering further discussions of this genre. Hence the variety of approaches used, hence also the diversity of critical points of view.

As always in such endeavours, the selection of authors and stories is ultimately subjective. The principle of selection is thus left to justify itself, or fail to, as the case may be.

Finally I wish to acknowledge the stimulating cooperation of all contributors who made it possible for this volume to appear.

P.B.
Münster/W., July 1977

Peter Bruck

BLACK AMERICAN SHORT FICTION
IN THE 20TH CENTURY
Problems of Audience, and the Evolution of Artistic Stances
and Themes

When James Baldwin, reviewing a volume of poetry by Langston
Hughes in 1959, spoke of the "all but irreconcilable war between
his [the black writer's] social and artistic responsibilities,"[1] he
gave voice to a dilemma that is as old as the history of black
literature. The problem he stated touches upon a conflict faced by
the black artist which is inherent in his spiritual universe. Hence
the black writer's attempts "to speak with two voices, one from
the stage of national culture and the other from the soul of ethnic
experience."[2]

As early as 1903, DuBois couched the ambivalent nature of
black existence in the following terms:

> It is a peculiar sensation, this double consciousness, this sense of always
> looking at one's self through the eyes of others, of measuring one's soul by
> the tape of a world that looks on in amused contempt and pity. One ever
> feels his two-ness, – an American, a Negro; two souls, two thoughts, two
> unreconciled strivings.[3]

DuBois' idea of "double consciousness" was to become the
central metaphor describing the existential predicament of the
black American. This metaphor was echoed over half a century
later by what Ralph Ellison termed "double vision"[4] as well as by
the prophetic words spoken by one of the characters in Richard
Wright's novel *The Outsider*: "Negroes are going to be gifted with
a double vision, for, being Negroes, they are going to be both inside
and outside of our culture at the same time. ... They will became
psychological men, ... centers of knowing, so to speak."[5]

From an anthropological point of view, the metaphor of "double
consciousness" refers to the unique "bicultural ambivalence" of
the Afro-American. As Ostendorf has pointed out, " 'double consciousness' ... refers to the awareness of cultural alternatives, kept
alive by social exclusion, and it refers to the awareness of a class

1

difference, often kept alive on the basis of color or poverty."[6]

This bicultural condition causes problems for the black artist in finding his proper audience and in determining his own stance as a writer. As James Weldon Johnson stated in 1928:

> The Aframerican author faces a special problem which the plain author knows nothing about — the problem of the double audience. It is more than a double audience; it is a divided audience, an audience made up of two elements with differing and often opposite and antagonistic points of view. ... To whom shall he address himself, to his own black group or to white America?[7]

Johnson's idea of the "divided audience" presents the socio-literary distillation of DuBois' imagery. It pinpoints a difficulty which seems to extend to all writers facing the problem of cultural ambivalence. As examples from contemporary African fiction demonstrate, the African writer faces an equivalent dilemma which, significantly, is also couched in the same terminology: "the dual nature of their public — African and European — ... means that the writer, from the very start, has got to conciliate antinomic requirements, given the two contrasting types of readers."[8] The consequences that this peculiar cultural context imposes on both the African and the Afro-American writer are indeed complex enough. They not only apply to the writer's self-definition and demand a difficult decision from him, but they also exert a crucial influence on the actual formation of the literary text itself, as Kane has convincingly demonstrated with regard to African fiction.[9]

With reference to Afro-American short fiction, this "socio-cultural gulf"[10] proved to be particularly cumbersome to the writer. If, as was often enough the case, he felt "that winning a white audience was the only adequate test of his talent and of his aesthetic standards, and that only the judgment of a white audience had meaning,"[11] he had, at least in the past, to succumb to the preconceived notions which the white audience had of his role and of his literary productions.

Some of these notion have been pointed out in detail by Saunders Redding, Sterling Brown, James W. Johnson, and Zora Neale Hurston. Redding, discussing several manifestations of the post-bellum period, notes that "the image of the Negro as chicken-thief, melon-stealer, incorrigible liar, ..., ravisher of women, irresponsible,

2

... and yet withal laughable grew until it came about that only within the pattern of this concept was the Negro acceptable and credible to a large portion of the white reading public."[12] Even in the 1920's, as Johnson indicated, these limiting conventions were still dominant. As he remarks, such topics as "the ideas of Negroes of wealth living in a luxurious manner," "the story of a Negro girl who rose ... to a place of world success," or "American Negroes as heroes"[13] had to be beyond the scope of black writing. More than a decade later, Brown had this to say about the exigencies of the publishing scene:

> The market for Negro writers, then, is definitely limited as long as we write about ourselves. And the more truthfully we write about ourselves, the more limited our market becomes. Those novels about Negroes that sell best, by Negroes or whites, ... are almost always books that touch very lightly upon the facts of Negro life, books that make our black ghettos and our plantations in the deep south idyllic in their pastoral loveliness. ... When we cease to be exotic, we do not sell well.[14]

Despite the change of racial politics, the core of limiting conventions in 1950 was as pervasive as half a century before. Thus Zora Neale Hurston deplored the lack of demand "for incisive and full-dress stories around Negroes above the servant class" and succinctly expressed the dominance of the following stereotype: "the non-morbid Negro is the best-kept secret in America [whose] revelation to the public is the thing needed."[15]

All these statements seem to suggest that the development of the thematic scope of black literature is functionally related to the expectations of white readers. From a functionally oriented socio-literary point of view,[16] the limiting conventions faced by the black writer may be seen as dependent variables of the ethnic consciousness of the white audience. This seems to be demonstrated by the gradual change of the conventions which underline the pre-conceived racial notions of white readers and of the publishers who catered to their taste.

Among critics of short fiction, it is now commonly agreed that the development of this genre was closely associated with that of the American magazine, notably the big family magazines. This fact is particularly relevant to the printing history of black short fiction at the turn of the century, where the impact of white expectations was only too obvious. Even though the short story "had become an established article of merchandise"[17] by that time, there were as yet "no magazines with a primarily Negro audience in which Negro writers could place their short stories."[18] Such important outlets for black authorship as *The Crisis* (1910) and *Opportunity* (1923) had not yet come into existence, so that the black short story depended entirely on such white journals as *The Atlantic Monthly, The American Mercury*, and *Esquire*. The intricacies growing out of this situation found paradigmatic expression in both the short fiction and artistic stances of Paul Laurence Dunbar and Charles W. Chesnutt.

I

Dunbar, the first black writer to publish a collection of short stories (*Folks from Dixie*, 1898), was also the first black to receive national acclaim for his writing. This success, however, depended entirely upon the approval of white critics — such as William Dean Howells — white publishers, and a white audience. Dunbar's most influential patron was undeniably Howells who, in an introduction to Dunbar's first volumes of poetry, had this to say:

> Paul Dunbar was the only man of pure African blood and of American civilisation to feel the negro life aesthetically and express it lyrically ... In nothing is his essentially refined and delicate art so well shown as in these dialect pieces ..., and it would be this which would most distinguish him, now and hereafter.[19]

Howells' rather favorable review proved to be hampering, however. As Dunbar was later to remark to James Weldon Johnson: "dialect is what people want. They don't let me do anything else, no matter how much I try."[20]

Dunbar was thus not only a victim of white paternalistic philanthropy and forced to play the role of the white man's concept of the black poet; he was also, in terms of the short fiction genre, compelled to accept the exigencies of the publishing scene. It demanded from the end of the Civil War to the turn of the century local-color fiction and plantation-tales, whose major champions were Joel Chandler Harris and Thomas Nelson Page. The so-called plantation-school with its emphasis on pastoral romance, idyllic life, and defense of slavery conveyed, politically, the "false image of the benevolent slave holder and his contended slave." It maintained, as Robert Bone reports, "the fiction that the black man was a helpless child unworthy to be free."[21] If these were the major terms on which editorial acceptance depended, the options left were indeed narrow enough. In order to sustain his status as the first professional black writer of short fiction, Dunbar chose to write primarily within the ideological limits of the plantation-school; this decision turned him, in the eyes of many critics, into something of a negative example of a black writer. In the words of Bone: "in so merging with his cultural surroundings, Dunbar was assured of popular success, but he paid an awesome price for this protective coloration. Like the black minstrels, he collaborated in the defamation of his own people."[22] This harsh judgment, however, tends to overlook Dunbar's own political activities,[23] his frequent use of revealing irony, and his last collection of short stories, *The Heart of Happy Hallow* (1904), in which he abandoned the plantation tradition. It is idle to speculate what direction his writing would have taken, because he died only two years later. What is noteworthy, however, is the fact that, despite the dominating strain of plantation-tales, local-color stories in a realistic manner as exemplified by the later stories of Dunbar and in particular by the fiction of Chesnutt had became a viable literary genre accepted by the white reading public.

Chesnutt's career as a writer is in many respects the reverse of Dunbar's. Although he published one of his first stories in the renowned *Atlantic Monthly* in 1887, his racial identity was not known either to his publisher or his audience for over a decade. Chesnutt, basically a satirist who attacked slavery and the racial practices of the Reconstructionist South, won his first audience with his "conjure tales." Their narrator, Julius, by skilfully manipulating his white audience, "provides a model of how to conjure or bewitch the white folks."[24] In contrast to Dunbar's stories which are primarily entertaining, Chesnutt in his short fiction plays the role of an ambassador from black culture to his white audience. As he had stated himself:

> The object of my writings would be not so much the elevation of the colored people as the elevation of the whites — for I consider the unjust spirit of caste ... a barrier to the moral progress of the American people.[25]

The attempt to create a moral revolution in the white man's consciousness failed almost by necessity; as Chesnutt's fiction became more and more bitter, as his racial identity was disclosed to the general public in a review by Howells in 1900,[26] he began losing his audience and, as a consequence, his economically secure position as a writer. His active concern with racial problems and the sense of injustice that he tried to convey to his white readership did not yet meet an accepted social ground. At the turn of the century, the racial consciousness of the white audience was not yet willing to let itself be questioned or even changed by a black cultural ambassador. In the words of Chesnutt, spoken in 1928:

> My books were written ... a generation too soon. There was no such demand then as there is now for books by and about colored people. And I was writing against the trend of public opinion on the race question at that particular time. And I had to sell my books chiefly to white readers. There were few colored book buyers.[27]

Both cases demonstrate the extreme difficulties of the early black short story writer who, handicapped by the preconceived notions of his white audience, had to succumb to their racist reading habits. Hence both writers became victims of the socio-literary exigencies of their time; Dunbar, by letting himself be confined to writing basically plantation-stories, and Chesnutt by being forced into silence, into virtually giving up writing. The examples of Chesnutt and Dunbar, like that of the novelist Sutton Griggs, serve as paradigms illustrating the options of the early black writer:

1. The writer could turn to protest fiction with the risk of having his works distributed only among his own people in the manner of Sutton Griggs;
2. if he did not want to write "door-to-door-literature," he was forced to stop writing on account of his limited reception like Chesnutt, or
3. he had to veil his protest and present happy characters in the plantation-tradition, as Dunbar did.

II

The emergence of the Harlem Renaissance together with the establishment of such black magazines as *The Crisis* and *Opportunity* provided the black short story writer with entirely new prospects

Although the writers of the 1920's concentrated primarily on poetry and the novel, a whole group of hitherto unknown short fiction writers appeared, among them Jean Toomer, Rudolph Fischer, Claude McKay, Eric Walrond, and Langston Hughes. The release of their artistic expression was decisively sponsored by the short story writing contests organized by *The Crisis* and *Opportunity* in the 1920's, by the growing interest of a larger white reading public in black culture, and, as a consequence, by the willingness of several white publishers to print black literature. Simultaneously, the 1920's saw the rise of a new feeling of ethnic identity and racial pride: blackness became the central theme in both fiction and poetry.

The incipience of a new ethnic consciousness was echoed in almost every statement by blacks. Thus for the first time, they publicly discussed "Criteria of Negro Art" and expressed their own cultural claims. As DuBois demanded in 1926:

> We are bound by all sorts of customs that have come down as secondhand soul clothes of white patrons . ... In all sorts of ways we are hemmed in and our new young artists have got to fight their way to freedom. ... We must come to the place where the work of art when it appears is reviewed and acclaimed by our own free and unfettered judgment.[28]

Similarly, Langston Hughes in his literary manifesto "The Negro Artist and the Racial Mountain" (1926) proclaimed the new cultural independence of the black writer, calling for an ethnically self-assured position:

> To my mind, it is the duty of the younger Negro artists ... to change through the force of their art that old whispering, 'I want to be white,' hidden in the aspirations of his people, to 'Why should I want to be white? I am a Negro and beautiful.'[29]

As these two representative samples suggest, the black short story writers of the Harlem Renaissance no longer intended to succumb to the stereotyped habits of the white reading public. Rather, following the stance taken by Chestnutt, they wanted "to act as truthful interpreters of the black race for the reading public."[30] To which public, however, was the writer to address his attention? Even though there were few black magazines, white magazines were obviously more attractive. A writer who envisioned himself as the cultural ambassador of the new race-feeling logically catered

7

to a white audience. On the other hand, the growing self-awareness needed to be spread among the blacks. The resulting intricacies formed what Johnson termed "the dilemma of the Negro author." The solution he proposed called for a combination of the two groups: "when a Negro author does write so as to fuse white and black America into one interested and approving audience he has performed no slight feat, and has most likely done a sound piece of literary work."[31]

Johnson's call, which clearly echoes the Whitmanesque ideal of the common bond between the artist and an ideal audience,[32] became the central concern of nearly all statements by black artists during the Harlem Renaissance. The idealized bond that these writers aspired to was to be realized in the shared experience of a new community life, with Harlem becoming the "Culture Capital." This new enthusiasm did not reckon, however, with the extreme socio-literary difficulties of finding just that audience, for, as Charles Scruggs has recently pointed out, "as the decade progressed, it became increasingly evident, that something was missing: the black audience."[33]

Jean Toomer and his collection *Cane* (1923) are here the case in point which help to illuminate the at that time still utopian character of Johnson's ideas. As the first true black avant-garde writer, the first to experiment with the genre, he was also the least successful in commercial terms. The light-skinned Toomer, who more than once lamented "the opposition the black artist faced in his own community," thus became the isolated artist, resolving, as it were, his own ambiguous existence by adopting the mask of the 'American' artist, by becoming the first classic racial fugitive.[33a] Hence the growing readership for Negro matter did not extricate the black short story writer from the racially motivated preconceptions of his audience. Rather, the growing demand for stories in black magazines exerted a new limiting convention, for, as Sterling Brown reported, the new popular taste, exemplified by the parochialism of the *Opportunity-Crisis*-story, called exclusively for the "lynching-passing-race-praising pattern."[34]

One important result of the fashionable interest in black culture was the emergence of "an audience that would know enough about Negroes not to be told everything."[35] The first short story writer to be able to take advantage of this new potential was Langston Hughes, who wrote more than thirty of his total of sixty-six short stories between 1933 and 1934. More important than this impressive figure, however, was the fact that Hughes was published by such noted magazines as *Scribner's, The American Mercury*, and *Esquire*, thus gaining a non-parochial platform and a primarily white audience. His first published collection, *The Ways of White Folk* (1934), contains the first genuine satirical short fiction pieces by a black writer which received favorable reviews and sold fairly well.[36] Needing no longer to succumb to the racially preconceived notions of a white reading public, he became the first black writer whose statements of the new ethnic pride and self-assertion were accepted.

The fusion of racially divided readership as advocated by Johnson still proved to be illusory, however. Yet, Hughes was not only the first to gain a large white audience; he also became the first to gain a genuine black audience outside the popular taste of the *Crisis-Opportunity* readers. The beginning of the publication of his Simple tales in the black weekly *Chicago Defender* in November, 1942, marked, in socio-literary terms, an important development of black short fiction. Hence the printing history of his short fiction demonstrates that the fusion of readership was all but unattainable at that time. However, in having "clarified for the Negro audience their own strength and dignity and in having supplied the white audience with an exploration of how the Negro feels and what he wants,"[37] Hughes set a model of how to leave behind the ethnic province and the literary ghetto of the black short story writer.

III

In his well-known essay "Negro Characters as Seen by White Authors" (1934), Sterling Brown insisted that the exploration of Negro life and character rather than its exploitation must come from Negro authors themselves. Discussing modes of presentation, he raised the question "whether Negro life and character were to be best interpreted from without or within."[38] With the exception of Toomer, black writers so far had primarily been concerned with physical aspects of racial conditions or, as in the case of Langston Hughes, with the satirical exposure of whites. As long as racial injustice in its physical manifestations was conducive to black writing, the view from "without" was the dominating literary technique. The realistic depiction of circumstance and convention, however, began to disappear in the late 1930's. In Brown's critical terminology, "listing" was replaced by "rendering,"[39] as the emphasis shifted from the external to the subjective, from the depicting of exterior events to the psychological exploration of inner tensions. The short fiction of Richard Wright is the case in point. His exploration of violence was no longer a list of discriminatory events, but rather the thoughts and emotions of his characters were revealed in complex symbolic settings: the manner in which he portrayed the effects of racism and the complexities of individual assertion opened up a new realm of literary imagination.

The 1930's saw the efforts of the Communist party to unite both the black and white writers under the objectives of proletarian realism and within the organizational framework of the John Reed Club. Under the influence of his sponsors, Wright developed a new theoretical stance for black writers which had close affiliations with the ideas of proletarian realism. In his "Blueprint for Negro Writing" (1937), Wright deplored "the fact that Negro writing has been addressed in the main to a small white audience rather than to a Negro one" and called for "Negro writers who seek to mould or influence the consciousness of the Negro people." Consequently, the aim of black literature was no longer the fusion of audience nor the "pleading with white America for justice"; instead, black literature was to be purpose literature, was to be educational and to concentrate on the depiction of the "whole culture" stemming from the Negro church and the folklore of the Negro people.[40] With the exception of "Bright and Morning Star" and "Fire and Cloud," which were both included in the 1940 edition of the collection *Uncle Tom's Children*, Wright's theoretical statements found no fictional expression in his short stories. Rather, as his later work — and in particular "The Man Who Lived Underground" (1944) — demonstrate, the distinct mark of his short fiction was to become a highly symbolic texture, written in the stream-of-consciousness manner. This symbolistic fiction made it possible to view the black as an individual with universal existential problems.

Although Wright's symbolistic short fiction remained almost unnoticed by critics for years, the collection *Uncle Tom's Children* was widely praised.[41] The public reception of this volume illustrates in a significant way the discrepancy between a writer's intention and his effect upon the reading public. For in contrast to Wright's ideas, the collection failed to reach a black audience. He publicly confessed in 1940:

> When the reviews of that book began to appear, I realized that I had made an awfully naive mistake. I found that I had written a book which even banker's daughters could read and weep over and feel good about.[42]

The reception of *Uncle Tom's Children*, despite its commercial success, presents the central dilemma of finding a black audience outside magazine publications. As Sterling Brown pointed out in 1941: "the likelihood of a Negro audience for books by Negro authors is not promising. Even this potential audience is less than it might be. There is on the part of many a dislike for books about Negroes and books by Negroes."[43] The black short story writer's failure to find a black reading public proved to have fatal consequences for the development of this genre. For the immense popular success of *Native Son* (1940) pushed, so it seems, the short story into the background. The published short fiction of Chester Himes and Ralph Ellison was thus to remain unnoticed for decades, and even Wright's own stories were all but neglected by critics and anthologies — a fact which Saunders Redding was to deplore as a "conspiracy of silence."[44]

The short fiction of Ellison is a case in point which helps to illuminate the socio-literary state of black short fiction in the 1940's as well as the state of criticism. Never published in book form, his short stories are still uncollected and, with few exceptions,[45] received almost no critical attention. In "Blueprint for Negro Writing," Wright had described the black American's folklore as the cultural source in which "the Negro achieved his most indigenous and complete expression."[46] It was Ellison who, in such stories as "Afternoon" (1940), "Mister Toussan" (1941), "That I Had the Wings" (1943), and "Flying Home" (1944), attempted "to conform to the precepts laid down by Richard Wright."[47] Ellison's extensive use of folklore in a highly symbolistic manner provided an important innovation for black literature and laid a truly nationalist ground for black fiction. As he pointed out, Negro folklore "announced the Negro's willingness to trust his own experience, his own sensibilities as to the definition of reality, rather than allow his masters to define these crucial matters for him."[48] It is indeed characteristic for the state of criticism that Ellison's role as the historical father of black cultural nationalism was never acknowledged, much less appreciated. Instead, he was either unnoticed as a writer of short fiction or wrongly denounced as being "wedded to the concept of assimilation at a time when such a concept has ceased to be the preoccupation of the black writer."[49]

The lack of critical attention to Ellison's and Wright's symbolistic short fiction was parallelled by the extraordinary impact of *Native Son*, which set the thematic scope of black writing for over a decade. Hence James Baldwin's attempts to define himself in opposition to Wright's protest novel; hence also his apparent lack of knowledge of the symbolistic short fiction of the 1940's, when he published his first story "Previous Condition" in 1948.

IV

James Baldwin, in his well-known essay "Many Thousands Gone" (1951), attacked Wright's *Native Son*, which, in his eyes, conveyed the idea that "there exists no tradition, no field of manners, no possibility of ritual in Negro life."[50] This rebuke implies, in part, the position adopted by Baldwin in his short fiction, which seeks to illuminate the influence of the past on the formation of black identity. Hence his concern with the theme of the quest for identity, which is always linked to the problem of how to overcome the historical past of the blacks.[51] The preoccupation with this theme, which runs as a leitmotiv through most of Baldwin's writings, elucidates his stance as a black artist. As he remarked in his "Autobiographical Notes":

> Social affairs are not generally speaking the writer's prime concern, whether they ought to be or not; it is absolutely necessary that he establish between himself and these affairs a distance which will allow, at least, for clarity, so that before he can look forward in any meaningful sense, he must be allowed to take a long look back. In the context of the Negro problem neither whites nor blacks, for excellent reasons of their own, have the faintest desire to look back; but I think that the past is all that makes the present coherent, and further, that the past will remain horrible for exactly as long as we refuse to assess it honestly.[52]

It follows that his fictional explorations of the past were not only written from his own experience,[53] but also "seek a white readership whose racial ignorance he wishes to correct."[54] In this respect, Baldwin still views his role as that of an interpreter of black life to white readers.

Fifteen years after Baldwin's attack on *Native Son*, another black writer voiced important criticism of this novel. In a piercing analysis, LeRoi Jones charged Wright's protest fiction with not having been able to move "into the position where he could propose his symbols, erect his own personal myths, as any great literature must."[55] Jones' criticism reads in many ways like a prolegomenon to the rise of the new black arts movements of the 1960's. The emergence of black cultural nationalism, the awakening of a new ethnic consciousness, the establishment of the Writers' Workshop of the Organization of Black American Culture, together with newly founded black publishing houses and other cultural media, signalled the arrival of important new outlets and activities. The literature growing out of the "Black Renaissance of the sixties"[56] turned out to be the reverse of Wright's prophecy, "as the Negro merges into the mainstream of American life, there might result actually a disappearance of Negro literature as such."[57] In contrast to Wright's beliefs, the sixties saw a great blossoming of black literature, which — in the words of Hoyt Fuller, editor of *Black World* — finally left the realm of protest fiction and became "a literature of affirmation."[58] Programmatic formulations of this new outlook cater to a black audience with the intention of reordering "the western cultural aesthetic." The role of the racial interpreter to whites has been replaced by that of the teacher to blacks. In the words of Larry Neal: "Black art is the aesthetic and spiritual sister of the Black Power concept. As such it envisions an art that speaks directly to the needs and aspirations of black America. ... It proposes a separate symbolism, mythology, critique, and iconology."[59]

So far, two different directions of the new literature of ethnic affirmation seem to have emerged. The one, exemplified by the writings of LeRoi Jones, explores the quest for authentic black identity. Unlike Baldwin, Jones tries to develop an ethnic consciousness that is no longer defined by the socio-cultural standards of the white, much less in opposition to it. This trend clearly marks the end of "double consciousness;" the writer is no longer

13

preoccupied with the fusion of his "divided audience" or with the preconceived notions of his white readership. Rather, his "role in America is to aid in the destruction of America as he knows it."[60]

The other direction of the contemporary short story is quite different from the political stance represented by Jones. For example, the short fiction of Ernest Gaines and William Melvin Kelley does not try to present solutions to the race problem. In Kelley's own words,

> let me say for the record that I am not a sociologist or a politician or a spokesman. Such people try to give answers. A writer, I think, should ask questions. He should depict people, not symbols or ideas disguised as people.[61]

Now for the first time, Zora Neale Hurston's lament that "the average, struggling, non-morbid Negro is the best-kept secret in America" is no longer valid. As the short fiction of Gaines and Kelley demonstrates, the black short story writer has finally extricated himself from those racially motivated preconceptions that used to limit his creative expressions to the prejudices of his predominantly white audience. Hence the fusion of the "divided audience" seems no longer to be illusory. Whether this course or the cultural nationalist stance of LeRoi Jones, Ed Bullins and others will set in motion more impulses and produce the more promising fiction, remains to be seen. The two antagonistic stances, however, seem to provide at least possible ways out of the "all but irreconcilable war between his [the black writer's] social and artistic responsibilities."

The evolution of the black short story from Chesnutt and Dunbar to Jones, Kelley, and Gaines presents a paradigm of the writer's changing audience and the changing ideas of that audience. The black writer is no longer confined to the role of an interpreter of an ethnic constituency to an ignorant, racist white audience, nor limited to the depiction of happy characters in the plantation-tradition or angry characters in the manner of the protest genre. For the first time in his history, he seems to have gained the privilege of choosing, according to his literary stance, between an ethnic-oriented black audience and a racially unrestricted double audience.

V

In the preface to the short story anthology *Cutting Edges* (1973), editor Jack Hicks has drawn attention to the fact that "earlier anthologies have slighted, however unintentionally, the talents of blacks and Third World artists."[62] Despite a growing number of black short story anthologies in recent years, Hick's observation accurately reflects the lack of interest in the black story. Peden's prophecy of 1964 that "the production of a vital Negro American literature is likely to be one of the major direction the short fiction of the next decade will take,"[63] has turned out to be far too optimistic. A similar reservation has to be extended to his latest prophecy of 1975: "Stories by and about American blacks are likely to grow both in number and quality ..."[64] Although Peden's remark "that the writer of short fiction has gradually emerged from obscurity .... and that more good volumes of short fiction get into print [and] increasingly achieve considerable popularity or critical recognition,"[65] is certainly correct in general terms, it does not apply to the black short story. As the novelist John A. Williams admitted in 1975: "There is a trend in New York, and that trend seems to indicate that 'Harlem Renaissance II' is over."[66] Still hardly considered in major anthologies, the short story as a genre has remained the cinderella of black fiction.

The black short story has also been widely neglected by modern critics. The remark of Emanuel and Gross in their anthology *Dark Symphony* (1968) is still as valid today as a decade ago: "no analytical criticism has yet defensibly identified the best short stories written by Negroes."[67] The silence of critics is in itself significant. It may be partly accounted for by the emergence of the 'black aesthetic,' which has left a good many critics insecure and baffled, like Richard Gilman, who has voluntarily suspended all critical faculties.[68] The need for a renewal of literary approaches to black literature has still not yet been met. In keeping with Abraham Chapman: "Western literary criticism has not come to terms in any recognized or satisfactory way with the far more complex question of ethnic writing generally, particularly the historical community of the literature of Africa and Blacks in the West."[69] Nor have the attempts of various representatives of the 'black aesthetic' to fill this void produced viable new approaches. For, if "the question for the black critic today is," as Addison

Gayle has asserted, "how far the work has gone in transforming an American Negro into an African-American or black man,"[70] we are left wondering what critical methodology could possibly find an answer to such a question.

The only notable attempt so far to fill this critical void is Robert Bone's *Down Home* (1975), which discusses the development of the black short story from its beginning to the end of the Harlem Renaissance. Unfortunately, this first full-length study lacks a precise critical framework and hence does not provide a really firm basis for further scholarly criticism of this genre. The categories he applies, pastoral vs. anti-pastoral, are so vague[71] that they enable him to present only a rather simplistic view. A sound framework for the interpretation of black short fiction is as much a *desideratum* today as it ever was.

NOTES

1. James Baldwin, "Sermons and Blues" *The New York Times Book Review* (March 29, 1959), 6.
2. Nathan Irving Huggins, *The Harlem Renaissance* (New York, 1971), p. 195.
3. W.E.B. DuBois, *The Souls of Black Folk* (New York, 1961), pp. 16-17.
4. Ralph Ellison, *Shadow & Act* (London, 1967), p. 132.
5. Richard Wright, *The Outsider* (New York, 1965), p. 129.
6. Bernhard Ostendorf, "Black Poetry, Blues, and Folklore: Double Consciousness in Afro-American Oral Culture," *Amerikastudien*, 20 (1975), 218.
7. James Weldon Johnson, "The Dilemma of the Negro Author," *American Mercury*, 15 (1928), 477.
8. Mohamadou Kane, "The African Writer and his Public," in G.D. Killam, ed., *African Writers on African Writing* (London, 1975), p. 55.
9. *Ibid.*, p. 60 ff.
10. J. Saunders Redding, "The Negro Writer and American Literature," in Herbert Hill, ed., *Anger, And Beyond: The Negro Writer in the United States* (New York, 1968), p. 19.
11. *Ibid.*, p. 8.
12. J. Saunders Redding, "The Negro Author: His Publisher, His Public and His Purse," *Publisher's Weekly* (March 24, 1945), 1287.
13. Johnson, "The Dilemma of the Negro Author," 479.

14. Sterling A. Brown, "The Negro Author and His Publisher," *Negro Quarterly*, 1-4 (1942-43), reprint (New York, 1969), pp. 14-15.

15. Zora Neale Hurston, "What White Publishers Won't Print," *Negro Digest* (April, 1950), 89.

16. See Lucien Goldmann, "The Sociology of literature: status and problems of method," *International Social Science Journal*, 19 (1967), 496.

17. Fred Lewis Pattee, *The Development of the American Short Story* (New York, 1923), p. 337.

18. Sterling A. Brown *et al.*, edd., *The Negro Caravan* (New York, rpt. 1969), p. 10.

19. William Dean Howells, "Paul Laurence Dunbar," *The Bookman*, 23 (1906), 184 ff.

20. Quoted in Virginia Cunningham, *Paul Laurence Dunbar and His Song*, (New York, rpt. 1969), p. 219.

21. Robert Bone, *Down Home: A History of Afro-American Short Fiction from its Beginning to the End of the Harlem Renaissance* (New York, 1975), p. 14.

22. *Ibid.*, p. 43.

23. See Jay Martin, ed., *A Singer in the Dawn: Reinterpretations of Paul Laurence Dunbar* (New York, 1975). In his introduction Martin discusses the hitherto unknown newspaper dispatches of Dunbar and concludes that he was "one of the most powerful spokesman around the turn of the century against the problem of the color line." (p. 30)

24. Bone, *Down Home*, p. 83.

25. Quoted in Helen M. Chesnutt, *Charles Waddell Chesnutt: Pioneer of the Color Line* (Chapel Hill, 1952), p. 21.

26. See William L. Andrews, "William Dean Howells and Charles W. Chesnutt: Criticism and Race Fiction in the Age of Booker T. Washington," *American Literature*, 48 (1976), 327-339.

27. Quoted in Robert M. Farnsworth's introduction to Charles W. Chesnutt, *The Marrow of Tradition* (Ann Arbor, 1969), p. xvi.

28. W.E.B. DuBois, "Criteria of Negro Art," in Daniel Walden, ed., *W.E.B. DuBois: The Crisis Writings* (New York, 1972), p. 289.

29. Langston Hughes, "The Negro Artist and the Racial Mountain," *The Nation* (July 23, 1926), reprinted in John A. Williams, ed., *Amistad 1: Writings on Black History and Culture* (New York, 1970), p. 304.

30. Margaret Perry, *Silence to the Drums: A Survey of the Literature of the Harlem Renaissance* (Westport, Conn., 1976), p. 63.

31. Johnson, "The Dilemma of the Negro Author," 481. See also Johnson's "Negro Author and White Publishers," *The Crisis*, 36 (1929), 228-229; his position is echoed by Redding, "The Negro Author," 1288.

32. Cf. Charles Scruggs, " 'All Dressed Up But No Place To Go': The Black Writer and His Audience During the Harlem Renaissance," *American Litera-*

ture, 48 (1976), 551.

33. *Ibid.*, p. 553.

33a. Cf. Charles Scruggs, "Jean Toomer: Fugitive," *American Literature*, 47 (1975/76), 84-96.

34. Brown, *The Negro Caravan*, p. 12.

35. Huggins, *The Harlem Renaissance*, p. 238.

36. Donald C. Dickinson, *A Bio-Bibliography of Langston Hughes 1902-1967* (Hamden, Conn., 1972), p. 75 ff.

37. *Ibid.*, p. 115.

38. Sterling A. Brown, "Negro Characters as Seen by White Authors," *Journal of Negro Education*, 2 (1933), 203.

39. Sterling A. Brown, *The Negro in American Fiction* (Port Washington, N.Y., rpt. 1968), p. 106.

40. Richard Wright, "Blueprint for Negro Writing," *New Challenge* (Fall, 1937), reprinted in Addison Gayle, ed., *The Black Aesthetic* (Garden City, 1972), pp. 315-326.

41. See Michel Fabre, *The Unfinished Quest of Richard Wright* (New York, 1973), p. 161 ff.

42. Richard Wright, "How 'Bigger' was Born," in Abraham Chapman, ed., *Black Voices: An Anthology of Afro-American Literature* (New York, 1968), p. 557.

43. Brown, "The Negro Author and His Publisher," 17-18.

44. J. Saunders Redding, *On Being Negro in America* (Indianapolis, 1951), pp. 126-27.

45. See Hartmut K. Selke, *A Study of Ralph Ellison's Published Work Viewed in the Context of the Theme of Identity in Negro American Literature* (Kiel, Diss., 1975), p. 69 ff.

46. Wright, "Blueprint for Negro Writing," p. 317.

47. Selke, *A Study of Ralph Ellison*, p. 72.

48. Ralph Ellison, "The Art of Fiction: An Interview," *Shadow & Act (London, 1967), p. 172.*

49. Addison Gayle, Jr., "The Function of Black Literature at the Present Time," in Gayle, *The Black Aesthetic*, p. 392.

50. James Baldwin, "Many Thousands Gone," *Notes of a Native Son* (London, 1965), p. 28.

51. See Peter Freese, *Die amerikanische Kurzgeschichte nach 1945* (Frankfurt, 1974), p. 295 ff.

52. James Baldwin, "Autobiographical Notes," *Notes of a Native Son*, pp. 3-4.

53. See Baldwin's statement, "One writes out of one thing only — one's own personal experience." *Ibid.*

54. Peter Bruck, *Von der 'Store Front Church' zum 'American Dream': James Baldwin und der amerikanische Rassenkonflikt* (Amsterdam, 1975), p. 143.

55. LeRoi Jones, "The Myth of a 'Negro Literature,'" *Home: Social Essays*

(New York, 1970), p. 112.

56. John Oliver Killens, "Introduction: The Smoking Sixties," in Woodie King, ed., *Black Short Story Anthology* (New York, 1972), p. xiii.

57. Richard Wright, "The Literature of the Negro in the United States," *White Man, Listen!* (Garden City, 1964), p. 104.

58. Hoyt W. Fuller, "The New Black Literature: Protest or Affirmation," in Gayle, *The Black Aesthetic*, p. 330.

59. Larry Neal, "The Black Arts Movement," in Gayle, *The Black Aesthetic*, p. 257.

60. LeRoi Jones, "state/ment," *Home*, p. 251.

61. William Melvin Kelley, in his preface to *Dancers on the Shore* (Chatham, N.J., rpt., 1973).

62. Jack Hicks, ed., in his preface to *Cutting Edges: Young American Fiction for the '70's* (New York, 1973).

63. William Peden, *The American Short Story: Front Line in the National Defense of Literature* (Boston, 1964), p. 162.

64. William Peden, *The American Short Story: Continuity and Change 1940-1975* (Boston, 1975), p. 187.

65. *Ibid.*, p. 186.

66. John A. Williams, "Black Publisher, Black Writer: An Impasse," *Black World* (March, 1975), 29.

67. James A. Emanuel and Theodore L. Gross, edd., *Dark Symphony: Negro Literature in America* (New York, 1968), p. 353.

68. See Richard Gilman, "White Standards and Negro Writing," in C.W.E. Bigsby, ed., *The Black American Writer*, 2 vols. (Baltimore, 1971), I, p. 40.

69. Abraham Chapman, "Concepts of the Black Aesthetic," in Lloyd W. Brown, ed., *The Black Writer in Africa and the Americas* (Los Angeles, 1973), p. 40.

70. Addison Gayle, intro., *The Black Aesthetic*, p. xxii.

71. See Darwin T. Turner's review in *American Literature*, 48 (1976), 416-418.

Hartmut K. Selke

CHARLES WADDELL CHESNUTT
THE SHERIFF'S CHILDREN
(1889)

Charles Waddell Chesnutt (1858-1932) vies with Paul Laurence Dunbar in being the first Afro-American author to be accepted by major American publishing houses and to win national recognition and fame. Both authors, in order to be published at all, had to come to terms with the literary forms and conventions of the Plantation Tradition whose chief exponents were Joel Chandler Harris, Thomas Nelson Page, James Lane Allen and Harry Stillwell Edwards. This literary convention stipulated that the black characters be presented as living contentedly in an Edenic South, that they be quaint, childlike and docile, tellers of exotic yarns for the entertainment of massa's children or for massa himself. It is this tradition which gave rise to the literary stereotypes of the "Contended Slave," the "Wretched Freeman," who, being deprived of the paternal care of his master, is unable to provide for himself, the "Comic Negro" and the "Local Color Negro."[1]

Since the black writer, who wanted to break into print with his accounts of the black experience in America, had to adapt his work to the prevalent tastes of the day and to present his characters in a pastoral, harmonious setting, the only freedom left to him was that of choosing "the genre or the countergenre," as Robert Bone points out.[2] By pastoral genre is meant the "idyllic posture toward experience," by countergenre the "ironic posture."[3]

Whereas Dunbar by and large conformed to the limitations of the idyllic posture, wearing, as it were, "the mask that grins and lies,"[4] Chesnutt never did, even when he made use of the established forms, as for example in his "conjure" stories, in which he subtly undercut the submissive message apparently inherent in the very form.[5]

Robert Farnsworth thus summarizes the relationship between Dunbar and Chesnutt:

In a sense Charles Chesnutt was to Paul Laurence Dunbar what W.E.B.

21

DuBois was to Booker T. Washington. While Dunbar demonstrated a shrewd ability to exploit the prejudices of his largely white audience and while he served an extraordinarily useful function by simply being black and achieving national literary prominence, yet his work does not look forward. He was not as alive to the currents of literary and social change as was Chesnutt. ... Dunbar seemed wistfully to believe in the near possibility of a truly colorless world. Chesnutt was more pragmatic, believing perhaps in the same ultimate vision, but recognizing more prominently the immediate problems of Southern disfranchisement, Jim Crow legislation, and racial intermarriage.[6]

Charles Waddell Chesnutt was born in Cleveland, Ohio in 1858, the son of free parents who had left the South two years previously to escape the narrow restrictions imposed even on the free members of their race. After the war, the family returned to Fayetteville, N.C., where Charles received his education in the newly established Howard School for Negroes. By the circumscribed standards of the South, he had a brilliant career: he was a pupil-teacher at fourteen, the principal of a public school at Charlotte at eighteen and at twenty-two he succeeded white Robert Harris as principal of the State Normal School at Fayetteville.

Chesnutt was the epitome of the self-made man. He read widely and, in the North Carolina backwoods, managed to study German, French, Latin and Greek besides acquiring, with no outward help, the then rather obscure art of shorthand which was later to be the basis of his livelihood in the North.

Despite his success, Chesnutt constantly chafed against the restrictions he encountered in the South. White enough to "pass," he toyed with the idea of joining the white race, as this entry in his diary for July 31, 1875 shows:

Twice today, or oftener, I have been taken for "white." At the pond this morning one fellow said he'd "be damned if there was any nigger blood in me." At Coleman's I passed. ... I believe I'll leave here and pass anyhow, for I am as white as any of them. One old fellow said today, "Look here, Tom. Here's a black as white as you are."[7]

Chesnutt had a very keen sense of what he was worth – "As I have been thrown constantly on my own resources in my solitary studies, I have acquired some degree of self-reliance"[8] – and he realized that prejudice, that "foul blot on the fair scutcheon of American liberty,"[9] would prevent him from obtaining the

22

education which he felt was due to him, and from reaping the rewards, both financial and emotional, that should naturally accrue from his abilities, if he were to remain in the South.

As early as 1880, Chesnutt felt the urge to aspire to a literary career. "I think I must write a book," he boldly confides to his diary on May 29, 1880, and he goes on to define the subject matter, the audience and the purpose of his projected writings:

Fifteen years of life in the South, in one of the most eventful eras of its history, among a people whose life is rich in the elements of romance, under conditions calculated to stir one's soul to the very depths — I think there is here a fund of experience, a supply of material, which a skillful pen could work up with tremendous effect. Besides, if I do write, I shall write for a purpose, a high, holy purpose, and this will inspire me to greater effort. The object of my writings would be not so much the elevation of the colored people as the elevation of the whites — for I consider the unjust spirit of caste ... a barrier to the moral progress of the American people; and I would be one of the first to head a determined, organized crusade against it. ...

The Negro's part is to prepare himself for recognition and equality, and it is the province of literature to open the way for him to get it — to accustom the public mind to the idea; to lead people out, imperceptibly, unconsciously, step by step, to the desired state of feeling.[10]

By 1883 Chesnutt sufficiently mastered shorthand to venture North, reassured that this knowledge would sustain him. After half a year's experience as a stenographer and journalist for Dow Jones in New York City, he settled in Cleveland, Ohio. In 1887 he was admitted to the bar. He ran a successful law and stenographer's business until, in 1899, he closed his office in the hope of embarking on a purely literary career. The absence of financial success forced him to resume his business as court stenographer in 1905, after which date he published only occasionally.

Chesnutt's first published story was "Uncle Tom's House," which appeared in 1885. This was followed by a steady flow of stories, which were published by the magazines of the McClure syndicate and other publications. When the renowned *Atlantic Monthly* printed the "conjure" stories "The Goophered Grapevine" and "Po' Sandy" in 1887 and 1888, Chesnutt not only won the friendship of George Washington Cable but also paved the way for the future publication of his first four books of fiction by Houghton, Mifflin and Co. In the summer of 1891 he submitted a manuscript of *Rena Walden and Other Stories* to Houghton, Mifflin and Co., erroneously advising his prospective publishers of the novelty of the "first contribution by an American of acknowledged African descent to purely imaginative literature," and going on to ask his publishers not to disclose his ethnic identity:

> I should not want this fact to be stated in the book, nor advertised, unless the publisher advised it; first because I do not know whether it would affect its reception favorably or unfavorably, or at all; secondly, because I would not have the book judged by any standard lower than that set for other writers.[11]

Houghton, Mifflin and Co. did not accept the manuscript but they kept his racial identity secret until after the publication of "The Wife of His Youth" in 1898 when a reviewer wrote in the *Critic* that Chesnutt "faces the problems of the race to which he in part belongs."[12]

In 1897 Chesnutt made a renewed attempt to publish a book when he submitted twenty-two stories to Walter Hines Page of Houghton, Mifflin and Co. After long deliberation his publishers again rejected the submitted materials but requested further "conjure" stories in the manner of "The Goophered Grapevine" for a collection of short stories. Within two months, Chesnutt wrote and submitted six new "conjure" stories, thus seemingly conforming to the requirements of a market which demanded the picturesque local color Negro. *The Conjure Woman* appeared in March 1899 and was favorably received by the critics.

A few months after the publication of his first book, Chesnutt suggested to Page that Houghton, Mifflin and Co. publish "a volume of stories along the line of 'The Wife of His Youth,'"[13] a story which had appeared a year previously in the *Atlantic Monthly* and which depicted the life of the "Blue Vein Society," so called because its members were so light-skinned that their veins were visible, in a city of the North. *The Wife of His Youth and Other Stories of the Color Line* appeared in the same year, as did a short biography of Frederick Douglass. "Rena Walden," a story of the psychological quandaries of "passing" which Chesnutt had written and rewritten many times, was extended to novel length and published as *The House Behind the Cedars* in 1900. *The Marrow of Tradition*, an ambitious novel attempting to give a broad perspective of socio-political and psychological problems faced by

Southern Afro-Americans at the turn of the century, followed in 1901. Chesnutt's last novel, *The Colonel's Dream* (1905), is an indictment of the moral and economic stagnation of the South and of the convict lease system which, as it were, continued slavery beyond Emancipation.

Among the themes treated most often in Chesnutt's works are (1) the inhumanity of the system of chattel slavery, (2) the incongruities of the color line as drawn within the black society itself, (3) the dual themes of passing and the ordeal of the double identity and (4) the injustices that Southern blacks have to suffer even after Emancipation, particularly during the restauration of white supremacy after Reconstruction.

At first sight, "The Sheriff's Children" might seem to be a treatment of the theme of the tragic mulatto. However, this is only one and, as shall be demonstrated, not the dominant theme of the story.

"The Sheriff's Children" was first published in the New York weekly magazine *Independent* in November 1889. The *Independent* then catered to an educated, liberal white audience. The first readers of the story were unaware of its author's racial identity. Earlier that year Chesnutt had moved into his own, rather spacious home in Cleveland. Yet, the other stories published or written during that year evince the same sombre and combative note that characterizes "The Sheriff's Children." In "The Conjurer's Revenge' (June 1889) the narrator, Uncle Julius, denounces slavery with unwonted explicitness, calling the slavetraders stealers and sellers of men and thus seeming to invoke the Biblical punishment for the manstealer.[14]

"Dave's Neckliss" (October 1889) is also an Uncle Julius story, although not a "conjure" story in the narrow sense. Like "The Sheriff's Children," this gruesome story exposes "the baleful influence of human slavery."[15] Indeed, the story bears close resemblance to "The Sheriff's Children": punished unjustly by an otherwise "kind" master (this fact is peculiarly insisted on in the story), Dave is driven to insanity and suicide. The "kind" master's recognition of his own guilt and his repentance come too late to undo the wrongs wrought by a system of chattel slavery. The third story, of which Chesnutt completed the first draft in 1889, was the often revised "Rena Walden." It deals with the problem of the tragic mulatto, which is also touched upon in "The Sheriff's Children."

25

Chesnutt's sombre outlook may be explained by the fact that at that time he was butting his head against the restrictions imposed by the tastes of the reading public and of magazine publishers. This went so far that he even toyed with the idea of migrating to Europe. In a letter written some six months after the publication of "The Sheriff's Children" he confided to Cable:

> If I should remain idle for two weeks, at the end of that time I should be ready to close out my affairs and move my family to Europe. The kind of stuff I could write, if I were not all the time oppressed by the fear that this line or this sentiment would offend somebody's prejudices, jar on somebody's American-trained sense of propriety, would, I believe, find a ready sale in England.[16]

Ten years after its original publication, "The Sheriff's Children" reached a wider audience through its inclusion in *The Wife of His Youth and Other Stories of the Color Line*. Whereas in the first collection of stories the superficial white reader could easily be deluded by Chesnutt's apparent adherence to the conventional forms of the Plantation Tradition, this second volume, at least in some of the stories, more openly strikes a note of poignant protest against the Afro-American's social and psychological predicament in the South.

In a letter to his publisher, in which he discussed promotion strategies for the volume, Chesnutt wrote:

> The book was written with the distinct hope that it might have its influence in directing attention to certain aspects of the race question which are quite familiar to those on the unfortunate side of it; and I should be glad to have that view of it emphasized if in your opinion the book is strong enough to stand it; for a *sermon* that is labeled a sermon must be a good one to get a hearing.[17]

Whereas the book was well received in the North, Southern critics, as was to be expected, did not fail to discover the elements of "crusade" and "sermon" and berated Chesnutt for his impropriety. One critic wrote: " 'The Sheriff's Children' furnishes, perhaps, the most shocking instance of his reckless disregard of matters respected by more experienced writers."[18] Criticism seems to have been directed primarily against "The Sheriff's Children" with its bold treatment of the tabooed subject of miscegenation, and not against "The Passing of Grandison," which effectively explodes the myth of the happy, docile slave, or against "The Web of Circumstance," which undermines Booker T. Washington's accommodationist contention that the acquisition of skills and property would automatically ensure recognition for the Afro-American even in the South.

The story opens with a description of the sleepy village of Troy, county seat of Branson County in North Carolina,[19] a district so isolated that the war seems to have passed it by, had it not been for the tribute of one generation of young men that the great conflict demanded. Some ten years after the war, the citizens of Branson County are shocked to learn that Captain Walker, an old soldier, "had been foully murdered" (63). A mulatto, a stranger in the area, is suspected of the crime and quickly apprehended. While the prisoner is awaiting judgment in the county jail, the citizens decide to lynch him. The sheriff is informed of the plan by a Negro and determines to do his duty and resist the lynch mob. He proceeds to the jail where he locks himself into the prisoner's cell. After having warded off the lynching party and having fired a shot in reply to a sniper's bullet, he is disarmed by the prisoner who then reveals his identity. The mulatto is Tom, the sheriff's son, his mother is a slave woman whom the sheriff had sold to a speculator. The son demands that the sheriff release him or else he will shoot him. At the very moment when Tom decides that he cannot trust his father and prepares to shoot him, the sheriff's daughter, Polly, who had worried about her father's long absence, comes up from behind and fires at the mulatto, wounding his arm. The sheriff dresses his son's wound, telling him that he will call a doctor on the following morning. He spends a restless night, passing his life and his failings in review and finally deciding to "atone for his crime against this son of his" (93). When he goes to the jail on Sunday morning, he finds that his son has committed suicide by tearing off the bandage and bleeding to death.

Chesnutt's story may be read simply as a carefully wrought suspense story, which moves in steadily increasing crescendo from the opening description of the dull and somnolent community[20] to the final twist at the end of the story. As the plot develops, the scene narrows: the first two pages are devoted to the county, the following six to the village of Troy and its inhabitants, the next seven focus on the sheriff's house as the sheriff is informed of the plot by Sam. The scene then moves to the captive's cell in the jail.

27

The next shift back to the sheriff's house seems to suggest that there is a break in the development delineated above. William L. Andrews sees in this supposed break a flaw of plot development: "The story ... lapses into argument and introspection which fail to sustain the tenseness of the action in the first half of the story."[21] However, this lapse into introspection is no more than a further narrowing of the scene along the pattern of the rest of the story, only this time to the sheriff's consciousness. The constant narrowing of the scene from the "sequestered district" (60) of Branson County to the "hamlet" (61) of Troy, from there to a prison cell and finally to the sheriff's mind conveys a feeling of claustrophobia, of inescapability.

This gradual restriction of space has its parallel in the gradual resolution of the question of identity, which was posed at the beginning of the story. The question is first raised in the speculations "upon the identity of the murderer" (63). But at that point in the story everything is vague, ill-defined. A "strange mulatto" (63) is suspected of the crime. The second central character, the sheriff, is only introduced at the beginning in his function as a public officer whose duty it is to arrest the suspect.

This vagueness is carried over into the next scene. As the design to lynch the prisoner assumes shape, the townspeople remain anonymous: no names are mentioned. Naturally, a major function of this scene is to demonstrate the genesis and anonymity of mob violence. By their very speech the townspeople are characterized as dumb-witted backwoods people[22] whose dull minds are helped along by illegally distilled whiskey and vague notions of "honor" to give birth to the dastardly plan.

The heavy hand of the omniscient narrator who edits and comments on his material makes itself felt particularly in this scene, driving home a point that does not stand in need of such commenting. The planned lynching is to the townspeople's minds "a becoming way in which to honor [Captain Walker's] memory" (66). Their perverted notion of justice is reflected in the mocking solemnity of the narrator's language as he describes the plan: "By agreement the lynchers were to meet at Tyson's store at five o'clock in the afternoon, and proceed thence to the jail ..." (67).

The following scene at the sheriff's house marks a first departure from the aura of anonymity which had characterized the first pages. The reader is informed of the sheriff's name and of his

28

appearance. Sheriff Campbell is a "tall, muscular man," he has "keen, deep-set gray eyes" and "a masterful expression" (68). His very stature and "attitude of a soldier" (69) as well as his language bespeak his determination and his superiority over the rest of the townspeople. Additional information provided by the omniscient narrator (71-73) corroborates this first impression. Campbell is a cultivated man, "far above the average of the community in wealth, education, and social position. ... He had graduated at the State University at Chapel Hill, and had kept up some acquaintance with current literature and advanced thought." (71f.).

The members of the lynch mob, too, are given a semblance of identity when the sheriff asks Sam who is coming. They are an array of self-styled doctors, majors and colonels: "'Dere's Mistah McSwayne, en Doc' Cain, en Maje' McDonal,' en Kunnel Wright, en a heap er yuthers.'" (69). But even this identity is fleeting, as well befits a mob setting out with this purpose in mind. It is wiped away by the sheriff who declares them all to be "strangers" to him because he "did not think it necessary to recognize anybody in particular on such an occasion; the question of identity sometimes comes up in the investigation of these extra-judicial executions." (74).

The question of identity comes up again in the confrontation between Campbell and his prisoner after the lynch mob has withdrawn. It is no longer the detective story question as to who was the murderer, a question which persists only as a vague hope of extricating the prisoner from his hopeless situation. In the course of the story every suspicion against him is dispelled in the reader as well as in the sheriff: "he no longer doubted the prisoner's innocence" (93).

Alone in his cell with the sheriff, the prisoner undergoes an almost miraculous transformation from a "cowering wretch" who provokes the sheriff's "contempt and loathing" (77) to a "keen-eyed,[23] desperate man ... a different being altogether from the groveling wretch" (81) of only a few minutes before. This transformation is possible only because Tom, the prisoner, is exclusively seen through the sheriff's eyes. He is never presented, except in his own utterances, in his own right, but remains a reflection in his father's eyes. Before the prisoner had gained control of the situation, he had remained a mere abstraction to the sheriff, a well-defined quantity that fitted into a prefabricated category. It is this

29

refusal to look upon the prisoner as an individual human being that prevents him from recognizing his son sooner than he does.

As Tom points out to him, they have the same features: "no man need look at us together twice to see that ..." (85f.). It is obvious that the sheriff had never looked at his son. Instead he had seen "the negro" in him: "He had relied on the negro's cowardice and subordination in the presence of an armed white man as a matter of course." (81). It is only this unwonted behavior that "caused the sheriff to look at him more closely" (81). Even then, however, he does not recognize the prisoner, and it is only after the question "Who are you?" (84) that the latter's identity is revealed to him.

This revelation initiates a new movement. It is the beginning of yet another question of identity. The confrontation with "this wayward spirit" who had come "back from the vanished past to haunt him" (91) forces the sheriff to see himself as he truly is, to explore his own smug identity.

This new and central theme of the story is prepared by a change of the point of view. The first two thirds of the story bear the mark of the omniscient narrator whose presence as editorial commentator is constantly felt. This is particularly true of the three-page introduction which leads up to the action proper. Here the author even appears in the first person, explaining his materials to the reader: "At the period of which I write ..." (62). In what follows, the omniscient narrator as editorializing agency is also felt, at times very directly, as in his remark that something "is immaterial to this narrative" (66), at times less so, as in the choice of scenes which are presented in the dramatic mode. In the last third of the story these editorial interventions do not cease altogether — they are particularly obvious in the description of Polly's stealthy approach, unnoticed by both the protagonist and Tom, in the authorial comments on the sheriff's character and in the imperative addressed to the reader: "Let no one ask what his answer would have been" (88) — but a new dimension is added. Starting with the sentence, "The sheriff mentally cursed his own carelessness for allowing him to be caught in such a predicament" (80), all subsequent events are mainly seen and evaluated through Campbell's consciousness. From now on, to apply Henry James' words to the sheriff, "It is *his* vision, *his* conception, *his* interpretation ... He therefore supremely matters; all the rest matters only as he feels it, treats it, meets it."[24]

This change of perspective is a necessary prerequisite for the soul-searching that is about to follow. The sheriff, who had hitherto appeared an impeccable character, now realizes that he "had yielded" (85) to the tempations of an evil system when he had sold his son and his lover to a speculator. This also throws a new light on a remark made earlier in the story. Yielding to his environment, to the force of circumstances, even against his better judgment, seems to be the sheriff's particular weakness: "At first an ardent supporter of the Union, he had opposed the secession movement in his native State as long as opposition availed to stem the tide of public opinion. Yielding at last to the force of circumstances, he had entered the Confederate service rather late in the war ..." (72).

This weakness also accounts for the sheriff's decision in favor of his sense of duty and against his human instincts, both when his own life is in danger and when he asks himself how he can extricate Tom from his predicament and make up for his own previous shortcomings: "It occurred to him, purely as a hypothesis, that he might permit his prisoner to escape; but his oath of office, his duty as sheriff, stood in the way of such a course, and the sheriff dismissed the idea from his mind." (92).

It is only after the initial shock of the confrontation has worn off that the full impact of the experience becomes clear to the sheriff. "Alone with God," he again experiences "a kind of clarifying of the moral faculty ... a state of mind in which one sees himself as God may be supposed to see him." (90). Seeing himself as he is, the sheriff decides to atone for his sin. It is interesting to note that neither Tom nor himself see his sin in the fact of miscegenation itself,[25] but rather in the fact that he has neglected his parental duties, his moral obligations in depriving his son of a true identity of his own: Tom has "no name, no father, no mother – in the true meaning of motherhood." (92).

The tragedy of the story lies in the fact that the circumstances are such that the father's recognition of the son comes too late. The sheriff's personal tragedy is that his attempts at atonement are only half-hearted and incomplete and that he is finally deprived of the "opportunity for direct expiation."[26]

As quoted above, Chesnutt had thought of *The Wife of His Youth* in terms of a sermon. "The Sheriff's Children" preaches a sermon in the sense that it induces the enlightened white reader, to whom it is addressed,[27] to identify with the sheriff who is presented in very positive terms as a courageous, law-abiding, conscientious and educated man. The sheriff's qualities make his moral shortcomings appear in an even cruder light,[28] and the reader, who had come to identify himself with him, is made to share in his fall and to experience a purging similar to that "clarifying of the moral faculty" (90) that the sheriff feels. Chesnutt's is a fire-and-brimstone sermon which shows no way out of the moral dilemma. The attempt to make amends comes too late. Injustice has been done and it seems irremediable. The impact on the reader who is required to go to task with himself, is all the greater.

Yet, even after the sheriff's failings have been revealed, the sympathetic narrator speaks out in his behalf in an authorial comment: "But the baleful influence of human slavery poisoned the very fountains of life, and created new standards of right. The sheriff was conscientious; his conscience had merely been warped by his environment." (88). Without denying any of the sheriff's guilt, he thus places it in a broader perspective, indicting a system to which Campbell has fallen prey. Again, the reader may be led to ask himself if the influence of the environment is truly a valid attenuating circumstance for Campbell and for himself.

By choosing the sheriff's point of view in the last third of the story, Chesnutt has diverted the reader's attention from Tom, the mulatto. The narrator does not perform the role of advocate for him, trying to explain his motives and soliciting compassion or understanding, as he had done in the case of the sheriff. Seen only from outside except in his own utterances, Tom's story remains untold, although the narrative offers some hints as to the dramatic potential of the theme.

Haslam detects one of the strong points of the story in the absence of this theme, which is indeed fraught with grave dangers: "By emphasizing the white father rather than the mulatto son, he [Chesnutt] partially avoided the melodramatic stereotypes which marred so much of his work."[29]

The theme which Chesnutt partially subdued in this story is that of the tragic mulatto, which came out of anti-slavery fiction, as Sterling A. Brown has shown. The mulattoes in fiction "are the intransigent, the resentful, the mentally alert, the proofs of the Negro's possibilities."[30] The theme harbors the danger of presenting the material in such a way that the Afro-American's humanity is measured in proportion to the "white" blood in his veins.

Upon the completion of his second draft of "Rena Walden" only a few months after the publication of "The Sheriff's Children," Chesnutt wrote to Cable on the subject of mulattoes in fiction:

> There are a great many intelligent people who consider the class to which Rena and Wain belong as unnatural. ... [a] gentleman remarked to me in substance that he considered a mulatto an insult to nature, a kind of monster that he looked upon with infinite distaste. ... I fear there is too much of the same sentiment for mulattoes to make good magazine characters.[31]

Chesnutt was doubtless prompted by these sentiments when he made the sheriff's moral dilemma the central concern of his story instead of choosing the equally available theme of the tragic mulatto. Tom's major function in "The Sheriff's Children" seems to be that of the spark which sets off the crisis.

Yet, there is more to him. When Tom first appears in the story, he is ambiguously called "a strange mulatto" (63), an epithet which is reminiscent of Chesnutt's letter. Tom is not only a stranger in his own land, unrecognized in all senses of the word and by everybody including his father,[32] he is also an abomination in the eyes of the whites.

The dilemma of the double-consciousness as defined by W.E.B. DuBois is particularly obvious for the mulatto. DuBois wrote:

> One ever feels his twoness, – an American, a Negro; two souls, two thoughts, two unreconciled strivings; two warring ideals in one dark body, whose dogged strength alone keeps it from being torn asunder.
>
> The history of the American Negro is the history of this strife, – this longing to attain self-conscious manhood, to merge this double self into a better and truer self. In this merging he wishes neither of the older selves to be lost. ... He would not bleach his Negro soul in a flood of white Americanism, for he knows that Negro blood has a message for the world. He simply wishes to make it possible for a man to be both a Negro and an American, without being cursed and spit upon by his fellows, without having the doors of Opportunity closed roughly in his face.[33]

Tom is obviously an individual who does not possess this dogged strength and who is torn asunder by the magnitude of the conflict. He is a tortured, warped character who has come to turn his aggression against the race that the custom of the country makes him a part of, and thus finally against himself. His attitude toward his mother, who, to his mind, has become synonymous with the black race, is highly ambivalent. While he pities her and admires her for having "had enough womanhood to call her soul her own" (86), he is at the same time ashamed of her blackness: "You gave me your own blood ... and you gave me a black mother. ... You gave me a white man's spirit, and you made me a slave, and crushed it out." (85f.). Tom has sought to flee his blackness, as by acquiring an education, but has found that his blackness stays with him as "a badge of degradation" (87).

Commenting on the inappropriately refined language used by Tom, Haslam asks himself "if Chesnutt has not, in this one respect, fallen again into his habit of trying to demonstrate that mulattoes are more white than Negro."[34] Similarly, Bone feels that "the story does not wholly escape from the stereotype of the tragic mulatto" but is redeemed by its pervasive irony.[35] Tom does indeed seem to conform to what Brown had called the present image of the tragic mulatto: "The mulatto is a victim of a divided inheritance; from his white blood come his intellectual strivings, his unwillingness to be a slave; from his Negro blood come his baser emotional urges, his indolence, his savagery."[36] We should, however, ask ourselves if Chesnutt did not intend to criticize Tom for his own interpretation of his situation, for his inability to turn his talents and his education to some good purpose, for his self-pitying despair.

Tom, then, is vaguely related to Tourgée's mulatto characters towards whom Chesnutt had no charitable feelings. In the above quoted letter to Cable he writes: "Judge Tourgée's cultivated white Negroes are always bewailing their fate and cursing the drop of black blood which 'taints' — I hate the word, it implies corruption — their otherwise pure race."[37] The only difference seems to be that Tom, distorted beyond recognition by the force of circumstance, is more sordid, his fate more sordid than that of Tourgée's characters.

This makes him very different from the saintly figures created by younger authors, figures who die a Christlike death on the cross, as in W.E.B. DuBois' story "Jesus Christ in Texas" or in Langston Hughes' poem "Christ in Alabama." Rather, Tom dies by his own hand, and the pattern of Crucifixion and Resurrection is thoroughly perverted. Yet, there is an obvious parallel in the story. The action takes place at a weekend, starting with a death on Friday morning (one page) and ending with another on Sunday morning (one page). The bulk of the story is devoted to the abortive attempt to lynch the prisoner and to the sheriff's soul-searching, which might be likened to a descent into the "hell" of his own mind where he has to face and overcome his own sinful self. But the parallel is not sustained by the characters. The whole story is pervaded by murder, near parricide, fratricide and, finally, suicide. The father cannot save the son. Instead of a resurrection, we witness the confirmation of death, of hopelessness. The Biblical allusion might be even further pursued. The death of the old soldier might be assumed to represent the sacrifice made by the nation as a whole — we are told that Branson County was robbed of "the flower of its young manhood" (61). The redemption of the nation, however, fails miserably, ending with the death of him for whom the sacrifice has ostensibly been made.

Tom's only triumph might be that he dies of his own free will and thus in a way asserts his manhood, but it is not much of a triumph. "The Sheriff's Children" is the first sign of an angry strain in Chesnutt, more often than not subdued by his gradualist, even accommodationist, philosophy. Tom, though not possessing any of the greatness, vaguely foreshadows a later Chesnutt character, Josh Green in *The Marrow of Tradition*, who would rather die like a man than live like a dog.

The choice of the title "The Sheriff's Children" seems to be at odds with the point of view used in the story, which clearly favors the sheriff as the central character. However, the relationship between the sheriff's children opens the way to a deeper, parabolical reading of the story.[38] It is important for this parabolical meaning that they should have no knowledge of each other's existence, or, to put it more precisely, that Polly should have no knowledge of the existence of a black half-brother. Tom and Polly do not come fully alive in the story precisely because they are made to represent more than themselves alone. They are both the heirs of a father who, by virtue of his ambivalence — he is torn between allegiance to the Union and the Confederacy —, very much resembles Thomas Jefferson who managed to reconcile his authorship of the Declaration of Independence with his status of slaveholder and progenitor of mulatto children.[39] Tom, the Afro-

35

American, is as much an heir to the political and cultural heritage left by Campbell, the Founding Father, as is Polly, the Anglo-Saxon. But whereas nobody will dare question the legitimacy of the latter's claim, the former's is generally denied. The original sin is the father's failure to recognize his son as his heir, his having left him out of the masterplan. Polly acts out a tragic role by being instrumental in the destruction of somebody who is in reality her brother.

NOTES

1. On these and other stereotypes see Sterling A. Brown, "Negro Character as Seen by White Authors," in James A. Emanuel and Theodore L. Gross, edd. *Dark Symphony: Negro Literature in America* (New York, 1968), pp.139-171.
2. Robert Bone, *Down Home: A History of Afro-American Short Fiction from Its Beginning to the End of the Harlem Renaissance* (New York, 1975), p. 17.
3. *Ibid.*, p. xix.
4. From Dunbar's famous poem "We Wear the Mask." Arna Bontemps, ed., *American Negro Poetry* (New York, 1963), p. 14.
5. See the following interpretation of the "conjure" stories: Richard E. Baldwin, "The Art of *The Conjure Woman*," *American Literature*, 43 (1971), 385-398. See also Bone, *op.cit.*, pp. 80f.
6. Robert Farnsworth, "Testing the Color Line — Dunbar and Chesnutt," in C.W.E. Bigsby, ed., *The Black American Writer. Volume I: Fiction* (Baltimore, 1968), p. 118. See also Bone, *op.cit.*, pp. 11f., 74.
7. Quoted in Helen M. Chesnutt, *Charles Waddell Chesnutt: Pioneer of the Color Line* (Chapel Hill, 1952), p. 13. For all biographical data I am indebted to Helen Chesnutt.
8. *Ibid.*, p. 16.
9. *Ibid.*, p. 17.
10. *Ibid.*, p. 21.
11. *Ibid.*, pp. 68, 69.
12. Quoted in Sterling A.Brown *et al.*, edd., *The Negro Caravan* (New York, 1969), p. 11. In his review of Chesnutt's stories, William Dean Howells comments on the recent disclosure of his racial identity: "Now, however, it is known that the author of this story is of negro blood ..." "Mr. Charles W. Chesnutt's Stories," *Atlantic Monthly*, 85 (1900), 699.
13. In a letter dated July 15, 1899. Helen Chesnutt, *op.cit.*, p. 112.

14. *The Conjure Woman*, Ann Arbor 1969, p. 121. The Bible demands the death penalty for him "that stealeth a man and selleth him." Exodus 21;16.

15. The quotation is from "The Sheriff's Children." *The Wife of His Youth and Other Stories of the Color Line*, Ann Arbor 1968, p. 88. All future page references to this story will be given parenthetically in the text.

16. Helen Chesnutt, *op.cit.*, p. 58.

17. *Ibid.*, p. 129. Italics added.

18. Nancy Huston Banks in *Bookman*, Feb. 1900; quoted by Helen Chesnutt, *op.cit.*, p. 136. See also Chesnutt's reaction to this type of criticism: *ibid.*, p. 129.

19. Branson County is a fictional name. The scene described in this story seems to be near that of the "conjure" stories. The Lumberton plank-road is mentioned repeatedly in *The Conjure Woman* (e.g. p. 10) and it appears in "The Sheriff's Children" (67).

20. Bone draws attention to the "studied parallel with the opening passages of Irving's 'legend of Sleepy Hollow.'" *Op.cit.*, p. 95.

21. William L. Andrews, "The Fiction of Charles W. Chesnutt," Diss., North Caro'~ *Dissertation Abstracts* 34 (1974), 6622-A – 6623-A; p. 80.

22. Gerald W. Haslam, " 'The Sheriff's Children': Chesnutt's Tragic Racial Parable," *Negro American Literature Forum*, 2 (Spring 1968), 23 has justly drawn attention to Chesnutt's "reliance upon levels of speech usage as a not too subtle *leitmotif*" in this story.

23. Cf. the reference to the sheriff's "keen ... eyes" (68).

24. Henry James, *The Art of the Novel: Critical Prefaces* (New York, 1950), p. 37.

25. Bone holds a different view. *Op.cit.*, p. 97.

26. Haslam, *op.cit.*, p. 25.

27. Chesnutt had no illusions about who his reading public was. See Helen Chesnutt, *op.cit.*, pp. 120, 127.

28. Cf. Haslam, *op.cit.*, p. 25.

29. *Ibid.*

30. Brown, *op.cit.*, pp. 158f.

31. Quoted in Helen Chesnutt, *op.cit.*, p. 57.

32. Bone draws attention to the verbal ironies centering around the words "stranger," "identity" and "recognize" as applied to Tom and to the lynch mob. *Op.cit.*, pp. 96f.

33. W.E.B. DuBois, *The Souls of Black Folk* (Greenwich, Conn., 1961), p.17. Cf. Chesnutt's remark that "the problems of mixed blood ..., while in the main the same as those of the true Negro, are in some instances much more complex and difficult of treatment." Quoted in Brown, ed., *The Negro Caravan*, p. 27.

34. Haslam, *op.cit.*, p. 24.

35. Bone, *op.cit.*, p. 97.

36. Brown, *op.cit.*, p. 160.
37. Quoted in Helen Chesnutt, *op.cit.*, p. 58.
38. Most critics have not failed to detect this. Walcott in this context develops a parallel to the story of Cain and Abel which is not very convincing but which, in depicting the sheriff's children as "heirs to the same fortune," contains the central issue of the parable. Ronald Walcott, "Chesnutt's 'The Sheriff's Children' as Parable," *Negro American Literature*, 7 (Fall 1973), 85. Haslam (*op.cit.*, p. 25) sees in the story "a parable for this nation's contemporary racial crisis and continuing moral atrophy" and goes on to ask himself who is the sheriff and who the son, but fails to mention the daughter. Bone (*op.cit.*, 97) also forgets the daughter (and the title of the story), but says that the central conflict in the story is "emblematic of a nation that will not face its historical responsibilities. The sheriff's repudiation of his paternal role is symbolic of America's rejection of her black minority. Chesnutt is thus the first black story-writer to employ the archetypal figure of the Negro as rejected child."
39. See J.C. Furnas, *Goodbye to Uncle Tom* (New York, 1956), pp. 140f. See also William Cohen, "Thomas Jefferson and the Problem of Slavery," *Journal of American History*, 55 (1969), 503-526.

BIBLIOGRAPHY

Chesnutt's books of fiction are all available in reprint editions:
The Conjure Woman. Ann Arbor, 1969 [1899].
The Wife of His Youth and Other Stories of the Color Line. Ann Arbor, 1968 [1899].
The House Behind the Cedars. New York, 1969 [1900].
The Marrow of Tradition. Ann Arbor, 1969 [1901].
The Colonel's Dream. Miami, 1969 [1905].
For a complete list of Chesnutt's work see William L. Andrews, "The Works of Charles W. Chesnutt: A Checklist," *Bulletin of Bibliography*, 33 (1976), 45-47, 52.
For a list of secondary sources see Joan Cunningham, "Secondary Studies on the Fiction of Charles W. Chesnutt," *Bulletin of Bibliography*, 33 (1976), 48-52.
Chesnutt's uncollected short stories are now also available in book form:
Sylvia Lyons Render, *The Short Fiction of Charles W. Chesnutt* (Washington, D.C., 1974).

John Wakefield

PAUL LAURENCE DUNBAR
THE SCAPEGOAT
(1904)

When Dunbar at the height of his fame, his contemporary Charles
W. Chesnutt quit work as a full-time writer. In a letter to his
publisher he observed, "My friend, Mr. Howells has remarked
several times that there is no color line in literature. On that point
I take issue with him."[1] Dunbar continued his career as a professional writer, and in so doing accepted the limits imposed upon
him by a publishing world dominated by white values. If we can
judge from what the leading editor of his age found attractive in
black writing, then we are led to the conclusion that a black writer
was required to play the role of what Howells called the "exemplary citizen."[2] The liberal editor was referring in this phrase to
the public image projected by the writings of Booker T. Washington.
Howells' approval indicates the kind of decorum required of a
black writer by his nineteenth century audience.

The kind of style that pleased Howells, he found in the writing
of Dunbar, Washington, and the early Chesnutt. He admired above
all its freedom from "bitterness." Unruffled by racial injustice,
they wrote in a style that he characterized as showing a "sweet,
brave, humor."[3] Dunbar's career depended upon his being able to
reproduce the desired tone.[4] By confining himself to the stereotype themes of plantation fiction — racial reconciliation, black
loyalty, and above all humour — Dunbar achieved this. He was,
however, well aware of the genre's limitations. When questioned
about the relationship of his work to his race, he replied, "I hope
you are not one of those who would hold the Negro down to a
certain kind of poetry — dialect and concerning only scenes of
plantation in the South?"[5] Dunbar's short stories showed that he
rarely followed his own advice.

Dunbar's conversation in this respect was largely dictated by the
hidden conventions of decorum ruling the black writer's relationship with his audience. While we can safely assume that a white
audience imposed severe restrictions of style and subject-matter on

a writer, we must not underestimate the demands of the black middle-class. James Weldon Johnson, Dunbar's friend and literary heir, claimed that both black and white audiences exerted pressures on the black writer. Dunbar, faced with what Johnson called — "the problem of a double audience" — had to be careful to respect the prejudices of both sides.[6]

Decorum then, may be defined as the writer's response to his audience's sense of "good behaviour." Translated into terms of Dunbar's prose this meant evolving a series of strategies. Foremost of course, Dunbar tried to evade portraying any open conflict between black and white. Secondly, he had recourse to irony and humour. Irony enabled him to distance himself from his material and so avoid any accusation that his intention was to complain or protest. Finally, Dunbar presented himself as an adept in the white literary code: an exemplary citizen supporting the values of white culture. The overall strategy appears to have been a form of self-defence for the writer. In terms of his relationship with his audience it amounted to a tacit agreement to forget the problem of race altogether.

Dunbar's readiness to subscribe to the demands of decorum can be partly explained by reference to his education. Dunbar belonged to the emerging middle-class. And it was after all the literate black who had contributed to the creation of the exemplary citizen. If we look at Dunbar's family we find an ambivalence, even a hostility, toward popular oral black culture. Dunbar first learned dialect and heard tales of the plantation from his mother, yet when he wrote his poem "When Malindy Sings" he feared to offend her by dedicating it in her name.[7] Mathilda Dunbar was a self-educated woman and spoke perfect English; dialect, though amusing, still reminded her of slavery. Thus Dunbar seems to have grown up speaking two languages, but with a certain reserve toward the black oral tradition. Later in life, Dunbar would encounter similar attitudes in his wife, Alice Dunbar. Alice did not wish Dunbar to take credit for the text of the musical comedy *Clorindy*. She did not wish her husband to be publicly known as one of the "coon song writers."[8]

It is not difficult to understand the attitude of Dunbar's mother and his wife. The spurious and degraded character of contemporary black minstrelsy could hardly have been their idea of fame. Unfortunately, the commercialization of black oral culture served to divorce the black middle-class from its cultural past. Dunbar found himself fluent in the language of two opposing cultures, but according to Alice Dunbar could only truly express himself in English:

> It was in the pure English poems that the poet expressed *himself*. He may have expressed his race in the dialect poems; they were to him the side issues of his work, the overflowing of a life apart from his dearest dreams.[9]

Dunbar's later aversion for dialect suggests that Alice's judgement must be respected. Dunbar's education had led to think of literature in terms of mastering the white literary code. Influenced by the black minstrel shows of his day, he was led to believe that the oral tradition could only serve as a vehicle for amusement.

Howells detected something of Dunbar's attitude toward the black tradition in his review of Dunbar's poems *Majors and Minors* in June 1896. Howells praises Dunbar's ironic tone. What Dunbar had in fact done was to signal his allegiance to the rules of decorum. As an educated black, Dunbar was carefully trying to avoid being identified with the blacks of his dialect poems. Irony served as a device by which the poet could distance himself from his material. His powers of oral mimicry must not be allowed to hide his mastery of the white literary code. Howells doubtless recognized in Dunbar's irony exactly what Dunbar hoped a white critic would:

> He reveals in these [poems] a finely ironic perception of the negroes' limitations, with a tenderness for them which I think so very rare as to be almost quite new.[10]

Howells' judgment of Dunbar's style coincides in some respects with Alice Dunbar's: black culture is inferior to white. The language of the former slave expressed his limitations. Howells makes this quite clear when he refers to how these poems reveal the narrow emotional "range of the race."[11] This, of course, is Howells' opinion but it is surely significant that Dunbar's irony seems to point in this direction.

Recent criticism of Dunbar's short stories has been rather influenced by the protest literature of the sixties. However, as Robert Bone has pointed out, there is not too much evidence that Dunbar was a frustrated protest writer.[12] Bone dismisses Darwin T. Turner's references to Dunbar's stories of lynching, and his occasional letters of protest to newspapers, as unconvincing.[13]

Bone's view of Dunbar as a typical product of the so-called age of Booker T. Washington seems to push the argument too far in the opposite direction. Dunbar was a more complicated man than that. More recently Bernhard Ostendorf has re-focussed discussion on Dunbar's social dilemma as a writer: "Thus Dunbar was caught between theme, form, and audience."[14] This seems to me a more promising appraoch to Dunbar, especially if the writer's style is related to the newspaper articles which Bone chooses to ignore.[15]

My own feeling is that instead of approaching Dunbar in terms of genre and content, as Bone and Turner try to do, we might consider how Dunbar manoeuvred within the narrow confines of decorum. What we discover will represent only marginal victories for Dunbar. It will, however, reveal some of the problems of audience-writer relations that Dunbar had to contend with, and some of the rhetorical devices Dunbar developed. The bulk of Dunbar's first collection of short stories *Folks From Dixie* (1898) is a study in evasion.[16] As the title suggests, it is a fight from contemporary problems to an idealized south, filled with stereotype blacks who scarcely ever refer to slavery. There is, however, one exception. The story of the mine strike "At Shaft 11" deals with a current conflict between black and white workers. Dunbar shows some ingenuity in dealing with this subject within the limits prescribed by decorum. Since this story was written in the same year as Dunbar had sent an article to a black newspaper defending the black miners' civil rights it might be instructive to compare how Dunbar presents his case to his two different audiences. In his newspaper article Dunbar had written in *propria persona*, his tone is both angry and idealistic:

> It is true, as has been insistently urged, that it would be expedient for the Negro to forego his suffrage and climb to worth and to the world's respect by other means: that is the cry of the miners when they ask him out of the mines. It is the word of the whole commercial world when they ask him out of everything – the American shibboleth. Relinquish! Relinquish![17]

Clearly this is not the language of a Booker T. Washington. Bone's view of Dunbar is too generalized. Be that as it may, when Dunbar handled this same topic in his short story, he put it in the mouth of a white man. This man's tone is quite different from Dunbar's own: he is neither motivated by passion or idealism, but by common sense:

"As for niggers, I ain't any friendlier to 'em than the rest of you; But I ain't the man to throw up a job and then howl when somebody else gets it. If we don't want our hoe-cake, there's others that do."[18]

Dunbar's altered tone reflects his effort to retain decorum by avoiding the language of protest. By playing the role of the white miner he tries to reconcile his audience to the reasonableness of the blacks. In a less interesting way he used this same strategy in at least three other stories from *Folks From Dixie*: "A Family Feud," "The Intervention of Peter," and "Nelse Hatton's Vengeance." Nelse Hatton is a typical example of Dunbar's conception of the exemplary black. Instead of revenging himself on his old master, who turns up at his home after the emancipation, Hatton overcomes his former hatred and treats the white with hospitality. Dunbar's idealism leaves little to be desired, but it does leave his hero somewhat devoid of any normal human responses. Decorum clearly required that blacks purge themselves of anger. And this was equally valid for both the writer and his characters.

With the publication of Dunbar's second collection of short stories, some of his hesitance disappears. Social injustice does get discussed, and blacks are allowed to show anger. *The Strength of Gideon* (1900) represents Dunbar's only real attempt to break directly with the rules of decorum. Characteristically, the small group of stories in which Dunbar allows himself this liberty all deal with scenes from contemporary life, and none of them are told in dialect. One character in particular merits our attention. The newspaper editor Courtney of "A Council of State" forgets the text of a rather tame speech he has prepared and bursts into anger on the question of racial injustice. Here Dunbar as a former editor of a black newspaper comes closest in his fiction to playing himself. The sense of frustration felt by Courtney in following a carefully prepared text that will offend no-one in his audience reflects perhaps some of Dunbar's own hidden emotions:

He started calmly, but as he progressed, the memory of all the wrongs, personal and racial that he had suffered; the knowledge of the disabilities that he and his brethren had to suffer, and the vision of toil unrequited, love rejected, and loyalty ignored, swept him off his feet.[19]

Another embittered black, the disappointed politician of "Mr. Cornelius Johnson: Office Seeke," is more direct still:

43

"Damn you! damn you! he cried. "Damn your deceit, your fair cruelties; damn you, you hard, white liar!"[19]

Dunbar, however, seems to have tired even of these momentary flashes of anger. In his next collection of stories *In Old Plantation Days* (1903) he reverted to the plantation fiction of his first publication *Folks From Dixie*.

In "The Scapegoat" which appeared in Dunbar's last series of stories *The Heart of Happy Hollow* he finally turned away from any direct treatment of the race problem. In this story Dunbar attacks the black middle-class, thus reversing most of the assumptions upon which his career as a writer had been based. Dunbar's displays of anger in *The Strength of Gideon* were the result of his ability to identify with the ideals of the emerging black middle-class: the story of Asbury's betrayal and defeat at the hands of these "idealists" suggests that he had changed his mind.

The hero of "The Scapegoat" is a man who does not derive his virtues from the middle class but from the poor blacks of Cadgers where he grew up. By emphasizing Asbury's shrewdness and cunning, Dunbar shows his determination to break with the image of the exemplary citizen:

> It was his wisdom rather more than his morality that made the managers after a while cast their glances toward him as a man who might be useful to their interests. It would be well to have a man — a shrewd powerful man — down in that part of the town who could carry his people's vote in his vest pocket and who at any time its delivery might be needed, could hand it over without hesitation. (p. 5)

Asbury's strengths enable him to ignore the rules of decorum. He has no obligations either to white patrons, or the black middle-class.

In the "Scapegoat" Dunbar appears to be drawing on the folk-tale. By taking the theme of intrigue and the black trickster-hero from his plantation stories and setting him in a contemporary urban situation, he could step outside the values imposed by the white literary code. The black folktale did not celebrate the values of the middle-class, but of the race. Robinson Asbury realizes that competing with the white man is but half the game. A talented black in a hostile society is a peculiarly vulnerable man. And so Asbury instinctively falls back on the wisdom of the black folktales

44

that teach the importance of subterfuge and cunning.

In escaping from the limiting influences of the white literary code Dunbar was able to drop that "fine perception of irony" which had vitiated his early writing. Irony is present in "The Scapegoat" but it is an irony directed at the false, élitist idealism of the black middle-class. Instead of decorum, there is a spirit of amoral mischief ruling this story. Asbury's virtues derive from the ethos of the folktale where, "It is not virtue that triumphs, but helplessness; not malice, but mischievousness."[21]

Asbury provides the black with a strategy for survival. Dunbar had already shown in *The Strength of Gideon* stories that the idealistic black was the natural prey of the unscrupulous white patron. Asbury, shrewd and resourceful, regards virtue as the questionable luxury of those born into the black middle-class. Asbury, who has been a former bootblack and barber, understands human nature. His rise to fame as a local ward politician does not change him. Instead of moving uptown where the black rich live, he stays with the poor and identifies with them. Asbury scorns "the better class" blacks that run the politics of the town, and draws his political strength from the people. By refusing to observe the ideas of social decorum that characterize the black middle-class, Asbury overcomes the divisiveness that weakens the black community in politics. In fact he embodies Dunbar's own earlier criticism of the black middle-class of New York City who destroyed racial solidarity through their inability to identify with the poor of the ghetto:

> So if the better class Negro would come to his own he must lift not only himself, but the lower men, whose blood brother he is. He cannot afford to look down upon the citizens of the Tenderloin or to withdraw himself from them; for the fate of the blacks there degraded, ignorantly vicious as they may be, is his fate.[22]

Asbury's character suggests, then, an implicit rejection of the politically impotent exemplary black. So thoroughgoing is his political realism, that Dunbar never allows him to discuss the subject of racial injustices. The empty rhetoric of the black press is not for him. Even the sign that hangs above his store "Equal Rights, Barber Shop" is designed primarily to attract custom, not to express an ideal. The ideals of the middle-class can be read any day in their newspapers, along with such trivia as "how Miss Boston

45

entertained Miss Blueford to tea." Asbury has more practical concerns, and helps his customers by keeping their "policy returns," which was wise, if not moral." (p. 5)

Asbury, unlike Dunbar's previous heroes, is not naive. The moral ambivalence of whites does not come as a suprise to him. Consider the following scene. After having passed his law exam Asbury asks for admission to the bar, but his old friend Judge Davis advises him against this. The judge is afraid that, should he fail, he will lose his esteem in the black community. On the other hand, if he passes, he will move uptown and, again, lose influence. Asbury, amused by the judge's underestimation of his shrewdness, smiles and whispers his plan in the old man's ear:

> "Asbury," he said, "you are — you are — well, you ought to be white, that's all. When we find a black man like you we send hom to State's prison. If you were white, you'd go to the Senate." (p. 7)

The first political campaign that Asbury enters brings him into immediate conflict with the black middle-class. Two lawyers called Bingo and Latchett, who also have political ambitions, hear news of Asbury's activities. Ironically, the innocent sign above the barber's shop angers them most of all. Political idealism, they feel, belongs properly to the middle-class:

> Is it any wonder, then, that they viewed with alarm his sudden rise? They kept their counsel, however, and treated with him, for its was best. They allowed him his scope without open revolt until the day upon which he hung out his shingle. This was the last straw. They could stand no more. Asbury had stolen their other chances from them, and now he was poaching upon the last of their preserves. So Mr. Bingo and Mr. Latchett put their heads together to plan the downfall of their common enemy. (p. 9).

Although as resourceful as Br'er Rabbit, Asbury has forgotten the art of the possum who lays low so as to avoid danger.[24] Mr. Bingo, who never does anything openly, understands the value of this subterfuge at this stage better than Asbury.

An appeal to black ideals becomes a central theme in Mr. Bingo's campaign against Asbury. Bingo, who is not in the least idealistic, finds a suitable front in the form of a Mr. Issac Morton, the unsuspecting principal of a local school. Morton exemplifies for Dunbar the ineffectual idealism of the middle-class:

46

Mr. Morton was really an innocent young man, and he had ideals which should never have been exposed to the air. When the wily confederates came to him with their plan he believed that his worth had been recognised, and at last he was to be what Nature destined him for – a leader. (p. 10)

Dunbar's attack on this form of idealism is recorded in the language of these worthy citizens. Their vocabulary is full of such terms as, "ideal," "moral," and "better class of people." Although this rhetoric is enough to win the support of the middle-class blacks, it fails to convince the black electorate as a whole. Mr. Bingo gives it up and goes downtown to pledge support to Ashbury's faction. The conversation that takes place between the two men helps us to define what kind of "morality" Ashbury stands for. Bingo begins by taking Asbury to task for living in the ghetto:

"Well, it was well done, and you've shown that you are a manager. I confess that I haven't always thought that you were doing the wisest thing in living down here and catering to this class of people when you might, with your ability, to be much more to the better class."
"What do they base their claims of being better on?"
"Oh, there ain't any use discussing that." (pp. 13-14)

Asbury ultimately wins the election for his side, but commits a few indiscretions in the effort. The losers challenge the legality of the ballot, and evidence of irregularity comes to light. Asbury, the most conspicuous black in the community, presents himself as the most obvious victim to quieten outraged public opinion:

They began to look around them. They must purify themselves. They must give the people some tangible evidence of their own yearnings after purity. They looked around them for a sacrifice to lay upon the altar of reform. Their eyes fell upon Mr. Bingo. No, he was not big enough. His blood was too scant to wash away the political stains. Then they looked into each other's eyes and turned their gaze away to let if fall upon Mr. Asbury. They really hated to do it. But there must be a scapegoat. The god from the Machine commanded them to slay him. (p. 16)

Thus Asbury is obliged to bear the collective sins of the entire community. Asbury's only consolation at the trial lies in unmasking those who really played a hand in the fraudulent ballot. Although not entirely innocent himself, Asbury has never laid claim to any moral superiority. There is, thus, a kind of poetic justice in his revealing the deeper immorality of those around him:

47

He did not mention the judge's name. But he had torn the mask from the face of every other man who had been concerned in his downfall. (p. 18)

In the second part of "The Scapegoat" Asbury returns from prison and starts playing possum. Although he is not a helpless animal from black folklore even an important black remains vulnerable. In the heat of his successful campaign Asbury had momentarily forgotten this. His first act on returning is to remove the sign "Equal Rights, Barber Shop" from his store. Doubtless he does this to openly demonstrate his retirement from the political scene, but there is another reason. Asbury has learned that conspicuous idealism — even if, as in his case, unintended — is the worst possible form of advertisement.

Like his vulnerable brethren from the black folktale, Asbury realizes that he is a natural prey to hostile forces and must behave accordingly. Indeed, as the story progresses he begins more and more to resemble the trickster-hero of the folktale. Despite the realistic setting of Cadgers and the details of the election campaign, Asbury is clearly a type. We neither know what he looks like, nor how he dresses. We know only that he is shrewd. The same may be said of Bingo. These two men act out a seemingly unequal contest of wit characteristic of the folktale. Bingo must lose because his social pretensions serve to identify him with the élite rather than the common people.

The exact relationship between "The Scapegoat" and black oral culture would probably be difficult to establish within clearly defined limits. And it would seem unwise to push the undoubted resemblances between them too far. What does seem to me more readily ascertainable is that Dunbar's rejection of decorum in favour of the black trickster's disguise can be traced to his early story "The Ingrate."[23] This story records how Dunbar's father, Joshua, tricked his master and escaped from slavery. The details of the plot are for us unimportant. The main point of reference between "The Scapegoat" and "The Ingrate" is that both the main characters resort to the old trick of a slave trying to outwit his master: they disguise their intelligence under a display of outward weakness and humility. Thus we are told of Asbury that, "He came back with no flourish of trumpets, but quietly, humbly." (p. 21) He remains "quiet," and when Bingo visits to check on Asbury, the barber-lawyer's demeanour fools him, "Mr. Bingo expressed the opinion that Asbury was quiet because he was crushed." (p. 22) Asbury has to display that his shrewdness no longer poses a threat to his political enemies. Dunbar has adapted the behaviour of Josh from "The Ingrate" to meet contemporary needs. The lore of surviving on the plantation still has relevance. Josh plays his role as follows:

> But he met his master with an impassive face, always silent, always docile; and Mr. Leckler congratulated himself that so valuable and intelligent a slave should be at the same time so tractable. Usually intelligence in a slave meant discontent; but not so with Josh.[23]

The one significant difference between the stories is that Asbury outsmarts a fellow black, and not a white man. But here I think we must note some apparent evasiveness on Dunbar's part. Open conflict between black and white was, according to the rules of decorum, impossible. Looked at more closely however, does not a hidden struggle exist between Asbury and the white man? It is true that Asbury declined to expose the corruptness of old Judge Davis at the trial. On the surface no overt conflict between Asbury and whites is to be seen. However, it was not the black middle-class that led to his downfall: the final decision to offer Asbury to the people of Cadgers as a scapegoat came from "The God of the Machine." Logically Asbury's desire for revenge should be directed at the white-black power structure behind the party. We will recall that Bingo was not big enough to satisfy the party managers. Why should he now provide a satisfactory target for Asbury's revenge?

This is born out by the end of the story. Dunbar's manoeuvre would appear to be to present Bingo as the surrogate victim of Asbury's revenge, for what are we to make of the story's conclusion?:

> The lawyer was not alone in seeing Asbury's hand in his downfall. The party managers saw it too and they met together to discuss the dangerous factor which, while it appeared to slumber, was so terribly awake. They decided that he must be appeared, and they visited him. (p. 29)

Dunbar could readily identify with his hero's triumph over the custodians of public opinion; their power was an ever present threat to his career as a writer.

It would not do to confuse the character of Asbury with Dunbar. Nevertheless, the similarities between the two are compelling.

49

Although Dunbar never faced his hero's defat, he ran the same kind of dangers. Like Asbury, Dunbar's silence on civil rights was part of a strategy. Only by an almost scrupulous adherence to decorum could he save himself from falling prey to public opinion. Only by developing a constant vigilance could he steer a course between the prejudices of both black and white. If the story of "The Scapegoat" helps us to understand some of the problems facing the black as a public figure, it also argues the need for a reappraisal of Dunbar in terms of his age.

NOTES

1. William L. Andrews, "William Dean Howells and Charles W. Chesnutt: Criticism and Race Fiction in the Age of Booker T. Washington," *American Literature*, 48 (November, 1976), 338.
2. *Ibid.*, p. 334.
3. Andrews, *loc. cit.*
4. This image of the black should be compared with the one created by Washington. Booker T. Washington, "Atlanta Exposition Address," in *Justice Denied: The Black Man in White America*, ed. by William M. Chace and Peter Collier (New York, 1970), pp. 201-204.
5. Benjamin Brawley, *Paul Laurence Dunbar: Poet of his People* (Chapel Hill, 1936), p. 77.
6. James Weldon Johnson, "The Dilemma of the Negro Author," *American Mercury*, 15 (1928), 477.
7. The biographical information I borrowed chiefly from Wagner. A great deal of material on Dunbar's life which is not readily available has been conveniently collected and re-examined by him. Jean Wagner, *Black Poets of the United States: From Paul Laurence Dunbar to Langston Hughes* (London, 1973), pp. 105-111.
8. *Black Poets*, p. 78.
9. *Ibid.*, p. 108.
10. William Dean Howells, "Life and Letters," *Harper's Weekly*, June 27, (1896).
11. Robert Bone, *Down Home: A History of Afro-American Short Fiction from its Beginning to the End of the Harlem Renaissance* (New York, 1975), p. 43.

12. Darwin Turner, "Paul Laurence Dunbar: The Rejected Symbol," *The Journal of Negro History*, 52 (1967), 5.

13. Bernhard Ostendorf, "Black Poetry, Blues, and Folklore: Double Consciousness in Afro-American Oral Culture," *Amerikastudien*, 20 (1975), 249.

14. Some of these letters and articles to newspapers have now been made available by Martin. Jay Martin, ed., *A Singer in the Dawn: Reinterpretations of Paul Laurence Dunbar* (New York, 1976).

15. Paul Laurence Dunbar, *Folks From Dixie* (Freeport, rpt. 1971).

16. *Singer in the Dawn*, p. 25.

17. *Folks*, p. 217.

18. Paul Laurence Dunbar, *The Strength of Gideon* (1900; reprint ed., New York: Arno Press, 1969), p. 333.

19. *Ibid.*, p. 227.

20. Paul Laurence Dunbar, *The Heart of Happy Hollow* (New York, 1904). All subsequent references in the text to "The Scapegoat" will be from this original edition.

21. Marshall Fishwick, "Uncle Remus vs. John Henry: Folk Tension," in *Remus, Rastus, Revolution!* (Bowling Green, Ohio, no date), p. 75.

22. *Singer in the Dawn*, p. 29.

23. *Strength of Gideon*, pp. 87-103.

24. *Ibid.*, p. 96.

Udo O.H. Jung

JEAN TOOMER
FERN
(1922)

"Fern" is from Jean Toomer's book *Cane*, which he published in 1923 and which to his chagrin sold no more than 500 copies.[1] However, if we are to believe the late Dr. Bontemps "a few sensitive and perceptive people went quietly mad"[2] about the book. The judgement of those readers who were more articulate was not unanimous. Some of the reviews that *Cane* drew and which have been collected by John M. Reilly in his bibliographical checklist[3] and partly reprinted in Frank Durham's *Studies in Cane*[4] were frankly hostile (although these constituted only a minority). Many people were frustrated because of the intricate pattern of the stories, poems, and sketches: When they praised the book they cloaked their confusion in highflying but meaningless rhetoric, like the well-known and respected critic Stanley Braithwaite who wrote: "Cane is a book of gold and bronze, of dusk and flame, of ecstasy and pain, and Jean Toomer is a bright morning star of a new day of the race in literature."[5] The majority of reviews hailed *Cane* as "a harbinger of the South's literary maturity"[6] or as the beginning of what "soon thereafter began to be called a Negro Renaissance."[7] From yet another point of view the book has caused the critics headaches. There has been some dispute as to which category *Cane* should be placed into. Is it a mere collection of poems, stories, and sketches or is it an, albeit, very experimental form of the novel? In 1958 Robert Bone argued the latter case, in order to be able to include *Cane* in his study of *The Negro Novel in America*, but the majority of scholars have refused to go along with him. There exists, however, an almost universal consensus that *Cane* is not wholly without design. We have Toomer's own testimony according to which the book's design is a circle: "Aesthetically, from simple forms to complex ones, and back to simple forms."[8] Regionally it also takes three steps to complete the circle, from South up to North, and back to the South again. "Fern" with its Southern setting clearly belongs in the first station

53

of this pilgrimage.

There has also been some dispute whether Jean Toomer should have a legitimate place in a *Negro* Renaissance, since he himself gave rise to the question of whether he was an Afro-American or not, when he refused James Weldon Johnson permission to include some poems of his in the second edition of *The Book of American Negro Poetry*, or when he declared, "Though I am interested in and deeply value the Negro, I am not a Negro,"[9] which led some people to declare that Toomer had — as the saying goes — "passed."[10] An authoritative biography of Toomer is a great *desideratum*. Fortunately several scholars are at work to provide just this.[11] The biographical material about Toomer that has been published to date is sufficient, though, to draw a rough and ready sketch of his person and personality.

The product of racial intermingling, Jean Toomer was tall, handsome, and what is more, fair-skinned. Chameleon-like he could take on "the color of whatever group"[12] he chose to belong to. In 1922 the editors of the *Doubledealer* and the *Liberator*, John McClure and Claude McKay, were uniformly advised by him that he had seven blood mixtures: French, Dutch, Welsh, Negro, German, Jewish, and Italian. However, Toomer believed, paradoxically and significantly, that he would be classed as a Negro by the American public. To the average American of Toomer's time, used to pigeon-holing people according to a handful of racial and other categories, this seemed only too natural, for Nathan Eugene Pinchback Toomer was born in 1894 to Creole-Negro parents. The boy spent most of his childhood and adolescence in the Washington D.C. home of his grandfather, the legendary P.B.S. Pinchback, who in his heyday had been acting governor of Louisiana and had accumulated considerable wealth. But in line with the political and economic post-bellum situation of the race as a whole[13] the fortune of Toomer's grandparents had slowly dwindled away.

At the outbreak of World War I Jean Toomer graduated from Dunbar High School and enrolled at the University of Wisconsin to study agriculture. Neither the University of Wisconsin nor agricultural studies were to his liking, so he quit. In rapid succession he tried the Massachusetts College of Agriculture, the American College of Physical Training in Chicago, New York University and the City College of New York, all to no avail. In the course of this odyssey, however, he became acquainted with the works of one of

America's leading sociologists, Lester F. Ward, whose *Dynamic Society* Toomer is said to have devoured, and with Socialist lawyer Clarence Darrow, who later acted as counsel for the defense of the famous Scottsboro boys. Finally giving up all thought of an academic career, Toomer worked at an amazing array of jobs: "selling papers, delivery boy, soda clerk, salesman, shipyard worker, librarian-assistant, physical director, school teacher, grocery clerk, and God knows what all,"[14] to use his own words. In the spring of 1920 Toomer came into the possession of some six hundred dollars.[15] The leisure time which this sum of money bought him, he spent in the company of a New York crowd of people, such as Waldo Frank, Lola Ridge and Edwin Arlington Robinson. The next year saw Toomer working at the Howard Theatre in Washington, and in the fall he made a trip to Georgia. For 4 months he taught school at the Georgia Normal and Industrial Institute in Sparta.

Toomer himself considered his experience in the South as "the starting point of almost everything of worth that I have done."[16] The eight months that followed upon his stint as a school-teacher he spent in Washington writing feverishly and mailing out manuscripts to the editors of literary magazines. John McClure of the New Orleans *Doubledealer* was the recipient of a batch of manuscripts that contained among others a short story: "Fern." McClure wrote back an apologetic letter, in which he explained: "'Fern' and 'Karintha' are excellent, more excellent than the other manuscripts. We would have been glad to print them, but we were frankly afraid. The bigotry and prejudice do permeate our subscription list to a great extent."[17] He went on to suggest that the editor of *The Dial* might be willing to publish the story or if Gilbert Seldes would not have it that *Broom* might accept "Fern." At long last Margaret C. Anderson's *The Little Review*, which had been founded with the intention of "making no compromise with the public taste,"[18] printed the story in the fall of 1922. What deterred the editors of several magazines from publishing the story and stunned some of the critics who gave it a more or less close reading in 1923 when it reappeared as part of *Cane* must have been the seemingly frank way of dealing with sex.

As first sentences are naturally of the greatest importance, let us turn our attention to how and by which means Toomer chose to initiate his readers into the world of his black heroine. "Face flowed into her eyes," the narrator informs us. Syntactically the sentence is well-formed, it is part of the system of the English language; semantically it is not or hardly so: people's faces do not normally flow into their eyes. In any event this is the kind of first comment you would get from a generative-transformational grammarian of the Chomskyan School in response to a sentence like the one above.[19] He might go on to tell you that modern linguistics is mostly a matter of retrieving the hypothetical deep structure of sentences from material in the surface structure. Asked for an example he could cite the following passage from James Joyce's *A Portrait of the Artist as a Young Man*,"It pained him that he did not know well what politics meant and where the universe ended," and he could point out to you that Joyce had deleted for stylistic reasons what was still present in the deep structure version of the sentence: "It pained him that he did not know well what politics meant and it pained him that he did not know where the universe ended."[20] According to this theory the reader's contribution to understanding a sentence often consists in adding information not immediately observable. There seems thus to be a natural tendency for readers to supplement the input signal.

What has been proven to be a very useful discovery procedure for the analysis of speech utterances in the case of the generative-transformational approach might easily turn out to be a fatal mistake if indulged in indiscriminately by the literary critic. For in a literary work of art surface can be of prime importance: alliteration is such a surface phenomenon, and Toomer certainly knew how to avail himself of the phonological properties of the English language: "*F*ace *f*lowed into her eyes." But the relevance of the argument does not stop here. The sentence could be expanded to something like "... wherever your glance may momentarily have rested, it immediately thereafter wavered in the direction of her eyes." As a matter of fact, this is the larger half of the second sentence. What has been purposely omitted from the first, viz. the observer, is explicitly reintroduced. In the first, however, any trace of a second individual as a necessary prerequisite of perception and narration has been deleted. Properly understood we are faced with the description of an autonomous process, autonomous in the sense that it does not obey the laws of physical nature. The language expressly denies the existence of an observer. He must not — unconsciously or otherwise — be superimposed by the reader.

Observer and object observed seem to be one, as if the former had been drawn in, so to speak, and was reporting from within this totality.

This short discussion of the first sentence has almost imperceptibly involved us in the intricacies of narrative technique. What is the narrator's position vis à vis the characters in the story? What rôle, if any, is the reader supposed to play in the matter of constituting the characters? And the characters themselves — what is their contribution of the total picture?

The woman Fern is the product of Jean Toomer's poetic mind, and what the reader should lawfully know about her is delimited by the information Toomer passes on through the mouth of his narrator and the amount of imagination the reader is able to command in interacting with the narrator. If this sounds trivial or like a contradiction let me explain that by interaction I do not mean the simple fact that a sensitive reader is always a necessary prerequisite if literary personae are to come alive. Interaction here means that the reader must draw on information from outside the story, as it were, and use it to build up the character of this woman by systematically collaborating with Toomer's narrator.[21] Looked at from this angle Fern has a simultaneous existence on at least two levels.

1. There is the Fern who emerges from the relation of an unnamed male person from the North on a visit to a small village in Georgia, and there is

2. the Fern whose characteristics change as the reactions of the reader changes in response to requests from the narrator to contribute his share: "Your thoughts can help me, and I would like to know."[22]

It is important to realize that the narrator himself — on whose testimony alone our own rendition of the plot itself will have to be based — is full of prejudices and stereotypes. He will dish up such platitudes as "A man in fever is no trifling thing to send away" (p. 25) or maintain that "when a woman seeks ... her eyes deny" (p. 24) and that "men are apt to idolize or fear that which they cannot understand, especially if it be woman," (p. 26). On occassion, too, he seems to be unable or unwilling to pass on information. He can pretend to be ignorant: "Why, after noticing it, you sought her eyes, I cannot tell you." (p. 24) Sometimes he is reduced to guessing and immediately afterwards he can disclose an extraordinary and intimate knowledge of a person's inner life. Or he will unashamedly interpose himself between the reader and Fern as if to indicate that only by solving the riddle of the narrator's personality first can the reader get closer to an understanding of the woman: "If you have heard a Jewish cantor sing," he says, "if he has touched you and made your own sorrow seem trivial when compared with his, you will know *my* feeling when *I* follow the curves of her profile, like mobile rivers, to their common delta." (p. 24) What, if the reader has not? In short, the partner that you, the reader, must make shift with, is certainly not thoroughly omniscient; on the contrary he is a prejudiced, partly ignorant, sometimes undisciplined everyday-type of a storyteller, and only after having detected these weaknesses can his report be put to good use. Perhaps it should be added that the narrator's account is full of interjections and other linguistic tokens of attempted dialogue; he really behaves like a story-teller most of the time, not like a (short) story writer.

To set the record straight then, Fern, short for Fernie May (Rosen), has a Jewish surname and she has an aquiline, Semitic nose; to state, however, that she "is the product of miscegenation, of a Jewish father and a Negro mother,"[23] on the basis of such scanty information would have to be called an unwarranted conclusion.

No longer young, with just a suggestion of down on her upper lip, Fern lives in a small Southern town sometime between the advent of the railroad and the nineteen twenties. Townspeople who walk up the Dixie Pike are accustomed to find her resting on the railing of her porch most any time of day. The Dixie Pike, it should be mentioned, as Toomer readers already know (from another story earlier in the book) has grown "from a goat path in Africa." (p. 18) From this quotation it is obvious that here physical appearance as well as the laws of matter and of time must cede precedence to the creative imagination of a people shaping their world. And it is equally obvious that this unorthodox bit of historical research is an attempt at re-evaluating the Afro-American's contribution to the development of the country, "Dixie" being the shibboleth of the old South. However, the railroad crosses the Pike near Fern's house and cuts the road in two. Fern lives at the intersection, both spatially and temporally, of the old and the new. And she does not seem to be actively engaged in changing her surroundings or earning a livelihood. She does not care to pull out a nail that sticks out of a porch post just where her head comes and which must have been a source of constant annoyance for one who sits on the porch most of the day. Instead, she tilts her head a little forward and endures.

The most remarkable feature about Fern is her eyes; they are strange eyes, we are told; and we've already seen in part what is meant by this; how a person who looks at Fern invariably fails to realize his own existence, how he forgets about himself, and how his personality seems to dissolve in the process. There is a report about a young Negro, who, "once was looking at her, spell-bound, from the road. A white man passing in a buggy had to flick him with his whip if he was to get by without running him over." (p. 27).

Men always have been and still are fascinated by Fern. They have approached her and taken her, because "Fern's eyes said to them that she was easy." (p. 25) It may be useful to point out that it makes no difference whether we stress the word "eyes," the word "them," or both in the preceding quotation. In any case, since it is not Fern, but Fern's eyes, which talk visually to the men, and since the message they receive is not necessarily identical with what Fern may have intended, misunderstandings are inevitable. Still, the men about town "were everlastingly bringing her their bodies," (p. 25) although they got no joy from it. Strangely enough, those same men become attached to Fern, feel "as though it would take them a lifetime to fulfill an obligation which they could find no name for." (p. 25) As a kind of *Ersatz* these simple-minded folk dream of sending Fern candy every week, of performing feats of valour to rescue her, or picture themselves as the owners of houses which they can deed over to her.

Of course, Fern is utterly, but innocently amoral. She – or rather her eyes – knows of no reason why she should withhold her body. In 1924, W.E.B. DuBois, the (at that time) bourgeois and respectable black editor of *The Crisis* wrote of Fern in a review that she was a wanton. He must have sensed the inappropriateness of such a label, for he prefixed it by the word "unconscious."[24]

What could have induced the critic to partly alter his stern judgement is the fact that according to our informant something inside of Fern got tired of being sexually exploited by the men and that he was certain that for the life of her she could not tell

59

why or how she began to turn them off. A force – unidentified – is at work in Fern, makes decisions for her, tortures her, as we shall see, and influences the people around her, too.

So, in time, Fern becomes [sic] a virgin, virgins according to the author being by no means the usual thing in a small Southern town. This metamorphosis has been brought about by the something in Fern that turns her would-be-lovers away and by the men who afterwards, out of superstition, set themselves up as her guardians and see to it that Fern, whom they believe to be somehow above them, is not approached by anyone. Fern will thus never be a mother of children. She is barren in a rather unusual way. Fern is the last in the line with no one to hand the torch to. One day everything she represents will be buried with her.[25]

It has been rightly observed that Toomer associates Fern three times with the song of a Jewish cantor.[26] In the second instance, just as in the first, the impression the narrator reports to have had at the sight of Fern is also a synaesthetic one. He informs us that at first sight of her he felt as if he heard a Jewish cantor sing, as if his singing rose above the unheard chorus of a folk-song. The emotional sensibility of the spectator thus detects points in common between Judaism and Negritude (in the sense Ralph Ellison uses the term),[27] the sorrow and the wisdom of many centuries in exile and the specific cultural output of a people in chains. The connection, of course, is not utterly new; it had been adumbrated by Negro Spirituals like "Go down, Moses," "Didn't Old Pharaoh get los'?," "Didn't my Lord deliver Daniel?" or "Joshua fit the battle of Jericho," to name only a few, which for their textual basis had expressly turned to the holy books of the Jews (the only ones the peculiar institution would allow the 'unknown bards' to study). Again Fern serves as a medium, as a person, whose limbs or colour are of lesser importance. People "see" through her and detect universal qualities behind and beside her.

Fern is unusual in yet another way. She serves as a receptacle for all kinds of things. For "like her face, the whole countryside seemed to flow into her eyes. Flowed into them with the soft listless cadence of Georgia's South." (p. 27) The visitor who wants to learn something about Georgia, about the atmosphere of the country and the people who live there, might equally well question Fern, who is Georgia's medium and embodiment.

So far, by relating the past history of Fern and hinting at some of the possible meanings we have relied mostly on the first of the three parts plus epilogue that the story is divided into.[28] By far the greatest portion of the second part has been reserved for a confession by the narrator of his feelings and sensations vis à vis Fern and an attempt at dialogue with the reader in order to channel the streams of consciousness of both.

Like the other black man — Fern does not seem to exert the same kind of attraction on the white men in town; they leave her alone, which is not the normal practice of the South in the judgement of the narrator, who sometimes speaks with the authority of a social scientist in order to enhance the credibility of his report — the narrator feels an obligation toward Fern. He, too, would do something for her.

All of a sudden, however, his reportage ends. The speaker abruptly changes the tense, switches to the present and heaves Fern out of time, so to speak. He does so by stepping out of the story himself. The narrator tries to strike up a conversation with us, his readers, who, it must be said, he asumes to be very knowledgeable in matters of race relations: "You and I know, who have had experience in such things, that love is not a thing like prejudice which can be bettered by changes of town. Could men in Washington, Chicago, or New York more than the men of Georgia, bring her something left vacant by the bestowal of their bodies? You and I who know men in these cities will have to say, they could not." (p. 29) In the course of this one-way communication (the 'dialogue,' of course, completely depends on the assumption that narrator and reader agree on each and every detail; that they are unanimous, that they are at one or get along with each other on rhetorical questions), Fern changes constantly; in the imagination of the two associates she assumes the roles of doctor's or lawyer's wife in a Northern town, prostitute in Chicago's State Street, white man's concubine, and solitary girl at a Harlem tenement window.

All the alternatives being unacceptable when compared with Fern's present status the exchange of ideas ends in a roll call for help with not even the whites excluded this time: "I ask you, friend (it makes no difference if you sit in the Pullmann or the Jim Crow as the train crosses her road), what thoughts would come to you — ... Your thoughts can help me, and I would like to know." (p. 29-30) It is worth noticing that the author has taken special

61

care to advertise and expose Fern's timelessness. Not only has he arranged for the frequent changes in her costume, which we have already mentioned; he also tries another device, though not unusual for a writer. He manipulates the reader's thoughts via the language in such a way that the reader is forced to desist from seeing Fern as a real person. Could anyone possibly think of a character instead of a type in response to the sentence: "Men in her case seem to lose their selfishness," (p. 29) especially if he remembers the very first sentence of our story (and what has been said about it in the way of interpretation); if he remembers how on another occasion it was said that the young Negro looking at Fern had completely forgotten about himself, had given up his identity, his "selfishness" vis à vis Fern? Fern, then, is someone every Black American, male or female, can identify with. But Fern has become a virgin: Fern will not procreate. Fern stands for and symbolizes the race at a certain moment in its history[29] in the South of the United States. Fern is a symbolic vision of the Afro-American's Alter Ego. "She is still living," we are told, and, ironically, the author gives her full name, Fernie May Rosen, in case some foolish or nosy person "might happen down that way" (p. 33) to try and see for himself in the spirit, at best of the singer in the poem that immediately precedes "Fern":

Now just before an epoch's sun declines
Thy son, in time, I have returned to thee,
Thy son, I have in time returned to thee. (p. 21)

C.S. Lewis had pointed out that other than allegory which is a mode of expression, symbolism is a mode of thought. Fern is symbolic in the sense that you "read ... something else through its sensible imitation(s) to see the archtype in the copy."[30] Other scholars have noticed this quality about Fern, but attributed other causes to it or criticized the author for it. David Littlejohn, for example, believes that the people in *Cane* "are drawn with the new honest artfulness of the Stein-Anderson-Hemingway tradition, so crisp and icily succinct that the characters seem bloodless and ghostly, ..."[31] Apart from the fact that the Stein-Anderson-Hemingway *tradition* can hardly be said to have been in existence when Jean Toomer wrote his stories, it has to be remembered that in the case of Fern the literary persona comes to life for long stretches of time only to the degree that the reader is willing to go along with the author and infuse Fern with the blood of his imagination.[32]

Part three of the story, one would suspect, is not subject to Littlejohn's criticism. For in it we learn of a dramatic encounter between the narrator and Fern. One evening he walks up to Fern's house on purpose and finds her on the porch. He tries all kinds of gambits to engage her in a conversation. The sequence of topics again sheds more light on the amount of delicacy the narrator is able to muster than it says about Fern. As an opener he clumsily tries a piquant bit of gossip, the rumour about the supposedly secret relations between "Mr. and Miss [sic] So-and-So," "people" ostentatiously being placed second, so as to exclude the lovers from this category. Fern gives a mere yassur or nassur to all of his attempts. At last, and at the end of his tether, he suggests a walk. To counteract the surpise that his proposal generates (men before him had suggested just that before offering their bodies to Fern), he tries to communicate with his eyes, presumably because verbal communication is often so full of semantic snares and pitfalls. This visual communication seems to be successful, for "the thing from her that made my throat catch, vanished. Its passing left her visible in a way I'd thought, but never seen." (p. 31) Once Fern has devested herself of this breath-taking quality of hers that formerly rendered her more or less invisible, she suddenly becomes visible in a new way. And immediately afterwards the chronicler records her first and only utterance: "Doesnt it make you mad?" (p. 31) We are told that "it" refers to the row of petty gossiping people, who represent the world. No wonder, Fern behaved so reticently when the town gossip was tried on her only minutes before this outbreak. They leave this "world" and through a canebreak enter another, the shadowy world of a Georgia landscape undergoing change at dusk. Dusk transforms the canebreak, sets it in motion, suggesting the almost imperceptible procession of giant trees. While they sit together under a sweet-gum tree the narrator's mind wanders, strays from Fern and turns on his own feelings. These suggest the idea that "things unseen to men were tangibly immediate." (p. 31)

When his mind returns to Fern he holds her in his arms. "Her eyes, unusually weird and open, held me. Held God. He flowed in as I've seen the countryside flow in. Seen men." (p. 32) This crucial scene is not well understood by the narrator, although he is a party to it. The report is studded with 'I-dont-knows' and the like. His excessive talkativeness (about how people in Georgia often have visions and that he would not have been surprised he had one), obstrusively urged upon the reader, may be taken as an index of his confusion. But he makes important discoveries without knowing it. Luckily, his language knows better than he.

Fern, we discover, is his alter ego. As a carrier of all things Negro she is also part of his personality.[33] We are told that things unseen to men are *tangibly* immediate, and then, when he comes to, he *holds* Fern in his arms, their union, the union of body and soul, having unconsciously been perpetrated. Mirrorwise Fern's eyes *hold* him and something else: God. Because our witness is unwilling to say more, except that there is something that he calls God, it is largely a matter of speculation as to what exactly this new element of the Trinity means. If some of Toomer's other stories and poems in *Cane* may legitimately be taken as a starting point it would seem that God is a term applied to the state of reunification a person achieves with his soul, his racial and/or cultural identity.[34] It ends a period of estrangement or anomy, as the sociologist would call it. Human beings seem to possess this faculty of bridging a gap that may have lasted for centuries. In "Fern" Toomer has only hinted at the innate psychic possibilities, on other occasions the people in his stories bring to bear on their problems this very faculty and conjure up their African heritage: jujumen, greegree, and witchdoctors.

As the sweet moment of union ends, with the narrator again ignorant of how he brought the end about, Fern runs away from him and into the darkness, her body painfully shaken by something it can not let out. The embodiment of all things Negro and at the same time someone who has become a virgin, Fern is unable to give birth in clear speech to the qualities she encompasses. She seeks release in song, in "plaintive, convulsive sounds, mingled with calls to Christ Jesus," (p. 32) not unlike the vocal pieces we are used to call Negro Spirituals. When he finds her she faints in his arms.

The epilogue is an attempt at ironically de-emphazing and intellectually counteracting the narrator's strong emotional involvement in an overpowering encounter with a Negro girl from a small town somewhere in the South. Nothing ever came to Fern, he tells us. At that high-pitched moment with Fern in the canefield he had used these same words and maintained that when one is on the soil of one's ancestors, most anything can come to one. However, for both him and her, the soil of the ancestors is in Africa. Cleverly he disclaims his spiritual engagement and steps in the line of men who would do some fine unnamed thing for Fern.

After the commercial failure of *Cane* Toomer did not simply stop writing. And he did publish some stories in magazines and anthologies.[35] But his full-length works were all rejected by the publishers. The years 1924 and 1925 are reported to have been sterile for Jean Toomer as an artist. Spiritually, however, these same years must have been richly stimulating. In 1924 he met George Ivanovitch Gurdjieff, who had founded his "Institut pour le développement Harmonieux de l'Homme" in Fontainebleau near Paris and attracted quite a number of the elite of Western Europe.[36] Katherine Mansfield, another disciple of Gurdjieff's had died at the institute a year before Toomer came there to be initiated. On his return to New York Toomer began proselytizing among those of his former associates who were willing to listen. Out of the pen of the champion of the lower classes, Langston Hughes, we have a rather unfriendly account of Toomer's missionary profession.[37]

When in 1929 the stock market collapsed the Negro Renaissance came to an abrupt end almost overnight. Its authors dispersed, went on a longish holiday, like Langston Hughes, stayed in their European exile, like Claude McKay, or returned, like Countée Cullen, to teach young Afro-Americans French in a New York High School. Incidentally, James Baldwin was a pupil at Frederick Douglas High School at that same time and on one occasion wrote about an interview with Countée Cullen in the school paper.

Jean Toomer, who in 1927 had gone to live in Chicago, on the 30th of October 1931 married the white novelist Margery Latimer. Margery Latimer died in childbirth a year later. When Toomer hit the headline again, it was a rather unfriendly report from *TIME* on his marriage to another white woman, Marjorie Content Toomer, in 1932.[38] Two years later the couple moved to Doylestown, Pa., where Toomer continued to write and receive rejection slips from the publishers. He did not live to witness the Toomer renaissance of the late sixties and early seventies. Toomer died on the 30th of March 1967, two years before *Cane* was reissued as a paperback.

NOTES

1. Robert Bone gives this figure in his study *The Negro Novel in America* (New Haven, 1958), p. 81.
"Fern" is an often-anthologized story. Cf. e.g., Langston Hughes, ed., *The Best Short Stories by Negro Writers: An Anthology from 1899 to the Present* (Boston & Toronto, 1967). Francis E. Kearns, ed., *The Black Experience: An Anthology of American Literature for the 1970s* (New York, 1973). The best buy probably is the paperback edition of *Cane* (New York, 1969).
2. Foreword to the paperback edition of *Cane* (New York, 1969), p. x.
3. John M. Reilly, "Jean Toomer: An Annotated Checklist of Criticism," *Resources for American Literary Study*, 4 (1974), 27-56.
4. Charles E. Merrill Studies (Columbus, Ohio, 1971).
5. Cf. Arna Bontemps, "The Negro Renaissance: Jean Toomer and the Harlem Writers of the 1920's," *Anger, and Beyond: The Negro Writers in the United States*, ed. by Herbert Hill (New York, 1966), p. 23.
6. Waldo Frank, e.g., in his foreword to the 1923 edition of *Cane*. The Quotation is from Arna Bontemps' "The Negro Renaissance: Jean Toomer and the Harlem Writers of the 1920's," p. 26.
7. *Ibid.*, p. 24. On the Harlem or Negro Renaissance the following books might be consulted: Alain Leroy Locke, ed., *The New Negro: An Interpretation* (New York, 1925), repr. with a new introduction by Allan H. Spear (New York, 1968). Jean Wagner, *Les Poètes Nègres des Etats-Unis: Le sentiment racial et religieux dans la poésie de P.L. Dunbar à L. Hughes 1890-1940* (Paris, 1963); engl. transl. by Kenneth Douglas, *Black Poets of the United States: From Paul Laurence Dunbar to Langston Hughes* (Urbana, 1973). Gilbert Osofsky, *Harlem: The Making of a Ghetto* (New York, 1966). Nathan I. Huggins, *Harlem Renaissance* (New York, 1971).
8. Cf. Mabel M. Dillard, *Jean Toomer: Herald of the Negro Renaissance (Ohio University,* 1967), p. 76.
9. Letter to Nacy Cunard, February 8, 1932, cf. Darwin T. Turner, *In a Minor Chord: Three Afro-American Writers and Their Search for Identity (Carbondale & Edwardsville,* 1971), p. 32.
10. Cf. Richard Bardolph, *The Negro Vanguard* (New York, 1961), p. 204.
11. Personal communication from Mrs. Marjorie Content Toomer, to whom special thanks are due for untiring and continued cooperation.
12. Jean Toomer in a letter to John McClure, June 30, 1922, cf. Turner, p. 30.
13. Cf. Rayford W. Logan, *The Betrayal of the Negro: From Rutherford B. Hayes to Woodrow Wilson* (London, 1969).
14. In a letter to Claude McKay, Summer 1922, cf. the introduction to the paperback edition of *Cane* (New York, 1969), p. ix.
15. I am giving these figures and most of the other details on the authority of

Darwin T. Turner's *In a Minor Chord*. Prof. Turner's biographical sketch is the one with the greatest amount of detailed information. Another dependable source is Mabel M. Dillard's unpublished doctoral dissertation.

16. Cf. the foreword to the paperback edition of *Cane*, p. ix.

17. In a letter dated June 30, 1922, cf. Dillard, p. 11. On the question of the prostitution of the integrity of aspiring young Afro-American authors by the American reading public, cf. Bontemps, "Jean Toomer and the Harlem Writers of the 1920's."

18. Cf. *The Oxford Companion to American Literature*, ed. by James D. Hart (New York, 1965), p. 485.

19. For a readable account of the approach to the study of languages connected with the name of Noam Chomsky cf. John Lyons, *Chomsky* (London, 1970).

20. The example is from Roderick A. Jacobs & Peter S. Rosenbaum, *Transformationen: Stil und Bedeutung* (Frankfurt a.M., 1973).

21. Again, what I have in mind is not the 'implied reader' of Wolfgang Iser. Cf. his *Der implizite Leser: Kommunikationsformen des Romans von Bunyan bis Beckett* (München, 1972). Although the 'implied reader' is often called upon to collaborate, he is at the same time being carefully guided in his responses by the author and he always remains within the confines of the fictitious world which the narrator has set up. This boundary must never be overstepped and the reader has no right to interfere with the author's plans, whereas Toomer readers are, as we shall see, expressly invited to do so.

22. *Cane*, p. 30. All references in the text are to the paperback edition.

23. Cf. Dillard, p. 48. It is not my intention to detract from Miss Dillard's merit by selecting her for reference. Others, too, have reproduced this error from an earlier source. And besides, Miss Dillard's account of "Fern" is among the best that has been written about this story to date.

24. Cf. his review of *Cane* in *The Crisis*, February 1924, p. 161.

25. It is important to realize that Fern does not *remain* a virgin. On the contrary, she *becomes* a virgin. There are undoubtedly references to the Black Madonna in *Cane*, but that seems hardly enough reason to establish a strong tie between Fern and the Virgin Mary. Since, as I have pointed out earlier, it is not warranted to say that Fern is of mixed parentage either, I cannot see how a specific Jewish genius for suffering (whatever that is; a very frivolous term it seems to me) could be said to be displayed by the heroine. In his latest book on the history of Afro-American short fiction Robert Bone has a fine interpretation of 'Fern' in the chapter on Toomer, and I agree with almost everything he says about the story. However, Prof. Bone states that "no one who has not made his pilgrimage to Nashville" (Fisk University i.e., where the Toomer manuscripts were deposited in 1967) "can expect to be taken seriously as a Toomer critic." Cf. Robert Bone, *Down Home: A History of Afro-American Short Fiction from Its Beginnings to the End of the Harlem*

Renaissance (New York, 1975), p. 204. For obvious reasons and out of theoretical considerations the present author has seen fit to adopt an approach that looks upon the work of art as a more or less self-contained unity.

26. Cf. Hargis Westerfield, "Jean Toomer's 'Fern'. A Mythical Dimension," *CLA Journal* 14 (1971), pp. 274-276.

27. Cf. his "Remarks at the American Academy of Arts and Sciences Conference on the Negro American," *New Black Voices: An Anthology of Contemporary Afro-American Literature*, ed. by Abraham Chapman (New York, 1972), pp. 401-408.

28. Parts one and three are of exactly equal length if the printed line is the unit to be counted. Part two surpasses them by something like a third.

29. To my knowledge Mable Dillard was the first to have noticed this. Cf. her doctoral dissertation, p. 50. In addition we have Jean Toomer's own testimony in a letter to Waldo Frank ca. 1922: "In my own stuff, in those pieces that come nearest to the old Negro, to the spirit saturate with folksong: 'Karintha' and 'Fern,' the dominant emotion is a sadness derived from a sense of fading, from a knowledge of my futility to check colution." Cf. Dillard, p. 19. Mrs. Marjorie Content Toomer feels certain that her husband was not aware of the meaning of fern as an adjective in German (personal communication). An interlingual play on words is thus out of the question. If the girl's name must have an interpretation at all, two ways are open: The name might be taken as an indicator of the seeming preponderance of the vegetative in Fern's existence. Such an interpretation would probably go into the niceties of reproduction in the life of a fern, which properly belongs in a botany handbook, despite certain parallels in the plot of our story. Or it might be understood, on the basis of the Jewish component, as a hint at how "the Negro is in solution, in the process of solution. As an entity, the race is loosing its body, and its soul is approaching a common soul." Jean Toomer in an undated letter to Waldo Frank, ca. 1922. Cf. Dillard, p. 19.

30. C.S. Lewis, *The Allegory of Love: A Study in Medieval Tradition* (New York, 1958), p. 45.

31. David Littlejohn, "Before Native Son: The Renaissance and After," *Studies in Cane*, compiled by Frank Durham (Columbus, Ohio, 1971), p. 101.

32. Robert Bone has drawn attention to the fact that Toomer was admittedly and heavily influenced by Sherwood Anderson's *Winesburg, Ohio*. This is undeniably so. At the same time it should be noticed that Toomer was, from a very early date, rather critical of Anderson's artistic capabilities. In a letter to Waldo Frank (ca. 1922) he remarks: "Sherwood Anderson has doubtless a very deep and beautiful emotion by way of the Negro. Here and there he has succeeded in expressing this. ... I expect artists to recognize the circle of expression. ... Sherwood's notes are very deep and sincere. Hence I attribute his attitude to a natural limitation. This limitation, extended, is noticeable in the bulk of his work. The range of his sensitivity, curiosity, and intelligence is not

very wide. One's admiration suffers, but one's personal liking need not be affected by this." Cf. M. Dillard, p. 18-19.

33. The concept of the alter ego as used here was introduced into modern psychological thought by C.G. Jung. Toomer had read extensively in the literature of psychoanalysis, especially Freud. Cf. the excerpt from Toomer's *Outline of Autobiography* as quoted in Dillard, p. 19.

34. Cf. e.g., my " 'Spirit Torsos of Exquisite Strength': The Theme of Individual Weakness vs. Collective Strength in Two of Toomer's Poems," *CLA Journal*, 19 (December 1975), 261-267.

35. The question of why Toomer, in the words of Arna Bontemps, turned his back on greatness, is one of some notoriety. It has been discussed by a variety of people, like Fullenwider and Bontemps, some crediting the publishers with an almost unfailing literary or commercial instinct, others falling victim to a biographical fallacy, which examines the private life of the author to find there the causes of failure and success. Cf. A. Bontemps, "The Negro Renaissance: Jean Toomer and the Harlem Writers of the 1920's," and S.P. Fullenwider, "Jean Toomer: Lost Generation, or Negro Renaissance," *Phylon*, 27 (1966), 396-403. As far as I can see from a distance and with the librarian of Fisk University closely guarding her treasure of Toomer manuscripts Darwin T. Turner has a fairly correct and nearly complete list of the published and unpublished works of Toomer. Cf. his *In a Minor Chord*, pp. 140-143.

36. On the teachings of Gurdjieff cf. his *Recontres avec des Hommes Remarquables* (Paris, 1966) and Louis Pauwels, *Monsieur Gurdjieff: Documents, Témoignages, Textes et Commentaires sur une société initiatique contemporaine* (Paris, 1954).

37. Cf. Langston Hughes, *The Big Sea: An Autobiography* (New York, 1940)

38. The article has been reprinted in *Studies in Cane*, pp. 15-16.

ADDITIONAL SOURCES

Cancel, R.A., "Male and Female Interrelationships in Toomer's *Cane*," *Negro American Literature Forum*, 5 (Spring 1971), 25-31.

Chase, P., "The Women in *Cane*," *CLA Journal*, 14 (March 1971), 259-273.

Spofford, W.K., "The Unity of Part One of Jean Toomer's *Cane*," *Markham Review*, 3 (May 1972), 58-60.

Starke, G.J., *Black Portraiture in American Fiction: Stock Characters, Archetypes, and Individuals* (New York, 1971).

Stein, M., "The Poet-Observer and Fern in Jean Toomer's *Cane*," *Markham Review*, 2 (October 1970), 64-65.

Peter Bruck

LANGSTON HUGHES
THE BLUES I'M PLAYING
(1934)

Langston Hughes (1902-1967), according to many critics "poet laureate of Harlem" and "Dean of American Negro Writers," began his literary career by winning a poetry contest sponsored by the black magazine *Opportunity* in 1925. "The Weary Blues" was noted by Carl Van Vechten, through whose sponsorship Hughes was able to get his first contract with the noted publisher Alfred Knopf. Van Vechten, who acted as a main ambassadorial advisor and patron of black literature to white publishing firms during the 1920's,[1] not only paved the way for Hughes' literary career but also became the "chief architect of his early success."[2] Just as with Dunbar and Chesnutt, white patronage played a decisive role in the literary emergence of Langston Hughes. The omnipresence of the white patron with his significant socio-literary influence on the black author was a discovery that the young Hughes was still to make; his gradual and painstaking emancipation from the grip of such white patrons was to become the major concern of his early phase and to play a dominant theme in his short fiction.

Starting to publish in the midst of the 1920's meant for Langston Hughes to be intrinsically involved in a debate over the function, theme, and aesthetic form of black literature. The problem became even more urgent when the 'Harlem Renaissance' period began and, at the same time, the widely acclaimed emergence of the "New Negro' confronted the black writer with the task of defining his role as a literary artist. In order to foster a critical discussion of these questions, the leading black magazine *The Crisis* organized a symposium, "The Negro in Art: How Shall He Be Portrayed?," throughout the March-November issues of 1926. Prior to this, Alain Locke, "father of the 'New Negro' and the so-called Harlem Renaissance,"[3] had attempted to define the cultural stance of the 'New Negro' in the following manner:

He [the New Negro] now becomes a conscious contributor and lays aside

71

the status of a beneficiary and ward for that of a collaborator and participant in Amercian civilization. The great social gain in this is the releasing of
our talented group from the arid fields of controversy and debate to the
productive fields of creative expression. The especially cultural recognition
they win should in turn prove the key to that revaluation of the Negro
which must precede or accompany any considerable further betterment of
race relationships.[4]

Locke, who clearly pursued DuBois' philosophy of a "talented
tenth," aspired to an attitude of cultural elitism that envisioned
art and culture to be a bridge across the racial barrier; hence his
calling for a "carefully maintained contact between the enlightened
minorities of both race groups."[5] This philosophy of culture undoubtedly presented a challenge to all those young black writers
who were primarily concerned with expressing the new feeling of
ethnic identity and racial pride. One of those willing to face this
challenge was the young Langston Hughes who, on June 23, 1926,
published an essay that may not only be viewed as an indirect
reply to Locke but also became known as the first significant
black literary manifesto.

The importance of the "Negro Artist and the Racial Mountain"
for the evolution of black literature cannot be overstressed. In the
words of Charles S. Johnson, former editor of *Opportunity*, none
other than Hughes with this essay "so completely symbolized the
new emancipation of the Negro mind."[6]

In outlining his stance as a black writer, Hughes placed particular
emphasis on racial pride and ethnic identity:

To my mind, it is the duty of the younger Negro artists ... to change
through the force of his art that old whispering, "I want to be white,"
hidden in the aspirations of his people, to "Why should I want to be white?
I am a Negro and beautiful."[7]

Hughes' emphasis on blackness, which anticipated the present-day
discussion of the possibilities of a black aesthetic, clearly signalled
the renunciation of the well-known problem of "racial" vs. "universal" art. Instead Hughes turned to depicting the ordinary black
American. As he recalled in his first autobiography *The Big Sea*,

I felt that the masses of our people had as much in their lives to put into
books as did those more fortunate ones ... I didn't know the upper class
Negroes well enough to write much about them. I knew only the people I had
grown up with, and they weren't people whose shoes were always shined.[8]

His extensive reliance on folk forms and rhythms and his application of oral folk culture to poetry highlight his innovating efforts[9] and mark the beginning of the "reconciliation of formal black poets to their folk roots and grass roots audience."[10] One of the most popular results of his preoccupations in terms of narrative fiction were the "Simple folk tales" that first appeared in the black weekly *Chicago Defender* in November 1942. Through the publication of these tales in a newspaper "which functioned as a sort of bible to many Negroes in every walk of Negro life,"[11] Hughes spoke directly to the ordinary black American; their sorrows, miseries, hopes, and folk wisdom were encapsulated in the figure of the black everyman, Simple, whose creation undoubtedly established much of Hughes' lasting fame.

From a socio-literary point of view, the Simple tales marked Hughes' first success in gaining a genuine black audience. In the late 1920's, however, this goal still proved utopian, as Hughes was trying to find a way out of his predicament:

> I did not want to write for the pulps, or turn out fake 'true' stories to sell under anonymous names. ... I did not want to bat out slick non-Negro short stories in competition with a thousand other commercial writers trying to make *The Saturday Evening Post*. I wanted to write seriously and as well as I knew about the Negro people, and make *that* kind of writing earn for me a living.[12]

Whereas the bulk of his poetry is usually associated with the Harlem Renaissance, whose "chief literary artist and most famous survivor"[13] Hughes is often called, his career as a short story writer did not begin before the wane of this epoch. Although his first stories, all reflecting the author's experiences as a seaman on a voyage along the West coast of Africa, were already published in Harlem's literary magazine *The Messenger* in 1927, it took another six years before Hughes really devoted himself to writing short fiction. From the spring of 1932 to the fall of 1933 he visisted the Soviet Union and the Far East. It was during his stay in Moscow that he had a decisive reading experience which prompted him to devote himself to the short story:

> I had never read anything of Lawrence's before, and was particularly taken with the title story ["The Lovely Lady"], and with "The Rocking Horse Winner." Both tales made my hair stand on end. The possessive, terrifying elderly woman in "The Lovely Lady" seemed in some ways so much like

my former Park Avenue patron. ... I began to write a short story. I had been saying to myself all day, "If D.H. Lawrence can write such psychologically powerful accounts of folks in England, ... maybe I could write stories like his about folks in America."[14]

The years to come were to see amazing results from this literary initiation. Between 1933 and 1934 he devoted himself exclusively to this genre. "More than half of his stories," as Robert Bone reports, "and nearly all of his best stories were written in this period;"[15] fourteen of them were published in the collection *The Ways of White Folk* in 1934.

This collection, which received rather favorable reviews,[16] presents, thematically, a close examination of black-white relationships. Mostly satirical in tone, the stories try to unmask several manifestations of the Harlem Renaissance. Specifically, the theme of white patronage, as displayed in "Slave on the Block," "Poor Little Black Fellow," and "The Blues I'm Playing," is used to demonstrate the dishonesty of whites and the absurd notion of their paternalistic philanthropy. In this context, it is of particular socio-literary interest to note that Hughes' fictional treatment of the incipient dissociation from white predominance caused him no setback in magazine publication. Instead, his new literary efforts soon found their way into leading periodicals. Whereas Hughes' poetry was usually printed in such black journals as *Opportunity* and *The Crisis* (he had complained in 1929 that "magazines used very few stories with Negro themes, since Negro themes were considered exotic, in a class with Chinese or East Indian features),[17] four out of his five stories written in Moscow were now accepted and published by such noted periodicals as *The American Mercury*, *Scribner's Magazine* and *Esquire*. This major breakthorugh provided him with a nation-wide, non-parochial platform, allowing him to escape from his predicament, and opened up the opportunity of gaining a primarily white reading audience.

The reading of Lawrence's *The Lovely Lady* not only prompted Hughes to concentrate on the short story but also persuaded him to use the story's protagonist Pauline Attenborough as a model for the creation of Dora Ellsworth, the fictional representative of his former white Park Avenue patroness. *The Blues I'm Playing*, written after his return from the Soviet Union and first published in the May 1934 issue of *Scribner's Magazine*, was thus subject to an interesting combination of influence.

74

The impact of Lawrence's story becomes apparent when one compares the opening description of both women. Lawrence describes Pauline Attenborough as a women who "could still sometimes be mistaken ... for thirty. She really was a wonderfully preserved woman, of perfect *chic*. ... She would be an exquisite skeleton and her skull would be an exquisite skull."[18] The narrator's mocking emphasis on her appearance, which she can change through a "mysterious little wire" of "will,"[19] exposes her artificiality. As a collector of art, Pauline is herself a "self-made objet d'art."[20] Dora Ellsworth is introduced in a similar way. Hughes' description, however, is more mocking and obviously aims at unmasking his character's self-deception from the very beginning. Hence one common denominator of both figures seems to be hypocrisy:

> Poor dear lady, she had no children of her own. Her husband was dead. And she had no interest in life now save art, and the young people who created art. She was very rich, and it gave her pleasure to share her richness with beauty. Except that she was sometimes confused as to where beauty lay. ... She once turned down a garlic-smelling soprano-singing girl, who, a few years later, had all the critics in New York at her feet.[21]

This passage reveals several central aspects of the narrative texture. The focus of interest, which is on Mrs. Ellsworth throughout the story, suggests that Hughes is primarily concerned with depicting the ignorance of the white philanthropist. This intention is underlined by authorial comments which, although sometimes quite devastating, are seldom strongly aggressive. Instead, Hughes pities his white character, thereby producing the particular reading process of *The Blues I'm Playing*. By undermining the cultural status of his protagonist and exposing the absurdity of her judgements, Hughes creates in the reader's imagination the illusion of witnessing the forthcoming degradation of so-called superior white culture.

Satire hence sets the emotional tone throughout the story. Its function, autobiographically, is to unveil the devastating influence that Hughes' former patroness had on his creative impulses: "She wanted me to be primitive and know and feel the intuitions of the primitive. But, unfortunately, I did not feel the rhythms of the primitive surging through me, and so I could not live and write as though I did."[22] On the cultural level, this conflict was representative of a whole range of dilemmas that had emerged during the Harlem Renaissance. The black writers' "search back to a national past,"[23] their literary journey of ethnic self-discovery, marked the beginning of a declaration of cultural independence, whose paradigm may be seen in Hughes' literary manifesto "The Negro Artist and the Racial Mountain." Satire as employed in *The Blues I'm Playing* signals the end of white paternalism, thereby demystifying the 'cult of the primitive Black' that many whites took for granted during the 1920's.

This historical conflict is reflected in the antagonistic relationship of Dora Ellsworth and her black protegée, the pianist Oceola Jones. Both women represent opposing points of view; this structural contrast manifests a clash between "two standards of morality," between a "white and a Negro code."[24] The conflict itself evolves throughout five stages, each dramatizing their incompatible positions: the financial sponsorship is followed by increasing efforts on part of Mrs. Ellsworth to dominate the private life of her protegée; Oceola's return to Harlem and the announcement of her engagement to a black medical student cause a severe crisis and finally lead to a dissolving of their relationship.

The mocking irony with which the narrator emphasizes Mrs. Ellsworth's ignorance prevails through all these scenes. Her ignorance of art and artists is even excelled by her total lack of insight into black life and, in particular, Harlem: "Before going to bed, Mrs. Ellsworth told her housekeeper to order a book called 'Nigger Heaven' ..., and also anything else ... about Harlem." (103) Here Hughes tries not merely to unmask the fakery of white patronage; he also scores Carl Van Vechten's *Nigger Heaven*. This novel, published at the height of the Harlem Renaissance in 1926, served as a kind of guide-book to Harlem for many white readers and was mostly rejected by blacks. DuBois' review perhaps sums up best the black reaction of that time: " 'Nigger Heaven' is a blow in the face. It is an affront to the hospitality of black folk. ... It is a caricature. It is worse than untruth because it is a mass of half-truths."[25] Although Hughes' own criticism of *Nigger Heaven* and Van Vechten was rather friendly,[26] the satirical connotation of the passage quoted above seems to suggest that by 1934 Hughes felt free enough do denounce Van Vechten's patronage in the same way as he did that of his former Park Avenue patroness.

Moreover, the same passage reveals another important feature of

76

Mrs. Ellsworth's personality. Her reliance on books instead of personal experience, her preference for a substitute for reality, demonstrates that she is unable to differentiate between substance and appearance. This failure is particularly emphasized in the scene where she drives Oceola to her Harlem home:

> Mrs. Ellsworth had to ask could she come in. "I live on the fifth floor," said Oceola, and there isn't any elevator," "It doesn't matter, dear," said the white woman, for she meant to see the inside of this girl's life, elevator or no elevator. (105)

Devoid of any emotional and psychological perception, she mistakes the exterior for the interior, form for being, and thereby reduces life to a mere artefact. This attitude is equally apparent in her conception of art. Having substituted art for life, Mrs. Ellsworth, like Pauline Attenborough, becomes a self-made *objet d'art*; her stress merely on the refining, cultivating, and sublimating function of art not only separates art from life, but also deprives it of its' vitality and reduces it to a dead object.

Mrs. Ellsworth's attitudes contrast with Oceola's character and music. Having grown up in the musical tradition of the black church, Oceola's life is firmly rooted in jazz and the blues. Her music, which derives its strength from her cultural identity, distinctly sets her apart from Dora Ellsworth, who conceives of art as essentially classical. The evolving conflict thus centers around the clash of two antagonistic modes of art, which are simultaneously representative of two antagonistic modes of life. In contrast to her patroness' understanding of music, Oceola has kept an original sense of it, one that "demanded movement and expression, dancing and living to go with it." (111) As an initial, spontaneous expression of black life and experience, the blues is devoid of "classical runs or fancy falsities." (110) Rather, it becomes, as Ralph Ellison once remarked, a form of individual therapy:

> The blues is an impulse to keep the painful details and episodes of a brutal experience alive in one's aching consciousness, to finger its jagged grain, and to transcend it, not by consolation of philosophy but by squeezing from it a near-tragic, near-comic lyricism. As a form, the blues is an autobiographical chronicle of personal catastrophe expressed lyrically.[27]

Oceola's music hence becomes not only an assertion and definition of her identity; it also links her, culturally, to that chain of black folklore tradition, which, as Ellison has pointed out, "announced the Negro's willingness to trust this own experience, his own sensibilities as to the definition of reality, rather than allow his masters to define these crucial matters for him."[28] Oceola's "sheer love of jazz" (107), her hatred of "most artists, ... and the word art in French or English," (109 gives voice to an attitude which considers music a manifestation of an experienced reality, thus merging both art and life. Her contempt for a philosophy that separates these two arises out of her primal emphasis on the affirmative and virile nature of music:

> Oeceola's background was too well-grounded in Mobile, and Billy Kersand's Minstrels, and the Sanctified Churches where religion was a joy, to stare mystically over the top of a grand piano like white folks and imagine that Beethoven had nothing to do with life, or that Schubert's love songs were only sublimations. (111)

The "bipartite structure"[28] of this story, emphasizing two opposing ethnic codes and philosophies of art, is also equally apparent in the different geographical settings of the various scenes. From the very beginning of their relationship, the Park Avenue patroness tries to alienate Oceola from Harlem: "I must get her out of Harlem at once. I believe it's worse than Chinatown." (105) Her efforts finally result in Oceola's moving to Greenwich Village, and then for two years' study to Paris. The effects of her trainig in classical music are not, however, as sublimating as Mrs. Ellsworth had hoped. Returning from Paris, Oceola is determined more firmly than ever not to give up the black musical tradition. This is especially shown in her decision to move back to Harlem: "I've been away from my own people so long, I want to live right in the middle of them again." (115) This symbolic rediscovery of her heritage, induced by a stay in Paris, is one of the earliest black reiterations of the Jamesian pattern. For it is in Europe that Oceola, to paraphrase a title of one of James Baldwin's essays, makes the discovery of what it means to be black.

The different settings hence express metaphorically the various stages of their relationship. The symbolic confrontation of Harlem with Greenwich Village and Paris ultimately demonstrates that the conflict is again dramatized on a personal as well as cultural plane. Her return to Harlem signals the attempt to preserve her black cultural identity. Significantly enough, it is only after she has accepted her lover's proposal that Oceola at a concert in a Harlem church suddenly lives up to her own musical intentions by "not sticking to the classical items listed on the program," for now she is able to "insert one of her own variations on the spirituals." (115)

The inevitable separation of Oceola and Mrs. Ellsworth takes place one evening in the patroness' apartment, where Oceola had come to play for the last time "with the techniques for which Mrs. Ellsworth had paid." (118) Again, the conflict is described in the contrasting images that are representative of the two different cultural spheres. Dora Ellsworth's position is almost entirely linked with exquisite, though lifeless antique objects, evoking the impression of her emotional sterility and deadness. These objects, acting as objective correlatives of her emotional state, cannot be reconciled with life. The vital, life-promising nature of Oceola's music, which grew "into an earth-throbbing rhythm that shook the lilies in the Persian vases of Mrs. Ellsworth's music room," (119) ultimately exposes her limited point of view and suggests the final triumph, as it were, of black over white culture.

Because of her limited point of view, Dora Ellsworth remains unchanged. Even though she is dressed at the end in the same black velvet that Oceola used to wear, Emanuel's reading this as "a symbolic fusion of herself and her protegée"[30] seems to be an unwarranted conjecture. Rather, the story's ending calls for a reading which views the two unreconciled positions as a re-emphasis of "the theme of cultural dualism which is basic to the Harlem Renaissance"[31] and Hughes' position therein.

Oceola's self-conscious revolt against her patroness, which has strong autobiographical parallels,[32] underlines historically the black's incipient ethnic assertion, his pride in his race and the rediscovery of his cultural heritage. Within this cultural context, The Blues I'm Playing may be considered a twofold satire. One of its objectives, of course, is to unmask the hypocrisy of white patronage. In addition to this, the philosophy of black cultural elitism and the 'New Negro' seems to be equally under attack. By refuting the 'high culture' of the Renaissance champions, Hughes satirizes through his fictional character those attempts to bridge the gap between the two races by means of art. For this must, as he demonstrates through Oceola, inevitably lead to servility and a loss of black identity. In contrast to Emanuel's general dictum that "Hughes as a writer cannot be explained by references to the

79

Harlem Renaissance,"[33] this particular short story echoes, both on the autobiographical and cultural plane, historical problems that were firmly rooted in this period; thus Hughes' delienation of Oceola may ultimately be conceived as a fictional representation of his own literary manifesto and the story as a satirical reaction to the Harlem Renaissance.

Within the bulk of Hughes' sixty-six published short stories, *The Blues I'm Playing* holds a unique position. In keeping with Emanuel, who classified Hughes' short fiction thematically, this story turns out to be his only genuine artist story. It marks one of Hughes' outstanding achievements in this genre and established him as a serious writer of satirical short fiction. Most stories in the collection *The Ways of White Folk* are retrospective, looking back to the 1920's and trying to unveil many of the manifestations of the Harlem Renaissance. The date of publication, however, suggests a further significance. For the year 1934 signals the end of Hughes' early phase. As Bone observed: "apart from a flurry of activity in 1941, he never made a sustained effort in the genre again. ... In point of fact, most of Hughes' significant production in the short story form falls within the chronological limits of the Harlem Renaissance."[34]

Despite favorable reviews, the first issue of *The Ways of White Folk* sold only 2500 copies.[35] This meagre success may be accounted for not only by the fact that Hughes had not yet gained, as he was to do later with his "Simple Tales," a genuine black reading audience; the commercial failure also seems to demonstrate that with the end of the Harlem Renaissance the potential white audience no longer shared a larger enthusiasm in black literary products. From a historical and socio-literary perspective, however, the stories of *The Ways of White Folk* caused a major breakthrough in paving the way for a racially unrestricted audience. By re-examining the black-white relationships of the 1920's and by unmasking the falseness of the enthusiasm of whites for the 'New Negro,' Hughes "clarified for the Negro audience their own strength and dignity and ... supplied the white audience with an explanation of how the Negro feels and what he wants."[36] Six years after the publication of this collection, Richard Wright, in a review of Hughes' autobiography *The Big Sea*, perhaps summed up the importance of the early works of Hughes best. In his eyes, Hughes, on account of his extensive publications, had served as a "cultural ambassador for the case of the blacks."[37]

NOTES

1. According to the publisher Alfred A. Knopf, Van Vechten used to be his sole advisor on black literature. Cf. Alfred A. Knopf, "Reminiscences of Hergesheimer, Van Vechten and Mencken," *Yale University Library Gazette*, 24 (April, 1950), 150-157.
2. Donald C. Dickinson, *A Bio-Bibliography of Langston Hughes 1902-1967* (Hamden, Conn., 1972), p. 25.
3. Nathan Irvin Huggins, *Harlem Renaissance* (Oxford/New York, 1971), p. 57.
4. Alain Locke, "The New Negro," in Abraham Chapman, ed., *Black Voices: An Anthology of Afro-American Literature* (New York, 1968), p. 523.
5. *Ibid.*, p. 518.
6. Charles S. Johnson, "The Negro Renaissance and its Significance," in Rayford Logan *et.al.*, edd., *The New Negro Thirty Years Afterward* (Washington, D.C., 1955), p. 83.
7. Langston Hughes, "The Negro Artist and the Racial Mountain," *The Nation* (July 23, 1926), reprinted in John A. Williams, ed., *Amistad 1: Writings on Black History and Culture* (New York, 1970), p. 304.
8. Langston Hughes, *The Big Sea* (New York, 1963), pp. 267-268.
9. See James A. Emanuel, "The Literary Experiments of Langston Hughes," in Therman B. O'Daniel, ed., *Langston Hughes Black Genius: A Critical Evaluation* (New York, 1971), 171-182.
10. Bernhard Ostendorf, "Black Poetry, Blues, and Folklore: Double Consciousness in Afro-American Oral Culture," *Amerikastudien*, 20 (1975), 250.
11. Blyden Jackson, "A Word about Simple," in Therman B. O'Daniel, ed., *Langston Hughes Black Genius*, p. 110.
12. Langston Hughes, *I Wonder As I Wander: An Autobiographical Journey* (New York, 1956), p. 5.
13. Margaret Perry, *Silence To The Drums: A Survey of the Literature of the Harlem Renaissance* (Westport, Conn., 1976), p. 45.
14. Hughes, *I Wonder As I Wander*, p. 213.
15. Robert Bone, *Down Home: A History of Afro-American Short Fiction from its Beginning to the End of the Harlem Renaissance* (New York, 1975), p. 247.
16. This fact is reported by Donald C. Dickinson, *A Bio-Bibliography of Langston Hughes*, pp. 75-76.

17. Hughes, *I Wonder As I Wander*, p. 5.

18. D.H. Lawrence, "The Lovely Lady," *Love Among The Haystacks And Other Stories* (Harmondsworth, 1960), p. 49.

19. *Ibid.*

20. Kingsley Widmer, *The Art of Perversity: D.H. Lawrence's Shorter Fiction* (Seattle, 1962), p. 96.

21. Langston Hughes, "The Blues I'm Playing," *The Ways of White Folk* (New York, 1971), pp. 96-97 (All page numbers in parenthesis refer to this Vintage edition).

22. Hughes, *The Big Sea*, p. 325.

23. Perry, *Silence To The Drums*, p. 14.

24. Bone, *Down Home*, p. 253.

25. W.E.B. DuBois, "Van Vechten's 'Nigger Heaven,' " *The Crisis* (1926), reprinted in Arthur P. Davis and Michael W. Peplow, edd., *The New Negro Renaissance: An Anthology* (New York, 1975), p. 193; contemporary criticism has particularly been voiced by Addison Gayle, Jr., *The Way Of The New World: The Black Novel In America* (Garden City, 1976), pp. 104-110.

26. As Hughes recalls in his first autobiography: "In his novel Mr. Van Vechten presents many of the problems of the Negroes of Harlem, and he writes of the people of culture as well as the people of the night clubs. He presents the problem of a young Negro novelist faced with the discriminations of the white editorial offices. And he writes sympathetically and amusingly and well about a whole rainbow of life above 110th street that had never before been put into the color of words." *The Big Sea*, p. 271.

27. Ralph Ellison, "Richard Wright's Blues," *Shadow & Act* (London, 1967), pp. 78-79.

28. Ralph Ellison, "The Art of Fiction: An Interview," *Shadow & Act*, p. 172.

29. Bone, *Down Home*, p. 253.

30. James A. Emanuel, *Langston Hughes* (New York, 1967), p. 142.

31. Bone, *Down Home*, p. 257.

32. Besides those already mentioned, note the incident where Hughes throws all his books into the sea, thus symbolically freeing himself from his 'white' past. *The Big Sea*, pp. 3-4.

33. Emanuel, *Langston Hughes*, p. 30.

34. Bone, *Down Home*, p. 256.

35. This figure is given by Donald C. Dickinson, *A Bio-Bibliography of Langston Hughes*, p. 130.

36. *Ibid.*, p. 115.

37. Richard Wright, "Review of 'The Big Sea,' " *New Republic*, 53 (October 28, 1940), 600.

BIBLIOGRAPHY

Short story collections:
>   *The Ways of White Folk*. New York, 1934.
>   *Laughing to Keep From Crying*. New York, 1952.
>   *Something in Common and Other Stories*. New York, 1963.

The most comprehensive information on Hughes' primary works and on secondary sources devoted to him can be found in:

>   Therman B. O'Daniel, "Langston Hughes: A Selected Classified Bibliography," in O'Daniel, ed., *Langston Hughes Black Genius: A Critical Evaluation*. New York, 1971.
>   Donald C. Dickinson, *A Bio-Bibliography of Langston Hughes 1902-1967*. Hamden, Conn., 1972.

Maureen Liston

CHESTER HIMES
A NIGGER
(1937)

Chester Himes is perhaps best known as the creator of Grave Digger and Coffin Ed. That he has also written and published short stories, a play, essays, novels other than detective, and a two-volume autobiography is little known, save to Black writers and Black literature scholars. During his writing career — which spans some forty-plus years — Himes has published "six major novels";[1] some twenty-two short stories in periodicals; a series of detective novels; essays on a variety of subjects; and a collection including a film scenario as well as short stories and essays, some of which had been printed earlier in *Esquire, Coronet, Crisis, Opportunity* and *Negro Study.*

Born 29 July 1909 in Jefferson City, Missouri, Chester Himes was the youngest of three sons. His mother was an octoroon; his father, Professor Joseph Sandy Himes — teacher at the Lincoln Institute, a Negro college — was "a short black man with bowed legs, a perfect ellipsoidal skull, and an Arabic face with a big hooked nose."[2] Several years after Chester's birth, the family moved to Mississippi, where Professor Himes became head of Alcorn A & M's Mechanical Department. Around 1917 Chester Himes also spent a year in Augusta, Georgia, when his mother taught at the Haines Institute.

Chester and his brother Joe were educated at home until 1917; both children were better educated than most blacks of the same age. In 1921, when Prof. Himes went to Branch Normal College, Pine Bluff, Arkansas, Joe and Chester enrolled in the college, later to be known as Arkansas A & M. About a year later, Joe was blinded by a chemistry explosion in a school demonstration; the family returned to St. Louis in order to get better treatment for him. This episode played an important role in Chester's development and he devoted several long sections in the first volume of his autobiography to his closest brother's accident, subsequent reeducation and success. In 1923 or 1924, motivated by unem-

85

ployment, racial inequality, and the inability of the Barnes Hospital to further help Joe, Prof. Himes moved his family to Cleveland, Ohio, where he had relatives.

In January of 1926, due to a clerical error, Chester Himes was awarded his high school diploma. In order to earn money for college, he took a job as busboy at Wade Park Manor, where malfunctioning elevator doors caused him to fall about forty feet down an empty elevator shaft; the result was three broken vertebrae, a broken jaw, shattered teeth, a broken left arm and a ruptured urethral canal. Hospital expenses were paid by the Ohio State Industrial Commission, as well as a pension.

In September 1926 Himes entered Ohio State University in Columbus. He quickly tired of university, and by the end of the second quarter was allowed "to withdraw for reasons of 'ill health'" (Himes, p. 31). On his return to Cleveland, he was introduced to gambling and, in 1928, participated in his first burglary. Himes' family was breaking up — his parents' quarrels, which had been going on for years, were becoming more violent — and he seemed to seek security and relief from emotional pressures in the gambling halls, with prostitutes, and in burglary. "I discovered that I had become very violent," writes Himes in his *Autobiography* (p. 47); by the end of 1928 he had been arrested in Chicago for first-degree armed robbery. Sentenced to twenty-to-twenty-five years of hard labor, Himes served only seven-and-a-half years of his sentence, in the Ohio State Penitentiary; here he began to write.

In 1936 Himes married his first wife, Jean, in Cleveland. He wrote a few short stories, and wrote for the WPA and the Ohio Writers' Project. Sometime after the beginning of the Second World War, perhaps in 1940, Himes and his wife travelled by Greyhound to Los Angeles. (*If He Hollers Let Him Go* concerns this period in his life.) Four years later he travelled east to New York City.

The next two years were spent in California and on the East Coast, Himes going from job to job, supported mostly by his wife. *Lonely Crusade* was published in 1947 and, with the total rejection of the book, a five-year-long writer's block set in. By 1952 Himes' marriage to Jean had broken up, and in 1953 he finally left America for France. The last twenty years have been spent mostly in Europe — with infrequent trips to the United States — mainly in France and in Spain; Himes and his second wife, Lesley, travel a lot, frequently to escape other "expatriate" black writers, and have recently completed a villa in Alicante, Spain.

These biographical facts are of importance for a writer such as Chester Himes, especially since Robert Bone assigns him to the "Wright School,"[3] a 1940's "urban realism" movement.[4] The following quote explains the need for autobiographical content in Himes' writings and the role of the Wright School.

> For the Wright School, literature is an emotional catharsis — a means of dispelling the inner tensions of race. Their novels often amount to a prolonged cry of anguish and despair. Too close to their material, feeling it too intensely, these novelists lack a sense of form and of thematic line. With rare exceptions, their style consists of a brutal realism, devoid of any love, or even respect, for words. Their characterization is essentially sociological, but it may contain a greater attempt at psychological depth than is usually associated with the naturalistic novel. Their principal theme, reminiscent of Sherwood Anderson, is how the American caste system breeds "grotesques." The white audience, on perceiving its responsibility for the plight of the protagonist, is expected to alter its attitude toward race.[5]

Bone also comments that "many of these authors served their literary apprenticeship as newspaper writers."[6]

Wright was the first black to approach the situation of the urban Black naturalistically.[7] The Wright School movement followed a decade after the social protest expressed most frequently in the American novel in the Depression years. Not only a journalist, "Himes, like Wright, is a product of the Great Depression, of association with the labor movement, the Federal Writers' Project, and the Communist Party."[8] Whitlow comments that "Most of the writers of the movement are mediocre."[9] John A. Williams, however, states that "Himes is perhaps the single greatest naturalistic American writer living today."[10]

Himes' "six major novels" are as follows: *If He Hollers Let Him Go* (1945); *Lonely Crusade* (1947); *The Third Generation* (1954); *The Primitive* (1955); *Cast the First Stone* (1952), and *Pinktoes* (1961/62 and 1965).[11] In 1966 Himes wrote that "the Negro novelist, more than any other, is faced with this necessity [to find justification for existence]. He must discover from his experiences the truth of his oppressed existence in terms that will provide some meaning to his life. Why he is here; why he continues to live. In fact, this writer's subject matter is in reality a Negro's search for truth."[12] The first two novels — both highly autobiographical — deal with race, sex, and the labor movement of the 1940's. (In Volume 1, Book 1, Section 2 of *The Quality of Hurt*, he writes about the composition and background of these two books.) The next three novels advance along the same lines: autobiographical, racial, sexual. Himes writes not only of the place of the Black in American (western) society, but of humanity in a diseased world. Of the six, only *Pinktoes* has had any real commercial succes.

Pinktoes, which was first published in Paris as *Mamie Mason*, is a sometimes successful satire on race. Compared to the other "serious" novels, it is the least well-written but also the least violent. It is at times funny, this story of an up-and-coming black Harlem hostess, whose sexual adventures are probably the selling point of the book. (Himes seems to have added sexual scenes for the American edition of the book; he claims the publishers asked for more explicitness.)[13]

Against these novels can be set the nine more successful — and much more readable — "detective" novels. Strangely enough, all but one of the nine were first published in France, in French: the first, *La Reine des Pommes* (Série Noire-Gallimard, 1957), won the *Prix du Roman Policier* in 1958 and appeared in the United States as *For Love of Immabelle* in 1959; the latest, *Blind Man with a Pistol*, was published in 1969.

Coffin Ed Smith and Gravedigger Jones, the "heroes" of the novels, are two black cops in Harlem. They are tough, violent, hated, feared, and beaten-up by the blacks among whom they work. They twist the law to keep the law, sometimes even committing crimes to catch the bad guy. The novels are all set in Harlem, and, with the possible exception of *Blind Man with a Pistol*, are relatively easy to read. Himes captures in his prose the spirit of Harlem — the violence, the brutality, the simple joys, the sexuality .... It is in these books, not in his more serious attempts as a writer, that his talent is revealed.[14] Descriptions of street-corner preachers, lesbian strippers, transvestite "sisters," sleazy prostitutes — descriptions of the street, with its thousands of different characters and the ever-present possibility for violence — jerk and jive into real life. The dialogue is a mixture of Black English, underground slang, dope colloquialisms, black dialects, and patois. Even the smallest details are not too small for Himes: pages are devoted, for example, to the different eating places and to the different kinds of food in Harlem. It is a terrible world Himes is presenting, filled with sex and violence, and the energy of Harlem life is caught on every page. This crazy life which is often out of control is controlled by Himes: the plots work; each mad incident somehow fits into the story being unfolded, each mystery is somehow solved, each bad guy is caught, or killed, or maimed, or punished. The violence which is always there suddenly abrupts into blood, and the blood flows until somehow the book — this one incident being related, not the violence and not Harlem — comes to an end. As Himes would say, the books are "titillating."[15]

It is in this setting that one can approach the short stories. In Himes' "Foreword" to *Black on Black* he writes the following:

These writings are admittedly chauvinistic. You will conclude if you read them that BLACK PROTEST and BLACK HETEROSEXUALITY are my two chief obsessions.

And you will be right. I am a sensualist, I love beautiful people, I have SOUL. At the same time I am extremely sensitive to all the humiliations and preconceptions Black Americans are heir to. But I think my talent is sufficient to render these chauvinistic writings interesting, or at least provoking. ...
. . . .
With the exception of "Tang," which I wrote in Alicante in 1967 when my thoughts had concentrated on a BLACK REVOLUTION, I wrote the first nine short stories during the Depression of the nineteen thirties and the first years of the Second World War.

. . . .
I wrote the last short story, "Prediction," in Alicante in 1969 after I had become firmly convinced that the only chance Black Americans had of attaining justive and equality in the United States of America was by violence.[16]

Many of the stories appear in varied forms in the detective novels, as do many of Himes' early characters.[17] The preacher in "Pork Chop Paradise" (1938) appears in some form in every Harlem novel; in the short story the preacher is recognized as God because he feeds his people with pork chops. In the novels he uses other ploys to make money or to become God, but he is still the preacher who "carried his pulpit about in his hand and set it upon street corners and wrestled with the sin of the world as ardently as if he, himself, had been forever sinless" (p. 165).

He rocked his congregations, he scared them, he startled them if by nothing else except his colossal ignorance, he browbeat them, he lulled them, he caressed them. He made hardened convicts want to shout, he made gambling addicts repent and give away their ill-gotten gains and stay away from the games for two or three whole days. He played upon people's emotions. His voice was like a throbbing tom-tom, creeping into a person's mind like an insidious drug, blasting the wits out of the witty and filling the hearts of the witless with visions of everlasting bounty.

It had an indescribable range, sliding through octaves with the ease of a master organ. It was like a journey on a scenic railway, dropping from notes as clear and high as Satchmo ever hit on his golden trumpet, like the sudden, startling dive of a pursuit plane, to the reverberating roar of heavy artillery. You could see hell, in all its lurid fury, following in its wake, and then with as abrupt a change the voice took you to green pastures lush with manna. (p. 164)

In "Pork Chop Paradise" Himes explores the personality of "an illiterate black man" (p. 161); in "Headwaiter" (1938; pp. 144-60) that of a black headwaiter willing to do anything to please the white customers; in "Da-Da-Dee" (1948, pp. 267-74) a drunken writer. "To the Negro writer who would plumb the depth of the Negro personality, there is no question of whether Negroes hate white people — but how does this hatred affect the Negro's personality? How much of himself is destroyed by this necessity to hate those who oppress him? Certainly hate is a destructive emotion. In the case of the Negro, hate is doubly destructive. The American Negro experiences two forms of hate. He hates first his oppressor, and then because he lives in constant fear of this hatred being discovered, he hates himself — because of this fear."[18] These sentences, written in 1966, could be a description of Himes' "A Nigger," written in 1937.

There are autobiographical elements in "Nigger": the setting, for example, is Cleveland, Ohio, probably sometime between 1935 and 1937. Joe Wolf, a writer between 24 and 26 years old, goes to visit his mistress Fay after her common-law husband leaves for the afternoon. Mr. Shelton, Fay's white John, appears on the scene, and Joe is forced to hide in the clothes closet. As Mr. Shelton leaves, he opens the closet door by mistake; Joe thinks he has been seen and, when Fay returns to the room, erupts into violence. After he escapes to his room, eight blocks away, Joe realizes he is an Uncle Tom.

The most interesting elements of "A Nigger" are neither the

simple plot line nor the narrative techniques employed but the main character's reactions to the situation. Fay is "kept by a rich white John out of Shaker Heights, and living with a fine-looking, hard-working, tall yellow boy on the side who dumped his pay-check to her as regular as it came, then cheating on them both with this broke, ragged lunger who claimed he was some kind of writer or poet or something" (p. 125). Himes' ironic view of what is possibly a recreation of himself continues throughout the piece, communicated not only through the narrator's retelling of the events but also through Joe's interpretation of what occurs. Joe's first reaction, in "the cluttered closet" (p. 126), is "laughingly, *what a bitch!*" (p. 126). Mr. Shelton's voice is "smug and con-descendingly possessive," and Joe thinks *"why, you old bastard"* (p. 126). Mr. Shelton is going East, and wants to leave enough money for Fay, who secretly uses it to support Joe, thus making him indirectly dependent on Mr. Shelton.

Joe begins to get angry when he hears Mr. Shelton insisting on the same respect for Mrs. Shelton that Fay demands from Joe for Mr. Shelton. The dialogue between the John and Fay is a sugary parody of a lovers' dialogue. While Mr. Shelton complains about Roosevelt, Joe is distracted by his thoughts on *"old sons of a bitches like this ....* (p. 127). When he again listens, Fay is obvious-ly trying to get Mr. Shelton to make love to her:

What in the hell is she trying to do? But Joe was too proud to bend down to the keyhole to see for himself. He stood sweating in the center of the closet between the two racks of close-packed garments bought for her by *Mr. Shelton* – he thought of him as *Mr. Shelton* without being aware of it – his stockinged feet cramped and uncomfortable among the scatter of shoes, suddenly overcome with the sense of having sold his pride, his whole manhood, for a whore's handout, no better than the pimps down on Central Avenue, only cheaper – so damn much cheaper. One flicker of light came through the keyhole to which he was too proud, even, to bend down and look at the man who had controlled his eating for the past five weeks, and now at this moment was controlling his movement and emotions and even his soul. Too proud to look even while accepting the position, as if not looking would lessen the actuality; would make it more possible to believe he hadn't accepted it. Sweat trickled down his face and neck and legs and body like crawling lice, and the mixture of the scent of the twelve bottles of perfume she kept on her dresser like a stack of thou-sand-dollar bills, along with the sharp musk scent of her body, stale shoe smell and underarm odor, in the dense sticky closeness, brought a sickish

91

taste to his mouth ... (p. 128).

At the same time, Joe tries to maintain an artistic distance from the situation: *"If I can only get it funny*, he thought."

> He tried to get far enough away from it to see it like it was. The guy was just another square. Just like all the other white squares he'd seen being debased by Negro women after their sex had gone from their bodies into their minds, no longer even able to give or receive any vestige of satisfaction from younger women of their own race, their wives long past giving or requiring. Turning to Negro women because in them they saw only the black image of flesh, the organ itself, like beautiful bronze statues endowed with motion, flesh and blood, instinct and passion, but possessing no mind to condemn, no soul to be outraged, most of all no power to judge or accuse, before whom the spirit of exhausted sex could creep and crawl and expose its ugly nakedness without embarrassment or restraint (p. 129).

Joe remembers an incident which occurred in 1928, an incident which was at the time funny. He had been a voyeur when a black prostitute had been paid to debase a white man. "But it wasn't funny now. He couldn't get it funny. The fact was, he, Joe Wolf, had been maneuvered by a whore into a spot too low for a dog" (p. 130). As Himes became aware in the 1920's of his growing violence, Joe becomes aware of his, and forms a garrote out of a hanger. "His breath oozed out and with it his determination — *God knows, I don't want to kill them*. But he knew that he would; he always did every crazy thing he knew he shouldn't do" (p. 130).

  The closet door opens and "Joe blinked into the light, and for one breathless instant he stared straight into the small blue sardonic eyes of a stout bald-headed white man with a fringe of gray hair and a putty vein-laced face" (p. 130). After Mr. Shelton leaves, Joe realizes: "All of a sudden it hit him that *Mr. Shelton* had opened the door deliberately, knowing he was there, and after having satisfied himself that he was right, had refused to acknowledge Joe's existence" (p. 131). *"Why he had not only refused to recognize him as a rival, not even as an intruder; why, the son of a bitch looked at him as if he was another garment he had bought for her*. It was the first time he had ever felt the absolute refusal of recognition" (p. 131). Fay's "Suppose he did see you — so what? He didn't let it make any difference" (p. 131) drives Joe to violence; he lashes out at her with the wire. *"Trying to make him accept it!*

The man refused to even acknowledge his existence. And she wanted him to accept it!" (p. 131). His rage disappears when the landlady shoots at him with a .38, and he flees to his boarding house.

> ... deeper than his resentment was his shame. The fact was he had kept standing there, taking it, even after he could no longer tell himself that it was a joke, a trim on a sucker, just so he could keep on eating off the bitch and people wouldn't know just how hard up he really was. Just to keep on putting up a cheap front among the riffraff on Cedar Street, just to keep from having to go back to his aunt's and eat crow, had become more important to him than his innate pride, his manhood, his honor. Uncle Tomism, acceptance, toadying – all there in its most rugged form. One way to be a nigger. Other Negroes did it other ways – he did it the hard way. The same result – *a nigger* (p. 132).

It is never ascertained whether or not Mr. Shelton saw Joe. In any case, it is this probability that drives Joe to action. "He stood there, unable to breathe, feeling as foolish and idiotic as a hungry man leaving a cathouse where he'd spent his last two bucks. Then rage scalded him from tip to toe. He flung open the door to spring into the room, slipped on a shoe and went sprawling, the wire garrote cutting a blister across the back of the fingers of his left hand" (p. 130). As Joe Wolf has tried to "get it funny," Himes presents a potentially slapstick scene less the irony of which is lost in the pathos. Joe's leap from the closet in which he has been imprisoned leads not into freedom but into a more existential confinement where he is both prisoner and jailer. The realization that he too is a "nigger" shames him; he wants "to just crawl away somewhere and die" (p. 132). His inability to act against oppression places him in the same position as the other blacks he knows. Keith Richards, the protagonist of "All God's Chillun Got Pride" (1944; pp. 239-46), becomes proud enough to react against being a nigger and ends up in a guardhouse. Joe Wolf is incapable of overcoming his oppression and his fear.

Joe's interior monlogues followed by a short but intense burst of violence make the ending somewhat anticlimatic. The sudden activity juxtaposed with Joe's final discovery deprive the truth of having the impact it deserves. The ineffectuality stems not from Himes' philosophy – he had already discovered his potential for violence – but from the way in which he tries to handle the theme. Joe's discovery of his imprisonment would have been much more powerful if he had not burst from the closet, taken a pratfall, and attacked Fay and Miss Lou.

"A Nigger" is perhaps most interesting as a psychological study and as an introduction to many of Himes' major themes: Uncle Tomism, violence, race, manhood. The elements of social protest, emotionalism, sociological and psychological characterization, and intensity are shared by the other members of the Wright School. And the reader, "on perceiving its responsibility for the plight of the protagonist, is expected to alter its attitude toward race."

The idea of "nigger" is developed well through the ruminations of Joe Wolf. But as a short story, just like all of Himes' short stories, "A Nigger" is a lightweight. Himes' ideas towards violence seem to constantly lead him towards some kind of writer's block; since 1969 he has published the collection *Black on Black* and his two-volume autobiography, but no fiction. As Margolies notes:

> There can be little question that the tone of Himes's work has changed since his departure for Europe. As he himself noted he can no longer bring himself to write protest novels. Which is not to say that any of Himes's intensely bitter racial feelings have waned. Perhaps the opposite is true. His years abroad have lent him time to brood about the injustices, the tragedy of it all .... And if we read these expatriate works correctly we see that, if anything, Himes's European perspective has left him even more pessimistic ....[19]

The violence which runs throughout *Blind Man with a Pistol*, his last published novel, and "Prediction" (1969; pp. 281-87), his last published short story, has been wholesale, random, futile; Himes now believes "that only organized violence on the order of Viet Cong violence can effect social change."[20] His pessimism and brooding — what is perhaps still hate — are not creative but, as Himes himself realized a decade ago, "destructive" emotions.

Himes will be 68 this year. It can only be assumed that the life he has led — or has been forced to lead — has finally destroyed whatever fictive powers he ever possessed. Perhaps Chester Himes has been exploited; the ideology he has adopted to combat this exploitation has led to an impasse in his creative powers. Most likely the evaluation of his writing will agree with Bone's criticism of *If He Hollers Let Him Go* as "an impressive failure" and with Margolies' limited view that the detective novels are "some of his best prose."[21]

1. Edward Margolies, *Native Sons: A Critical Study of Twentieth-Century Black American Authors* (New York, 1968), p. 87.
2. Chester Himes, *The Quality of Hurt: The Autobiography of Chester Himes* (London, 1972), p. 5.
3. Robert Bone, *The Negro Novel in America* (New Haven, 1965), p. 157.
4. Roger Whitlow, *Black American Literature: A Critical History* (Chicago, 1973), p. 115.
5. Bone, p. 158.
6. *Ibid.*, p. 157.
7. *Ibid.*
8. Bone, p. 173.
9. Whitlow, p. 117.
10. John A. Williams, "My Man Himes," in *Amistad 1* (New York, 1970), p. 27.
11. *A Case of Rape*, published only in French, is a novel virtually unknown to the American reading public.
12. Chester Himes, "Dilemma of the Negro Novelist in the United States," in John A. Williams, ed., *Beyond the Angry Black* (New York, 1966), pp. 74-75.
13. Edward Margolies, "Experiences of the Black Expatriate Writer: Chester Himes," *College Language Association Journal*, 15 (1972), 426.
14. "In certain respects I think Himes's works about a couple of hardboiled detectives represents some of his best prose. Possibly because he thought he was writing potboilers, possibly because he could relax more within the framework of the detective genre, writing for a French audience about the kind of life he knew very well." Margolies, p. 426. Himes claims he started writing detective fiction because he needed the money. See Williams, p. 32.
15. "Titillating,:: "one of Himes' favorite words in describing the effect black people have on white people." Williams, p. 28.
16. Chester Himes, "Foreword," *Black on Black: Baby Sister and Selected Writings* (New York, 1973), pp. 7-8. Further references to this volume will appear in the text.
17. In response to Williams' question concerning Himes' memory of detail:
> Well, some of it comes from memory; and then I began writing these series [Série Noire] because I realized that I was a black American, and there's no way of escaping forty some odd years of experience, so I would put it to use in writing, which I had been doing anyway ....
> Well, then, I went back — as a matter of fact, it's like a sort of pure homesickness — I went back, I was very happy, I was living there, and it's true. I began creating also all the black scenes of my memory and my actual knowledge. I was very happy writing these detective stories, especially the first one, when I began it. I wrote those stories with more

pleasure than I wrote any of the other stories. And then when I got to the end and started my detective shooting at some white people, I was the happiest.
Williams, pp. 49-50.

18. Himes, "Dilemma of the Negro Novelist," pp. 78-79.
19. Margolies, pp. 426-27.
20. *Ibid.* Margolies also refers to an interview with Himes "granted to Michel Fabre on June 12, 1970 and then edited and translated into French for *Le Monde*." P. 426, footnote 6.
21. Bone, p. 173; Margolies, p. 426.

PRIMARY SOURCES

See Michel Fabre's "Chester Himes' Published Works: A Tentative Check List" in *Black World*, 21 (March 1972), 76-78, for a complete listing.

Fuller, Hoyt W. "Traveler on the Long, Rough, Lonely Old Road: An Interview with Chester Himes." *Black World*, 21 (March 1972), 4-22, 87-98.

Himes, Chester. *Black on Black: Baby Sister and Selected Writings.* New York, 1973.

— "Dilemma of the Negro Novelist in the United States," *Beyond the Angry Black*. Ed. John A. Williams. New York, 1966.

— *My Life of Absurdity: The Autobiography of Chester Himes.* Volume 2. New York, 1977.

— *The Quality of Hurt: The Autobiography of Chester Himes.* Volume 1. London, 1973.

Williams, John A. "My Man Himes: An Interview with Chester Himes," *Amistad 1*. Ed. John A. Williams and Charles F. Harris. New York, 1970. pp. 25-93.

SECONDARY SOURCES

Becker, Jens-Peter. " 'To Tell It Like It Is': Chester Himes." In *Sherlock Holmes and Co.: Essays zur englischen und amerikanischen Detektivliteratur.* München, 1975.

Bone, Robert. *Negro Novel in America.* New Haven, 1965.

Fabre, Michel. "*A Case of Rape.*" *Black World*, 21 (March 1972), 39-48.

Lundquist, James. *Chester Himes.* New York, 1976.

Margolies, Edward. "Experiences of the Black Expatriate Writer: Chester Himes." *College Language Association Journal*, 15 (1972).

—— "Race and Sex: The Novels of Chester Himes." In *Native Sons: A Critical Study of Twentieth-Century Black American Authors*. Philadelphia, 1968.

Milliken, Stephen F. *Chester Himes: A Critical Appraisal*. Columbia, 1977.

Reed, Ishmael. "Chester Himes: Writer." *Black World*, 21 (March 1972), 24-38, 83-86.

Whitlow, Roger. *Black American Literature: A Critical History*. Chicago, 1973.

Wolfgang Karrer

RICHARD WRIGHT
FIRE AND CLOUD
(1938)

The works of Richard Wright (1908-60) roughly belong to three different periods: the early communist phase till 1940, the existential (and anti-communist) phase to 1954, and the late civil-rights phase after the Supreme Court decision on desegregation. This division partly coincides with the important turning points in his life: the poverty and discrimination he experienced in Mississippi and Chicago during the 30's; his status as the first bestselling black writer after the success of his *Native Son* in 1940, and his expatriate life in Paris since 1947, surrounded by Sartre's friends and relative prosperity.[1]

Fire and Cloud belongs to the early communist phase. It was a prize winning entry in *Story, The Magazine of the Short Story* in 1938 and won Wright a contract with Harper to publish in the same year *Uncle Tom's Children. Four Novellas*, one of which is *Fire and Cloud*.[2] Wright joined the Communist Party in 1932 and was expelled in 1944.[3] *Fire and Cloud* is an example of proletarian realism as proposed by the party and raises interesting aesthetic and political problems in adapting the proletarian model of black writing, especially the problem of black speech in black writing and of finding a black audience.

The Great Depression in the 30's radicalized many American writers, and the Communist Party devised two main strategies to win over intellectuals: the use of *The New Masses*, a magazine, as a critical organ and stage for proletarian writing and the organization of writers in John Reed Clubs.[4]

In *The New Masses* (1930) the leading Marxist critic Michael Gold outlined the objectives of "proletarian realism":[5]

1. Skilful techniques using the Hemingway model.
2. Real conflicts of men and women as a theme.
3. Social themes serving a purpose.
4. Simplicity of style.
5. Proletarian instead of decadent bourgeois milieu.

6. Swift action — cinema in words.
7. Revolutionary élan instead of pessimism.
8. Scientific analysis of thought and feeling.
9. Real world instead of melodrama.

Wright began to write and publish after joining the Chicago John Reed Club where the ideas of proletarian realism seem to have reached him. When the party dissolved the John Reed Clubs in 1935 to form a League of American Writers in accord with the new Popular Front strategy — a broad, mass-based (not only proletarian) front against fascism and war — Wright went along with the new policy. His position is reflected in *Blueprint for Negro Writing* (1937).

Wright's *Blueprint* is an adaptation of proletarian realism for the black writer:[6]
1. Black writers so far have represented "the voice of the educated Negro pleading with white America for justice."
2. Black writers have failed to write for blacks.
3. Writings for blacks have to deal with their culture "centered around the Church and the folklore of the Negro people."
4. The writer has to use the ideology of his readers (in this case black nationalism) to lead them to a larger vision.
5. "It is through a Marxist conception of reality and society that the maximum degree of freedom in thought and feeling can be gained for the Negro writer."
6. After Marxism has laid bare "the skeleton of society," the writer should aim for a complex simplicity.
7. "Perspective is that part of a poem, novel, or play which a writer never puts directly upon paper."
8. The theme has to embody the *whole* black culture.
9. Black and white writers have to work together.

Wright's careful revisions in 4, 6, and 7 show his awareness of narrowing doctrinaire tendencies of Zhdanovism in the Communist Party. His use of "black people" instead of "black workers" and point 9 show influence of the Popular Front line.

Fire and Cloud is the last of the four novellas in *Uncle Tom's Children*. All of them were written around the time the *Blueprint* was published. More than a collection of stories *Uncle Tom's Children* was originally planned as a novel and then changed to "a series of short stories, all having similar treatment, theme and technical handling."[7] All stories are subjected to a similar treatment by adopting the novelistic convention of chapters, probably the reason why Wright prefers to call them novellas or long stories. The technical handling is modelled on Hemingway; less obviously, the thematic development also owes something to *In Our Time* (1925) in tracing a growing awareness of the protagonists through different ages of life. Giles characterizes the thematic progression in the enlarged edition *Uncle Tom's Children, five long stories* (1940) as follows:

> There is Big Boy the youth who runs, then Mann the adult who runs, then Silas who meets a heroic but lonely death, then Taylor the minister who will not openly endorse Marxism but who acts out its implications, and finally there is Sue who dies a martyred convert to Communism and thus triumphs over all the forces which have limited the characters in the first four stories.[8]

That the first edition (1938) ends with *Fire and Cloud* suggests the importance of that story and its last line *"Freedom belongs t the strong,"* but the original four stories do not fully develop the implication of Communism as the way to this freedom.

In Wright's own words:

> The fourth story in the book came about as a desire on my part to try to depict in dramatic fashion the relationship between the leaders of both races. Of course, among the Negro people, the preacher is the acknowledged leader. The preacher speaks for the people, he faces other races, he carries their cases to 'court,' and presents their pleas, and returns to them with the verdict of good or ill. This position carries with it a certain prestige, and naturally, a Negro preacher would want to rear his son to be a preacher. I represented the preacher in a very crucial moment, a moment in a relief crisis, when he had to tell his starving flock that the relief people would give them no food. What happens to him, and how his character underwent a change, will be found in the fourth story 'Fire and Cloud.'

The time is roughly the 1930's (the Great Depression and the local relief programs of the New Deal); the place, a small town in the South. As in a medieval morality play (or T.S. Eliot's *Murder in the Cathedral* for that matter), Reverend Taylor's conflict about whether or not to join a Communist sponsored demonstration is externalized in various voices trying to tempt or persuade him: a church committee of poor blacks looks for his leadership; Green and Hadley, the Communist organizers, want him to sponsor the march; Mayor Bolton, the Police Chief, and the head of the

"Industrial Squad" want him to call off the march; the Deacons of the Church are militant but divided (Deacon Smith playing Judas to Taylor's Christ); six white men (possibly members of the Industrial Squad) try to whip him into obedience and prayer. Only after the whipping has brought the fire and the sign he has been waiting for, does Taylor become a true leader of his people: he stops his son Jimmy from individual violence, calms his wife's fears, and leads the discouraged Deacon Bonds, his church, and the poor whites into the successful demonstration for food relief. The moral is clear and outspoken: "All the will, all the strength, all the numbahs is in the people!" and (by implication) the people are God. Uncle Tom piety yields to social and possibly revolutionary awareness.

The story thus combines three of the stereotypes of proletarian fiction outlined by Walter Rideout:

(1) those centered about a strike; (2) those concerned with the development of an individual's class-consciousness and his conversion to Communism; (3) those dealing with the 'bottom dogs,' the lowest layers of society; and (4) those describing the decay of the middle class.[9]

The story plays minor variations on (1), (2), (3), and adds the conventional sloganized ending. It also follows Gold's objectives fairly closely and adds some of the points made in the *Blueprint*: use of black culture (church, folklore), transformation of religious ideology into a socialist view, and Marxist class analysis. All in all, it obeys a set of conventional rules. Critics have rated *Fire and Cloud* accordingly low.[10] But it is exactly its status as a blueprint story — in many ways typical for the state of the short story in the 30's — that sharpens the aesthetic and political problems about the black adaptation of proletarian realism. In particular the points made by the *Blueprint* about "complex simplicity" and "perspective" raise interesting questions.

A close look at the first fifteen lines of *Fire and Cloud* reveals three elements that add up to the complex simplicity of the story: speech, description, and thought. If we code speech as A, description as B and thought as C we get something like this:

"*A naughts a naught* ..." (A)
As he walked his eyes looked vacantly on the dusty road, and the words rolled without movement from his lips, each syllable floating softly up out of the depths of his body. (B)

"N five a figger ..." (A)

He pulled out his pocket handkerchief and mopped his brows without lessening his pace. (B)

"All fer the white man ..." (A)

He reached the top of the slope and paused, head down. (B)

"N none fer the nigger ..." (A)

His shoulders shook in half-laugh and half-shudder. He finished mopping his brow and spat, as though to rid himself of some bitter thing. He thought. (B) Thas the way its awways been! (C)

The whole story can be analyzed as a concatenation of these three elements (in fact, this fairly simple method can be applied to almost any type of fiction).[11] Certain combinations of these three elements then emerge as particularly frequent:

1. Speech with description or regular dialogue (AB) has the highest frequency. A special subtype — the cutting up of a verse, song or coherent text by inserting description (AB) as in the example above — occurs only four times in the story.

2. Description with thought or interior monologue (BC) has the second highest frequency. The possible combination AC occurs only twice in the story.

If we map these combinations into the thirteen chapters of the story, certain structures emerge. Dialogue (AB) dominates in all chapters except I and IX. This parallel between I and IX is further underlined by contrast in thought (C) and description (B). The chapters usually open with speech or description (except IV, VIII) and end in description (significant exceptions XII, XIII). The chapters follow each other "in dramatic fashion" (enter or exit a person). So the thought openings in IV and VIII follow from the descriptive endings in III and VII (BC combination).

Within the individual chapters certain structures are equally significant. The decomposition of the verse in the first lines of the story is mirrored not only in the title song in XIII but also in the prayer toward the end of VIII. The dialogue is usually uninterrupted by interior monologue but the direction of the discussion in IV, VII, VIII turns on pivotal thoughts of Taylor.

Description (B) carries (together with the final hymn) the central symbolism: the fire of the inflicted wounds is the sign Taylor has been waiting for; it leads to the "pregnant cloud" (XIII) of the marching men. The story runs from sunset (I) to sunrise (XIII). The fire is whipped into Taylor by night, the "cloud" marches by day. Description, usually preparing for thought or dramatizing dialogue, rises from static settings to individual gestures and reaches its climax in collective action (I, IX, XIII).

Thought (C) implements this symbolism through Taylor's growing awareness of the need for collective action. Taylor's thought is couched in biblical imagery of Samson, Christ and Moses who led his people out of Egyptian bondage following a pillar of fire and a cloud. In the end even God becomes an image for the people: "*Gawd ain no lie! He ain no lie! ... Freedom belongs t the strong.*" Taylor has made the first step to a fuller understanding of society but he stops one step short of Marxism. (This is probably why Wright added *Bright and Morning Star* as a fitter ending to *Uncle Tom's Children* in 1940.) Thought usually follows description and is interrupted by speech in the earlier parts, but becomes an integrated part of action in XIII (ABC instead of BC or AC).

Speech (A) finally dramatizes the "real conflict of men and women." The positions taken are fully argued; the final moral is embedded in speech and confirmed by preceding action. The fire-whipping frees Taylor's speech from social, religious or situational constraints and links it to more painful but truer levels of his thought. Underlying the superficial simplicity of the story is a fairly complex structure of elements that support the thematic progression from passive individualist meditation to collective social action.[12]

The second problem, that of perspective, can also be better understood through this structural method, if we analyze the distribution of Black English and Standard English (SE) over the three components, speech (A), description (B) and thought (C). Following the *Blueprint* and Hemingway, Wright eliminates all personal references to narrator and reader within the third person narrative. The partisan point of view and the manipulation of the reader, however, are obvious and determined by far more than the fact that the only thought reproduced is Taylor's.

Black and white speech — in accordance with realist conventions — are clearly distinguished in dialogue. Black speech dominates and is again differentiated in various situations: ritualized prayer and response (III), spontaneous discussion with blacks (VIII) and a restricted code with whites (VI), that clearly reveals the underlying social constraints. (Thus Taylor adds "suh" to his sentences, when he addresses Bolton; Bolton calls Taylor "Dan" instead of "Reverend"). The typography tends to transcribe the rich variety in emphasis, loudness and intonation of Black English. Black and white speech are transliterated without apostrophes: they are not deficient states of SE.

Thought, whether presented as direct interior monologue or indirectly reported by the narrator, is reproduced partly in Black English and partly in SE. This distinction deserves some closer scrutiny. In some passages SE reproduction of thought seems to function as a transition from description to thought through imagination as in: "For a moment an array of soft black faces hovered before his eyes. N whut kin Ah tell em?" (I). But this explanation does not account for some long passages of thought reproduced in SE (I, IX). These passages together with the central whipping scene are really the key to the point of view taken by the author and supposed to be taken by the reader of the story. The six white men torture Taylor and force him to pray. The point is ironic and crucial: obedience to white supremacy and praying "Our Father" are one and the same. The archaic language of Our Father is in extreme contrast with the description of the whipping and Taylor's genuine feeling:

> "Ooour Fffather ..."
> The whip cut hard, *whick!* pouring fire and fire again.
> "Have mercy, Lawd!" he screamed.
> "Pray, nigger! Pray like you *mean* it!"
> "... wwwhich aaaaart in hheaven ... hhhallowed bbe Tttthy nname ..."
> The whip struck, *whick!* "Ahm prayin, Mmmmistah!"

The pastoral reminiscenes in Old Testament language (I) are also false consciousness, white consciousness. Wright makes this clear by bookish capitals and abrupt shift into Black English when Taylor begins to think of the Communist position:

> ... it was that joy and will and oneness in him that God had spoken to when He had called him to preach His word, to save His black people, to lead them, to guide them, to be a shepherd to his flock. But now the whole thing was giving way, crumbling in his hands, right before his eyes. And everytime he tried to think of some way out, of some way to stop it, he saw wide grey eyes behind icily white spectacles. He mopped his brow again. Mabbe Hadley n Greens right ...

Again, in IX under the biblical phrasing of Taylor's regained consciousness, there arises a tiny inner voice that grows stronger and stronger as the fire sinks in:

> It seemed he could hear a tiny, faraway sound whispering over and over like a voice in an empty room: Ah got fever ... His back rested on a bed of fire, the imprint of leaves and grass searing him with a scalding persistence. ... The voice whispered again, this time louder: Ah gotta git home ...

Thought has now become interiorized black speech, beyond the control of those conventions that regulated Taylor's speech and thought so far. His struggle to find the right words for Jimmy and the people leads to a new freedom of speech.

If we identify the narrator with the descriptive parts of the story (B), the perspective and the final frame of reference for the reader would be white. The descriptive language is closer to Mayor Bolton's speech than to Reverend Taylor's. But the perspective of the story arises from the interplay (corroboration or denial) of the three elements and here black speech and collective song not only outweigh SE description and triumph over contaminated thought but are also born out by the descriptive parts, while Taylor's white thought is refuted by the description of his real situation. In other words, Taylor's speech and thought have to be measured against the description of his real situation, and here his white thought fails. Anticipating the problem of dual consciousness in *Native Son* the story deals with its own aesthetic problem: the adaptation of white thought to black consciousness. The black preacher — long a symbol for Uncle Tomism[13] — has freed himself from subtler chains than those of slavery. And with him the intended black audience is supposed to undergo the same purification by fire.

The contrasts in language and perspective finally point to the underlying class conflict in this anonymous Southern town of 15,000 whites and 10,000 blacks. The analysis of "the skeleton of society" is clearly Marxist with a Popular Front touch. Black and white are segregated, the Chamber of Commerce, that is, the local capitalists, use the Mayor and the police to keep control over the labor force without land (unused because of agricultural overproduction) and without food (denied by the local relief program). The coexistence of unused land and starving people is an obvious image of the contradictions of capitalism. In the past the Mayor has used the black leader Taylor against his own people with bribes of small favors. This corruption of the black middle class is analyzed

106

in the same setting in Wright's novel *The Long Dream* (1958). Racist violence and the Industrial Squad show the fascist potentialities of capitalist rule. Only a popular front of black and white people, a coalition of democratic consultation and communist organization will be able to stop fascism. Not the individual speech of the leader but the collective singing and marching unites white and black: "Ain nobody leadin us nowhere." (XIII).

In 1942 Wright called *Uncle Tom's Children* "an awfully naive mistake": "I found I had written a book which even bankers' daughters could read and weep over and feel good about."[14] The reviews had shown Wright that this study of the gradual liberation from Uncle Tom mentality had failed to reach the black audience aimed at in the *Blueprint* and had been understood by a dominantly white audience as a sequel to the melodramatic conventions of Harriet Beecher Stowe's social criticism. Not the development of a new socialist consciousness in blacks, but the plight of poor Southern blacks, not the speech or thought but the description formed the final frame of reference for the contemporary reader. Wright took the blame for this and wrote *Native Son* deliberately to shock a white audience into a new response: the killing of one of the sentimental "bankers' daughters" cut off any stereotyped response of pity for Bigger Thomas. Wright abandoned his aim to write for a black audience rooted in church and folklore. Here lay a real problem for a writer like Wright, as Sterling Brown pointed out.[15] Not many blacks read books in the 30's, the number of college educated blacks was hardly the audience aimed at in the *Blueprint*, and the problem of winning blacks for the revolution was far more difficult than Wright had thought.

If the main dilemma for the black writer in the 30's was finding his audience, part of the problem lay also in the acceptance of realist conventions. Though keenly aware of the oral character of black culture and giving black speech a dominant position in *Fire and Cloud*, Wright limits its use mainly to the accepted slots of speech and interior monologue and retains the conventional descriptive framework in SE. Though the typographical innovations bring the story closer to the real speech of black people, Wright's transposition of proletarian realism in the *Blueprint* and in *Fire and Cloud* left SE and book conventions intact. It would take another audience and another generation of writers like Ishmael Reed or Sonia Sanchez to free black speech from the constraints of the

107

realistic conventions that Wright accepted.

As any even cursory glance at an anthology shows[16] revolution, rebellion, defeat or victory of the black cause were to remain standard ingredients of the black short story. So was the realistic model of Wright's fiction. With them remained the problematic role of the black preacher as Uncle Tom or as a revolutionary leader for blacks. Though the lynchings that figure so prominently in *Uncle Tom's Children* are largely a thing of the past, life is still dangerous for black leaders. In recent years the novels by Ralph Ellison, James Baldwin, and William Melvin Kelley have dealt with this problem and John A. William's *The Man who cried I am* analyzes the murder of Malcolm X in 1965 very much along the lines of *Fire and Cloud.*

According to documents made available in 1976 Martin Luther King, before his assassination in 1967, was harassed by the FBI with tapes of bedroom conversations and anonymous letters asking him to commit suicide. This harassment was part of a secret counter intelligence program (COINTELPRO) to disrupt liberal, left, and black groups by infiltration and to discredit or intimidate their leaders.[17] Reverend Taylor's problems are far from being a thing of the past.

NOTES

1.   The standard biography is Michel Fabre, *The Unfinished Quest of Richard Wright* (New York, 1973).
2.   Harper republished the collection as a paperback in 1965 and since kept it in print. The renewed interest in *Uncle Tom's Children* is closely connected with the political events of the 60's.
3.   Daniel Aaron, "Richard Wright and the Communist Party," *New Letters*, 38 (Winter 1971), 170-81.
4.   Walter Rideout, *The Radical Novel in the United States 1900-1954: Some Interrelations of Literature and Society*, repr. (New York, 1966), 144ff.
5.   In Daniel Aaron, *Writers on the Left*, repr. (New York, 1969), 225 f.
6.   *The New Challenge* (Fall 1937), 53-65. The numbering of arguments is mine.
7.   This and the next Wright quote come from Richard Wright, "How 'Uncle Tom's Children' Grew," *The Writers Club Bulletin* [Columbia University] (May 1938), 16; 17 f.

108

8. James R. Giles, "Richard Wright's Successful Failure: A New Look at *Uncle Tom's Children," Phylon*, 34 (1973), 266. Compare Edward Margolies, *The Art of Richard Wright* (Carbondale, Ill., 1969), 61-70. For the stylistic influences of the Hemingway stories see Edwin Berry Burgum, "The Art of Richard Wright's Short Stories," *Quarterly Review of Literature*, 1 (1944), 200 ff.

9. Rideout, 171 ff. and 223.

10. For instance Margolies, 68.

11. Complications arise in some narratives with various indirect forms of reporting speech and thought. In *Fire and Cloud* every sentence can be coded without difficulty. For the whole problem see Boris A. Uspenskij, *Poetik der Komposition*, transl. G. Mayer (Frankfurt, 1975).

12. Campbell Tatham, "Vision and Value in Uncle Tom's Children," *Studies in Black Literature*, 3 (1972), 19-21 misreads this structure and distorts the story to an individualist interpretation. Tatham calls Taylors ideas about the people phony and makes Jimmy the true hero of the story.

13. Ronny E. Turner, "The Black Minister: Uncle Tom or Abolitionist," *Phylon* 34, (1973), 86-95.

14. Richard Wright, "How 'Bigger' was Born," in *Native Son*, repr. (New York, 1973), xxvii.

15. "The Negro Author and His Publisher," *Negro Quarterly*, 1 (1942), 16 ff.: "We should expect the potential Negro book-buying audience to come largely from the ranks of college graduates. In the hundred years between 1826 and 1936 there were, according to Charles S. Johnson, only 43,821 college graduates, of whom 18,918 are living. Three thousand more graduates could be expected in 1940, according to this authority ... The number of those who buy books about Negro life by Negro authors is certainly low."

16. I checked Langston Hughes' (ed.), *The Best Short Stories by Negro Writers: An Anthology from 1899 to the Present* (Boston, 1967): out of 35 short stories published after 1940, 5 deal with revolt, 3 with defeat after revolt, 7 with conversion of some kind and 13 with violence or death.

17. David Wise, "The Campaign to Destroy Martin Luther King," *New York Review of Books* (Nov. 11, 1976), 38-42 an excerpt from David Wise, *The American Police State* (New York, 1976).

BIBLIOGRAPHY

Wright is the author of the following works of fiction:
   Uncle Tom's Children. New York, 1938.
   Native Son. New York, 1940.
   Black Boy. New York, 1945.
   The Outsider. New York, 1953.

Savage Holiday. New York, 1954.

The Long Dream. New York, 1958.

Eight Men. Cleveland, 1961.

Lawd Today. New York, 1963.

American Hunger, New York, 1977.

Nonfiction works:

12 Million Black Voices: Folk History of the Negro in the United States. New York, 1941.

Black Power. New York, 1954.

The Color Curtain. Cleveland, 1956.

Pagan Spain. New York, 1957.

Information on secondary sources:

Russel C. Brignano, "Richard Wright: A Bibliography of Secondary Sources,' *Studies in Black Literature*, 2 (Summer, 1971), 19-25.

Theresa Gunnels Rush *et al., Black American Writers Past and Present: A Biographical and Bibliographical Dictionary.* 2 vols. (New York, 1975), II, 786-91.

Willi Real, "Richard Wright," in Peter Bruck, *et al., Der moderne Roman des amerikanischen Negers* (Darmstadt, 1977, in print).

Willi Real

RALPH ELLISON
KING OF THE BINGO GAME
(1944)

It is not uncommon to regard short stories as precursors of more
comprehensive fictional works or even merely as by-products of a
novelist's career. This view seems to be confirmed by some of Ralph
Ellison's pieces of short fiction. His first story, "Slick Gonna
Learn," is an excerpt from an unpublished novel,[1] the famous
"Battle Royal," first chapter of Ellison's novel *Invisible Man*, goes
back to an earlier short story of that name,[2] and his stories
"Flying Home" and "King of the Bingo Game" are said to anticipate major themes of *Invisible Man* as well.[3] Yet it is still difficult
if not impossible to say whether Ellison will be remembered as a
novelist or as a novelist *and* a short story writer. *Invisible Man*
(1952) which has so far been Ellison's only fictional full-length
work, is definitely the book which won him fame.[4] The interpreters of this novel are legion,[5] whereas his short stories have up
to now received little critical attention.[6] Ellison's *oeuvre* as it is
now before us, is surprisingly small for an author having attained
65 years of age. In an interview held by Allen Geller, Ellison calling
himself "a highly conscious writer,"[7] pointed out: "I have a certain
distrust of the easy flow of words and I have to put it aside and
wait."[8] Perhaps the small scope of his work can also at least partly
be explained by the fact that originally Ellison's musical interest
prevailed over his literary ones and that he, instead of becoming
a writer, would have preferred to be a musician, and despite his
predilection for jazz, a symphony composer.[9]

Ellison was born in Oklahoma City on the first of March, 1914,
where he also grew up.[10] His father died when he was three years
old. Oklahoma had only joined the Union in 1907 so that this
Southern state had no tradition of slavery which meant that caste
lines were not so rigidly drawn as in other parts of the South.[11]
In spite of the comparatively favourable social climate there,
Ellison had to attend the usual segregated schools,[12] but it must

111

be said that he was able to develop his interest in music at an early age. From 1933 to 1936 he attended Tuskegee Institute in Alabama, studying composition under William Dawson who, in Ellison's own words, was "the greatest classical musician in that part of the country."[13] In 1937 he moved to New York City where in the same year he met Richard Wright who was soon to publish his first collection of short stories, *i.e. Uncle Tom's Children* (cf. chapter VI of this book). It was Wright under whose guidance and encouragement Ellison started his own literary career.[14] Though Ellison was fascinated by Wright's open manner in which he discussed the problems of writing,[15] he never lost his strong sense of individuality.[16] According to his own testimony, he gave up Wright's way of writing as early as 1940: "By 1940, I was not showing Mr. Wright any of my writing because by that time I understood that our sensibilities were quite different; and what I was hoping to achieve in fiction was something quite different from what he wanted to achieve."[17] This was not the only time that Ellison objected to being called dependent on Wright. In the famous controversy between Baldwin and Wright concerning the possibilities of protest literature, he refused to acknowledge Wright as his "spiritual father."[18] On the other hand Ellison repeatedly emphasized the importance of literary tradition for his own work.[19] Among his favourite authors were Malraux, Dostoevsky, T.S. Eliot, Joyce, Faulkner and especially Hemingway. Calling Hemingway his "true father-as-artist Ellison stated: "I read him to learn his sentence structure and how to organize a story."[20]

Within a few years Ellison had several short stories published. His first two, "Slick Gonna Learn" (1939) and "The Birthmark" (1940), were written in the protest tradition and stay close to the level of literal realism.[21] Then followed a series of three stories featuring the two boys Buster and Riley, namely "Afternoon" (1941), "Mister Toussaint" (1941) and "That I Had the Wings" (1943). These are characterized by overt conflict between the generations because its youthful characters and the adults take different attitudes towards the white world.[22] Three more stories were published in 1944: "In a Strange Country," Flying Home"[23] and "King of the Bingo Game," all of them were caused by wartime experiences. After his service as a cook in the Merchant Marine, Ellison started writing *Invisible Man* in 1945 which took him five years to complete.[24] Between 1954 and 1956 he published several other stories.[25] In 1964 he brought out a collection of important essays and interviews entitled *Shadow and Act*, which reveal his political, social and aesthetic views during the past two decades.[26] In 1955 he was given a chance to begin work on a second novel through a Prix de Rome Fellowship of the American Academy of Arts and Letters.[27] After more than two decades it has yet to appear.

"King of the Bingo Game," which together with "Flying Home" has been ranked among Ellison's "finest stories,"[28] is the last short story before the publication of *Invisible Man*. This is one reason why for Edward Guereschi, author of the only critical study which is exclusively devoted to an analysis of "King of the Bingo Game," this story provides a revealing comparison with the later more comprehensive work:

> It is his last work (published in 1944) before the appearance of the novel in 1952. ... The protagonist ... has kinship with an early model. Nameless, recently transplanted from the South, he has a low psychic "visibility" ("Who am I?") and a high social "invisibility" ("Don't take too long, boy.") that render him vulnerable and easily victimized. More significant are the series of transformations he undergoes to effect self-knowledge.[29]

This quotation taken from the introductory passage is open to several objections:

(1) Guereschi himself draws attention to the fact that after the publication of "King of the Bingo Game" eight years were to pass until *Invisible Man* finally appeared in 1952. What he does not mention, however, is that Ellison in 1944 had not yet started writing his novel at all.

(2) There is no logical connection between the quotation from Ellison's story "Don't take too long" and social invisibility, even if the form of address ("boy") is thought to imply contempt or at least condescension on the part of the white man. The white master of ceremonies is just admonishing the black protagonist not to waste his time and that of everybody else present.

(3) Certainly Guereschi is right in assuming a close relationship between psychic visibility and the problem of finding one's personal identity. The familiar question "Who am I?" can be interpreted as a sign of the hero's quest for ego-identity, which normally is, as social psychologists assure us, a life-long process. This view has

also been adopted by Ellison himself: "If you aren't on an ego trip from the cradle to the grave, you aren't nobody."[30] The problem is that the quotation from Ellison's story, isolated as it stands in Guereschi's argument, does not imply a value judgment: it does not mean that the protagonist's psychic visibility is *low*; nor does it mean that the protagonist doubts his psychic visibility altogether. It only means that he has not yet found his personal identity.

(4) The statement that he undergoes a "*series* (my italics) of transformations," is certainly true for the hero of *Invisible Man*; it cannot be applied, however, to "King of the Bingo Game." The story is about one single attempt by the hero at effecting self-knowledge. Guereschi, then, does not take into account the difference in quantity which exists between a full-length novel and an extremely short story of less than ten pages. As both are epic genres, this difference does not forcibly imply a difference in quality.[31]

Guereschi's assumptions, then, are questionable, and in some respect, even erroneous. The approach chosen in this essay is different. With the aid of some categories borrowed from both social and individual psychology (e.g. accommodation or identity formation), with the aid of some utterances by the author and by a close reading of the text itself this paper tries to achieve a threefold aim: to analyse the structure of the story, to analyse its social background, and, in relationship with this, to discuss the psychosocial problem of trying to find one's ego-identity.

Ellison's story[32] does not yield its whole content after one reading only. Yet to the attentive reader its structure becomes clear fairly soon. As there is very little action in the story, the conflict occurs within the protagonist himself. The story consists of one basic situation which can be divided into two parts with a perfectly smooth transition between the two. The first part (pp. 271-273) relates how the protagonist, after going to a movie house and after providing himself with some bingo tickets in the hope of winning enough money to pay a sorely needed doctor for his wife Laura, is rather inattentively watching the same film for the third time. In the second part (pp. 273-279) the protagonist is on the stage, *i.e.* in the very centre of action: after scoring bingo, he is allowed to try for the jackpot of $36.90.

Though both parts are told from the protagonist's point of view

114

(he is the narrator of the story), they differ in character which can be seen from the manipulation of acting time and narrating time in both parts. In the first part (about 30% of the text) acting time and narrating time are almost identical; the scene is viewed through the protagonist's eyes and described realistically. In the second part (about 70% of the text) narrating time is longer than acting time. As a result, this part represents a rather rare example of expansion, which is typical of the stream-of-consciousness technique.[33] This handling of time which indicates the introspective way of depicting events in the second part of the story, is also a proof of the narrator's feverish state of mind. Ellison does not describe things now as they exist in reality, but as they exist in the protagonist's consciousness which thus becomes the focus of the story. Events are conceived rather than perceived. The scene becomes surreal rather than realistic.

The protagonist of "King of the Bingo Game" is neither an ideal hero nor an anti-hero. Like all other characters both black and white, he is unnamed (his wife Laura being the only exception in the story). He was reared in the South and, like so many other people during the Great Migration, he walked the traditional road to freedom:[34] like the protagonist of *Invisible Man* and like Ellison himself, he left the rural South where black solidarity was greater (cf. p. 271) but white domination also more rigid, for the more industrialized North. But instead of finding the Promised Land there, he has to experience the depersonalizing influence of Northern slums where human emotions are crippled and where folk ties are eroded. As he possesses no birth certificate which is called by Deutsch a petty, bureaucratic technicality,[35] he is officially a non-person, a nobody unable to get a job. Thus his personal situation which is also that of the protagonist in "Slick Gonna Learn,"[36] is representative of that of so many people living in a slum. It means being caught in a vicious circle which is characterized by poverty, denial of individuality, denial of work, denial of medical care, death.

The protagonist's situation is desperate. As a consequence of Laura's disease and his own predicament he tries his luck in the bingo game for the third time already. The implication that two unsuccessful attempts must lie behind him, clearly shows that there is no other way out of his dilemma. And to some extent his plight as well as his bad luck account for the fact that the prota-

115

gonist has probably given himself up to stealing five bingo cards which means that he is determined to cheat during the game: "The guy at the door wouldn't like it if he knew about his having *five* cards. Well, not everyone played the bingo game; and even with five cards he didn't have much of a chance." (p. 273) For him, the function of the game has been reversed from the very beginning: instead of representing some kind of entertainment, it is deadly serious for him.

This is the social and personal background against which the story must be seen. It has an open beginning and sets in in the movie theatre: "The woman in front of him was eating roasted peanuts that smelled so good that he could barely contain his hunger." (p. 271) Among the several comments on this location of the story, the interpretations of the movie house as darkened womb or as modern psychic confessional[37] are rather far-fetched. Less ambitious, but more convincing is the view of Marcus Klein who calls the movie theatre "a cave of muffled noises and shadowy images, presentiments of reality."[38] The impact the film exerts on the audience, is powerful: "wide-eyed" (p. 271) two men beside the protagonist watch a scene where a woman almost in the nude (at that time all major parts were played by white people) is finally discovered and tied loose by her saviour. This scene is certainly in sharp contrast with the taboo placed upon white womanhood.[39] Moreover, as it is the only scene selected for description by Ellison, it may be supposed to be symptomatic of the whole film: made up out of clichés, it is just an effective means of extracting money from the black audience. The inferior quality of the film corresponds to the extremely realistic presentation of other details: "Yesterday he had seen a bedbug on a woman's neck as they walked out into the bright street. But exploring his thigh through a hole in his pocket, he found only goose pimples and old scars." (p. 272) Thus for Ellison, two sentences are sufficient in order to characterize the movie house, its lack of hygiene, and the protagonist's dishevelled state.

The effect of the film on the protagonist is somewhat different. Though he is less fascinated by it than the other visitors, "the movie provokes his fantasy and he imagines what would happen if the people on the screen refused to play their assigned roles."[40] But he realizes at once that this is sheerly impossible: "But they had it all fixed. Everything was fixed." (p. 272) Again the personal

116

and the social levels are connected. Not only are the film and the significantly white beam from the projection room fixed, "all fate is fixed and fixed against him."[41] Without going into further details, the author alludes to the fact that in a society governed by whites a black man is denied freedom. He has no possibility of escaping to fulfil the role expectations held by the whites – a fact which to some degree foreshadows the outcome of the story. Ellison's exposition, his depiction of place, characters and social background (black-white relationship), then, is highly condensed.

While the film is shown, Laura is steadily on the protagonist's mind: "Laura 'bout to die 'cause we got no money for a doctor" (p. 271); "Laura was on his mind" (p. 271); "For Laura, though, he had to have faith" (p. 273); "Wonder how much Laura's doctor would cost." (p. 273) Holding the five bingo cards in his hands, he is trying to keep just ahead of his hopelessness.[42] This feeling only leaves him when, after scoring bingo, he is on the stage. Whereas in the first part he was completely invisible in the crowd black like himself, he is now clearly visible to everybody. He is filled with hope: for once, "the fear had left, and he felt a profound sense of promise, as though he were about to be repaid for all the things he'd suffered all his life." (p. 274) The bingo wheel gains "a paramount importance"[43] for him: still doubtful, he presses the button and thus "he is for the first time embracing his own destiny,"[44] realizing that "as long as he pressed the button, he could control the jackpot. He and only he could determine whether or not it was to be his." (p. 275)

The experience of feeling power leads him to an unexpected insight: with his finger on the button, he thinks to have his own fate in his hands. With a sudden "burst of exaltation" he exclaims: "This is God," thinking to possess "the most wonderful secret in the world." (p. 275) "For the protagonist it is a great spiritual experience, a moment of epiphany."[45] The audience is rigid, even hostile, as if in conspiracy with the white master of ceremonies against the black protagonist's strange behaviour, either of them incapable of understanding his message or his strange behaviour. The protagonist in his all-obliterating ecstasy is absolutely convinced that it is their fault they cannot understand him.

Feeling power gives him a new sense of self. Power had been denied to him all his life long, especially in the South. For survival's sake, he like all black people, had to adopt an attitude of accom-

117

modation which John Dollard, in his classical study *Caste and Class in a Southern Town*, defined as "the acceptance of frustrating circumstances without open resistance."[46] As soon as the protagonist feels power, he is no longer a prisoner of anxiety but has courage to defy the white man. When the master of ceremonies tells him "to make a choice because he has taken too long," he, in the ensuing dialogue (p. 275), interrupts the white man twice, putting leading questions to him. He who is used to deference forms, who is practiced in saying "yes, sir, no, sir" to white people, is the one to determine the situation: he takes the white man by surprise and finally leaves him speechless. (p. 275f) The traditional roles in white-black relationship, those of master and slave, have thus completely been reversed.

The hero's behaviour is still motivated by his desire to help Laura, but this desire is gradually transformed into a quest for his self: "The vague faces glowing in the bingo lights gave him a sense of himself that he had never known before ... This is *me*, he thought. Let the bastards yell." (p. 277) Then he becomes aware of the fact that he is undergoing a transformation which is thus indicated in the text: "Somehow he had forgotten his own name ... That name had been given him by the white man who had owned his grandfather a long lost time ago down South." (p. 277) Forgetting one's name is a familiar, if not obstrusive symbol of an identity crisis: the same occurs to Fred Daniels, protagonist of Richard Wright's "The Man Who Lived Underground." (1944)[47] In the context of "King of the Bingo Game," this motif is at the same time a symbol of the protagonist's probably unconscious wish of repressing the past, of forgetting the previous condition of servitude. Forgetting his name, Hartmut K. Selke writes, is forgetting "the very symbol of the determination of his life by others."[48] As name and Negro tradition are issues of identity, the hero is thus necessarily confronted with finding a new identity for himself which is expressed by the crucial question: "Who am I?" (p. 277), which leads to the very core of the story: "Well, he didn't need that old name; he was reborn. He as The-man-who-pressed-the-button-who-held-the-prize-who-was-the-King-of-Bingo." (p. 277)

This is the climax of the protagonist's development towards ego-identity, but it represents also the turning point of the story. The protagonist seems to have achieved a new identity, but for several reasons, appearances are deceptive. First of all, he is ashamed of his race. (cf. p. 276) For him it is impossible to become one with his own folk: it is far from providing a necessary identification model. And an obstacle to racial integration is also a major obstacle to ego-identity, for it is impossible for any man to find a particular identity without relation to a common identity. Second the protagonist's isolation from his own folk is transferred to his personal sphere: "... he'd have to press the button even if nobody understood, even though Laura did not understand." (p. 277) Thus he is not only deprived of group solidarity, he is moreover isolated from the only human being he loves: "I got nobody but YOU." (p. 277) His isolation is complete: he is caught in solipsism. Sooner or later, such a situation becomes, as can be seen from Richard Wright's "The Man Who Lived Underground," utterly unbearable for man, for everybody is dependent on contact with other human beings.[49]

The problem of racial and personal identity and the relationship between them is also dealt with by Ellison in his story "Flying Home." Its protagonist Todd tries to win the recognition of the whites by becoming a pilot in the U.S. Air Force. Striving ambitiously for integration into white society, is an erroneous pattern of behaviour in Ellison's eyes. In the end, Todd, after changing his attitude as a consequence of experiencing black solidarity, achieves racial identity,[50] for, according to Ellison, only after accepting his folk legacy will he discover his identity as an American. Thus being accepted by the blacks, is at least a relative triumph: "And it was as though he had been lifted out of his isolation, back into the world of men. A new current of communication flowed between the man and boy [old Jefferson and his son, i.e. other black characters in the story] and himself."[51] The importance of Negro tradition is also emphasized by Ellison in an interview: "I have to *affirm* my forefathers and I *must* affirm my parents or be reduced in my own mind to a white man's inadequate — even if unprejudiced — conception of human complexity."[52] And elsewhere he states: "There's no doubt that we were slaves, both of my grandparents on both sides were slaves ... But, nevertheless, part of the music of the language, part of the folklore which informed our conscious American literature came through the interaction of the slave and the white man."[53] Thus Ellison certainly does not identify himself with the development which the character of the story created by him has taken at this stage.

It might be expected, then, that the protagonist's exaltation will be short-lived. His legitimate endeavours to assert himself as a human being are doomed to failure, his hopes will be unfulfilled. He has the impression that his whole life is determined by the bingo wheel; in his view, it becomes his fate which reminds the reader of the metaphor of the "wheels of fortune" and of Fortune as an arbitrary and capricious Goddess. In the course of the story, it becomes increasingly obvious that it is impossible for the protagonist to control the wheel endlessly: while the hero thinks to control the wheel, it actually controls him. He becomes a tool at the very moment he thinks to possess power. In reality power is connected with powerlessness; his hope is based on self-delusion, triumph is followed by defeat, elation gives way to depression. According to Marcus Klein the protagonist's stumbling search for the source of power is determined by hubris.[54] It is hubris for him to think that he holds God in his hand. Before man can aspire to divinity he must first realize and accept the full responsibilities and limitations of being human. Moreover Klein states: "His apprehension of the source of creation can only be a brief ecstasy after which he is resettled in confusion."[55]

As a matter of fact, the protagonist has no longer a firm grip on reality. He imagines events rather than watches them in reality so that the borderline between clearly visible and audible impressions and fantasy products is blurred: "He felt as though the rush of blood to his head would burst out in baseball seams of small red droplets, like a head beaten by police clubs. Bending over he saw a trickle of blood splashing the toe of his shoe." (p. 277) This passage not only anticipates the outcome of the story when the protagonist is beaten to unconsciousness, it also indicates that he is near a psychological breakdown[56] or even on the verge of insanity. Further evidence of his mental disorder is provided by a nightmarish vision of the protagonist which, slightly varied, occurs for the second time in the story. (p. 272 and p. 277) As he clings to the button, the protagonist feels persecuted by the wheels of a train which finally seem to crush him; his state of mind is formally indicated in the elliptical sentence structures. (p. 277) If it is true that dream situations which sometimes haunt men, bear a close affinity to real situations or even originate in reality, it may be concluded that the protagonist, as this nightmare occurs before and after scoring bingo, again is a victim of anxiety.

120

Depressing as this picture of a disintegrating personality may be, it is not without some grotesque traits. Even more: the pervasive power of the grotesque in the final scene can be felt everywhere. The behaviour of the protagonist who has completely lost control of the situation, is an endless source of pleasure for the audience. Their reaction is no longer hostile. Being unable to understand the scene, they make fun of the hero, singing, applauding, clapping their hands alternately, trying to enjoy the show as much as possible. (p. 277f) In this scene, there is that kind of mixture of tragic and comic elements which, according to Ellison, is typical of the blues: "The blues speak to us simultaneously of the tragic and the comic aspects of the human condition and they express a profound sense of life shared by many Negro Americans precisely because their lives have combined these modes."[57] As it is certainly well-balanced,[58] it is not only a source of suspense for the reader, but it also adds to the literary merit of the story.

The protagonist, however, is still fighting, clinging to the button, for it is "his life." (p. 279) In the movie theatre staff's eyes he is degraded to a trouble-making nigger. When two men approach him, he starts running: "He slipped them, and discovered by running in a circle before the wheel he could keep the cord from tightening." (p. 278) Thus his movement, like that of the white projection beam, is fixed and, like that of the bingo wheel, both fixed and circular: it does not lead anywhere. As he has no alternative of acting, no other possibility of flight, he cannot run anywhere else: he is trapped in a circle. His movement around the wheel is literally and metaphorically aimless. Besides, the structure of the story as a whole may also be called circular, for the story does not go anywhere either: in the end, the protagonist finds himself in the same kind of vicious circle as before. Moreover, the most important metaphor, the wheel image is placed in the centre of the story. And the hero's two nightmarish visions, decisive clues for his inner state, are placed at an equal distance from it: as grotesque variants they anticipate and take up again the wheel image. Thus the repetition of the same motif can be interpreted functionally and justified in formal respect.

Disillusionment is both brief and painful. The protagonist is brutally knocked down. Although this outcome might be supposed to be typical of a protest story, Ellison's way of writing does not confirm this view. The reader is spared any shocking details; the author merely concentrates himself on describing the effects of brutality on the protagonist. This procedure not only corresponds to the narrator's limited point of view, it is also sufficient to make clear that both his willingness to help and his attempt at self-discovery have been futile.

The aimlessness and senselessness of the protagonist's way of acting, the cyclic structure of the story is enhanced by a literary device whose full effect is only revealed by considering the context of this piece of short fiction as a whole: irony. A first example of irony is furnished by the title of the story: Ellison's protagonist, of course, is the winner of the bingo game, he is even king for a short period of time, but he quickly becomes a king dethroned, powerless and pitiable. Just before feeling "the dull pain exploding in his skull," (p. 279) the protagonist realizes that the wheel stops at double zero, and he is "very, very happy," (p. 279) thinking he has been successful. But for the reader there is the ironic revelation that double zero is twice nothing. The protagonist is convinced that he will "receive what all winners received." (p. 279) This must again be interpreted as irony, for the quotation is an allusion to Ernest Hemingway's collection of short stories "Winner Take Nothing," by which the author described people's disillusionment after wartime experiences.[59] This idea was once again taken up by Ellison in a different context. Arguing that the achievement of colourlessness by the Negro would constitute a loss for the world, he stated: " 'Winner take nothing' that is the great truth of our country or of any country."[60]

The conclusion and the title are not the only examples of irony in the story. Elements of the plot as well take an ironic tinge. First, the location of the story may be said to be not without ironical overtones: the movie house invites the audience to escape temporarily into an imaginary dreamworld. Though it has no attraction for the protagonist any longer, he is provoked to produce and to nurture illusions about himself. Second, when the protagonist is on the stage, the master of ceremonies calls him to be "one of the chosen people." (p. 273) This is an ironical allusion to the biblical saying recorded by St. Matthew that "many are called, but few are chosen."[61] Even apparently insignificant details may be seen in an ironic light: the protagonist intends to press the button very briefly, as he knows from experience the wheel is most likely to stop then at double zero. Ironically he presses the button because it gives him power apparently, as long as possible, almost against his will and against the white man's admonition: "Don't take too long, boy." (p. 275)[62] This does not annihilate his chances in the game, for the wheel does rest at double zero. Though he is the winner, he is brutally knocked down. Another instance of what may be called double irony, is the hero's feeling of rebirth which in reality twice means death: it means physical death for Laura, and if he himself survives, he will be reduced to a state of permanent self-denial; his death will be psychical. Marcus Klein goes as far as maintaining that the bingo wheel which dominates the protagonist, "ironically is a kind of suicide for him."[63] Thus it may be concluded that Ellison's remark, "We Negroes are the most ironic observers of the American scene,"[64] can be traced in his literary work.

To sum up: The protagonist is not recognized as an individual. It was impossible for him to achieve individual autonomy.[65] He failed in attaining and preserving positive self-images, the consequences of which Stuart T. Hauser describes as identity diffusion.[66] Eventually the protagonist will even be fixed upon those identifications and roles that have been presented to him as most undesirable: he is bound to identify himself with the oppressor which only occurs after all other forms of ego-defenses have failed.[67] The protagonist has thus not only become invisible to the whites, but invisible as an individual to his own eyes as well: his identity is negative.[68]

To conclude: "King of the Bingo Game" as well as "Flying Home" are variations on the theme of the quest for identity. But whereas Todd in "Flying Home" achieves a relative triumph, the unnamed protagonist's desperate search in "King of the Bingo Game" is characterized by a total defeat. The theme itself is thus commented upon by Ellison: "It is *the* American theme. The nature of our society is such that we are prevented from knowing who we are."[69] It is no wonder, then, that Ellison was to treat it again more fully in *Invisible Man*. In this sense both stories contain the seeds of the later novel, but this does not necessarily mean they are parts of a larger unit. It should be clear that the motifs in "King of the Bingo Game" are not only inextricably intertwined, but sometimes are also deliberately ambiguous as they take an ironic significance when viewed in the context of the whole story. "King of the

Bingo Game" is not marred by any inconsistencies, nothing super-imposed detracts from the value of the story. It represents a coherent work which may be said to exist in its own right.

NOTES

1. Cf. Hartmut K. Selke, *A Study of Ralph Ellison's Published Work Viewed in the Context of the Theme of Identity in Negro American Literature* (Kiel, Diss., 1975), p. 69.
2. Cf. Fritz Gysin, *The Grotesque in American Negro Fiction* (Bern, München, 1975), p. 328.
3. Cf. Selke, *op. cit.*, p. 84.
4. Cf. James A. Emanuel and Theodore L. Gross, edd., "Ralph Ellison (1914 -)," in *Dark Symphony: Negro Literature in America* (New York, 1968), p. 249.
5. Cf. Jacqueline Covo, *The Blinking Eye: Ralph W. Ellison and his American, French, German and Italian Critics, 1952-1971* (Metuchen, 1974).
6. Cf. Leonard J. Deutsch, "Ellison's Early Fiction," *Negro American Literature Forum*, 7 (1973), 53-59. Cf. also Edith Schor, *The Early Fiction of Ralph Ellison: The Genesis of Invisible Man* (Columbia University, Ph.D., 1973).
7. "An Interview with Ralph Ellison," *Tamarack Review*, 32 (1964), 6.
8. *Ibid.*, p. 4.
9. Cf. Ralph Ellison, "That Same Pain, that Same Pleasure: An Interview," repr. in *Shadow and Act* (New York,[5] 1966), p. 28. (Signet Q 3022)
10. Gysin, *op. cit.*, p. 165.
11. Edward Margolies, *Native Sons: A Critical Study of Twentieth-Century Negro American Authors* (Philadelphia and New York, 1969), p. 129.
12. Emanuel and Gross, *op. cit.*, p. 249.
13. "The World and the Jug," in *Shadow and Act, loc. cit.*, p. 141.
14. Margolies, *op. cit.*, p. 129.
15. Cf. R. Ellison, "That Same Pain, that Same Pleasure: An Interview," repr. in *Shadow and Act, loc. cit.*, p. 33f. Cf. also Gysin, *op. cit.*, p. 166.
16. Cf. Emanuel and Gross, *op. cit.*, p. 250.
17. Robert H. Moore, ed., "On Initiation Rites and Power: Ralph Ellison Speaks at West Point," *Contemporary Literature*, 15 (1974), 185.
18. "The World and the Jug," in *Shadow and Act, loc. cit.*, p. 124. Ellison was contradicting Wright's advocate Irving Howe; cf. his "Black Boys and Native Sons," *Dissent*, 10 (1963), 353-368.

19. Cf. "A Very Stern Discipline," *Harper's Magazine*, 234 (March 1967), p. 94: "I've been reading the classics of European and American literature since childhood."

20. "The World and the Jug," in *Shadow and Act, loc. cit.*, p. 145; "The Art of Fiction: An Interview," *ibid.*, p. 169f.

21. Deutsch, *op. cit.*, p. 54.

22. Schor, *op. cit.*, p. 16.

23. For an interpretation of this story cf. Bernhard Ostendorf, "Ralph Ellison, 'Flying Home' (1944)," in Peter Freese, ed., *Die amerikanische Short Story der Gegenwart* (Berlin, 1976), pp. 64-76. Cf. also Joseph F. Trimmer, "Ralph Ellison's 'Flying Home,'" *Studies in Short Fiction*, 2 (1972), 175-182.

24. Cf. Ralph Ellison, "The Art of Fiction: An Interview," repr. in *Shadow and Act, loc. cit.*, p. 177.

25. Among these was "A Coupla of Scalped Indians" which has been interpreted by Karl Dietz in Frieder Busch, Renate Schmidt-v. Bardeleben, edd., *Amerikanische Erzählliteratur 1950-1970* (München, 1975), pp. 197-206.

26. Emanuel and Gross, *op. cit.*, p. 253.

27. Gysin, *op. cit.*, p. 167.

28. Emanuel and Gross, *op. cit.*, p. 251.

29. Edward Guereschi, "Anticipations of *Invisible Man*, Ralph Ellison's 'King of the Bingo Game,'" *Negro American Literature Forum*, 6 (1972), 122.

30. David L. Carson, "Ralph Ellison: Twenty Years After," *Studies in American Fiction*, 1 (1973), 9.

31. Cf. Paul Goetsch, "Probleme und Methoden der Short-Story-Interpretation," in Paul Goetsch, ed., *Studien und Materialien zur Short Story* (Frankfurt am Main, [2]1973), p. 27.

32. The story was originally published in *Tomorrow* 4 (November 1944), 29-33. Since then it has been anthologized at least three times: cf. William Adams, Peter Conn and Barry Slepian, edd., *Afro-American Literature: Fiction* (Boston, 1970), pp. 128-137; cf. Marcus Klein and Robert Pack, edd., *Short Stories: Classic, Modern, Contemporary* (Boston, [3]1967), pp. 487-496; cf. also Emanuel and Gross, *op. cit.*, pp. 271-279. Quotations will be taken from this anthology. Page references are given in the text itself in (...).

33. Cf. Peter Freese, "Die Short Story im Englischunterricht der Sekundarstufe II: Entwurf eines Interpretationsverfahrens," *Der fremdsprachliche Unterricht*, 37 (Februar 1976), 10.

34. Cf. R. Ellison, "The Art of Fiction: An Interview," repr. in *Shadow and Act, loc. cit.*, p. 174.

35. Deutsch, *op. cit.*, p. 57.

36. Selke, *op. cit.*, p. 82.

37. Guereschi, *op. cit.*, p. 122.

38. *After Alienation: American Novels in Mid-Century* (Cleveland & New

York, 1964), p. 106.

39. Cf. Calvin C. Hernton, "The White Woman," in *Sex and Racism* (1965) (Paladin Books, 1970), pp. 20-54.(08032)

40. Selke, *op. cit.*, p. 82.

41. Klein, *op. cit.*, p. 105.

42. *Ibid.*

43. Selke, *op. cit.*, p. 82.

44. Klein, *op. cit.*, p. 106.

45. Deutsch, *op. cit.*, p. 58.

46. (Yale University Press, 1937), p. 61.

47. *Eight Men* (New York, 1969), p. 49. (Pyramid Books 02034)

48. *Op. cit.*, p. 82.

49. Cf. Willi Real, "Richard Wright, 'The Man Who Lived Underground' (1944)," in Peter Freese, ed., *op. cit.*, p. 59.

50. Cf. Ostendorf, *op. cit.*, p. 65 und p. 73.

51. Emanuel and Gross, *op. cit.*, p. 270.

52. "A Very Stern Discipline," *loc. cit.*, p. 83.

53. Robert H. Moore, ed., *op. cit.*, p. 174.

54. *Op. cit.*, p. 106f. Cf. also Selke, *op. cit.*, p. 83: "His freedom, however, is of necessity only an ephemeral illusion."

55. *Op. cit.*, p. 107.

56. Emanuel and Gross, *op. cit.*, p. 252.

57. "Blues People," repr. in *Shadow and Act, loc. cit.*, p. 249.

58. Cf. Emanuel and Gross, *op. cit.*, p. 253.

59. For the genesis of the title cf. Carlos Baker, *Hemingway: The Writer as Artist* (Princeton, New Jersey, cop. 1957), p. 142.

60. Cf. Gene Bluestein, "The Blues as a Literary Theme," *The Massachusetts Review*, 8 (1967), 615.

61. Cf. Mat. 22, 14; cf. also 20, 16.

62. This motif occurs several times in Hemingway's work: cf. "Snows of Kilimanjaro," in *The First Forty-Nine Stories* (London, new edition, 1962), p. 72; cf. also "An Alpine Idyll," *ibid.*, p. 280.

63. *Op. cit.*, p. 106.

64. Carson, *op. cit.*, p. 13.

65. Selke, *op. cit.*, p. 83.

66. *Black and White Identity Formation: Studies in the Psychosocial Development of Lower Socioeconomic Class Adolescent Boys* (New York, 1971), p. 34.

67. Gordon W. Allport, *The Nature of Prejudice* (Doubleday Anchor Books, 1958), p. 147f. (09374)

68. Hauser, *op. cit.*, p. 35.

69. "The Art of Fiction: An Interview," repr. in *Shadow and Act, loc. cit.*, p. 178. Cf. also Geller, *op. cit.*, p. 10.

BIBLIOGRAPHICAL NOTE

An extensive bibliography of Ellison criticism may be found in the books by Selke (cf. note 1) and by Covo (cf. note 5). For a summary of secondary sources devoted to *Invisible Man* cf. Rolf Franzbecker, "Ralph Ellison," in Peter Bruck, Rolf Franzbecker, Willi Real, *Der moderne Roman des amerikanischen Negers* (Darmstadt, 1977, in print).

David Galloway

WILLIAM MELVIN KELLEY
THE POKER PARTY
(1961)

Critics and book reviewers were unanimous in greeting William Melvin Kelley as one of the most accomplished and versatile young writers to appear in the turbulent decade of the 1960's. They also recognized that, while Kelley explored the problem of being black in America with immense energy and imagination, his vision was less militantly political than that which claimed so much attention in the international press of the day. Kelley wished, above all, to establish his credentials as a writer of fiction, a dedicated, innovative craftsman. The fact of his own skin color was secondary to that sense of vocation, and even when he spoke directly of race relations, of the subtle interdependencies locking black and white Americans together, he did so without the searing anger of Eldridge Cleaver or Amiri Baraka.

The characters in Kelley's novels and short stories suffer none of the violent terrors and persecutions that once seemed the inevitable heritage of the black protagonist. Despite their modest beginnings, they often manage to carve a reasonably secure niche for themselves within the American system; the trials to which they are submitted have as much to do with being human as they do, specifically, with being black, though it might be argued that Kelley's own sense of racial consciousness has become more troubled and more radicalized during the course of his career. Nonetheless, we can recognize in his writings the voice of a relatively comfortable, secure, well-educated black community which will no doubt make itself even more frequently heard in the decades to come.

Born in New York City in 1937, Kelley was educated at the prestigious Fieldstone School, and from there went to Harvard University, where he studied with Archibald McLeish and John Hawkes. Both of these distinguished teachers were important influences on his development as a writer, and significantly, both combined intellectual-academic careers with creative writing.

129

From John Hawkes, Kelley absorbed something of the fabulist manner, and from MacLeish, no doubt, he learned the lesson that art must serve and be involved in society as a form of knowledge the state urgently needs. Kelley graduated from Harvard College in 1959, but during his undergraduate days he had already begun the early version of what would become his first novel, *A Different Drummer* (1962). Harvard's Dana Reed Prize helped him complete the book, which in turn won the Rosenthal Foundation Award of the National Institute of Arts and Letters in 1963. Meanwhile, Kelley was publishing articles and short stories in *The Saturday Evening Post, Esquire, The Negro Digest, The Dial*, and *Mademoiselle*. The best of the short fiction of this period was collected in *Dancers on the Shore* (1964), from which "The Poker Party" is taken.

Kelley's early, dramatic success clearly set him apart from former generations of black American writers, but it also played a role in establishing one of the central concerns of his fiction. The dilemma he frequently underscores is that the black's destiny is in many ways indistinguishable from the destiny of the entire post-modern American society, but that participation in such a destiny must not be allowed to submerge entirely the ethnic, cultural, and personal identity of the black. Success in America is largely definied in white terms; black "success" is, therefore, often a tormenting paradox — as it is shown to be in James Baldwin's "Sonny's Blues," John A. Williams' *Sissie* or in Kelley's second novel, *A Drop of Patience* (1965). Kelley's own future successes included a period as writer-in-residence at the State University College of New York, fellowships to both the New York Writers Conference and the famous Breadloaf Conference, and a grant from the John Hay Whitney Foundation. He has taught writing at the New School as well as the University of Paris, Nanterre, and with his wife Karen has lived in New York, Rome, Ibiza and Paris; they now make their home in the West Indies. In 1967 Kelley published *dem*, a raucous satire of white America and its synthetic culture, and in 1970 a linguistic *tour-de-force* entitled *Dunfords Travels Everywheres*. Since that time, no new work by Kelley has appeared, and none is scheduled to appear in the near future. Given the extraordinary productivity of his early years as a writer, this amounts to a very long silence. Perhaps Kelley himself has been caught on the horns of that dilemma known as success; and perhaps he pushed his formal experiments so far, and so fast, that a necessary silence had to succeed his exhausting foray into the intense verbalizations of *Dunfords Travels Everywheres.*

In the "Preface" to *Dancers on the Shore* Kelley observed that

An American writer who happens to have brown skin faces this unique problem: Solutions and answers to The Negro Problem are very often read into his work. At the instant they open his book, his readers begin to search fervently, and often with honest concern, for some key or answer to what is happening today between black and white people in America.

At this time, let me say for the record that I am not a sociologist or a politician or a spokesman. Such people try to give answers. A writer, I think, should ask questions. He should depict people, not symbols or ideas disguised as people.

I am an American Negro. I hope I am a writer, but perhaps the latter statement is not mine to judge.[1]

Kelley's brief but significant career clearly establishes his credentials as a writer; his work reveals him not merely as an accomplished technician, but as a true pyro-technician. In *A Different Drummer* Kelley portrayed a poor Southern black named Tucker Calliban, the descendant of a legendary African slave, who one day pours salt on his fields, sets fire to his house, and walks away with his pregnant wife and child. Others follow him, and within forty-eight hours an entire fictitious state has been emptied of its black population. Kelley's title is taken from Thoreau's famous assertion that "If a man does not keep pace with his companions, perhaps it is because he hears a different drummer. Let him step to the music which he hears, however measured or far away."[2]

In placing Tucker Caliban within the tradition of American individualism, of grass-roots political activity, Kelley suggests one possible course for black liberation. In the person of a wealthy Northern reformer, a Negro preacher who comes to study Tucker's revolt, he depicts another — the educated, somewhat cynical liberal reformer. More importantly, in the reactions of the astonished whites who witness Tucker Caliban's rebellion, Kelley first begins to explore the subtle, complex, often painful symbiosis of black and white America. In its use of fantasy, the novel also points ahead to Kelley's further experiments in the fabulist tradition, represented by *dem* and *Dunfords Travels Everywheres.*

At first glance, *A Drop of Patience* seems more conventionally realistic than Kelley's other novels. It episodically chronicles the

131

life of a blind jazz musician, Ludlow Washington, who after eleven years in a home for handicapped children, leaves at the age of sixteen to join a band as a trumpeter. Ludlow marries his landlady's daughter but later falls in love with a white student. When she discovers herself pregnant with his child, she refuses to accept the problems of a mixed marriage, and her rejection is the beginning of a long period of torment for Ludlow. Much of the next seven years is spent in mental hospitals, and his sanity is finally saved only by the dedication of a friend named Hardie and by Harriet, a young black journalist who falls in love with him. Any summary of the novel's action inevitably overstresses its realistic framework; in fact, the book is wonderfully innovative in technique. Ludlow Washington is Kelley's central consciousness, the sensitive register through which the author reflects on race relations, on the different life styles of the blacks, on North and South, on the perils of success and the meaning of art. But Washington is blind, and with immense technical virtuosity Kelley communicates his experiences through tacticle and auditory sensations. Visual images rarely occur, and the reader is subtly drawn into the dark but delicately responsive world of the blind character. The novel's technique is clearly etched in the opening paragraph:

> The house was too quiet. His little sister should have been running, screeching in the hallway; behind the house his brother should have been batting stones with a stick; his mother should have been singing. At least there should have been the short, heavy hiss of her broom. Instead the house was so still that the dripping of the kitchen pump was as loud as rocks dropping in a pond.[3]

Having established his unique point of view, Kelley is able to proceed to describe a rite of passage into the adult world of sex, love, racism, and fame which might otherwise have seemed entirely conventional.

Kelley's third novel is prefaced by the phonetic transcription næʊ, lɛmi tɛlje hæʊ dɛm foks liv ... ("Now lemme tellya how dem folks live ..."). "dem folks" are, of course, the white folks, and they live with their feeble myths of white superiority, masculine prerogative, and soap-opera escapism. The novel's white protagonist is an advertising executive, Mitchell Pierce, whose wife Tam takes a black lover, eventually becoming pregnant by both lover and husband and giving birth to fraternal twins, one black and one white. The white baby soon dies, and Mitchell Pierce sets out on a surreal journey through Harlem in search of the black infant's father. Completely misinterpreting the folkways and the argot of this world, he becomes the dupe of a black confidence man who is, in fact, his wife's lover. Here, far more than in Kelley's earlier work, the common enemy is Whitey, Mister Charlie, the man, a theme stressed by the novel's dedication to "The Black people in (not of) America." The white world seems so empty, frivolous, and morally decayed that it can no longer offer a serious threat to black people, but in celebrating the continuing vitality of the black community, Kelley is also warning against the malaise that could come with the assumption of middle-class standards; hence, he adopts an Ashanti proverb to preface the novel: "The ruin of a nation begins in the homes of its people."

Dunfords Travels Everywheres is Kelley's most ambitious attempt to bridge the gap between academic and "populist" mores, between black and white cultures, between the burden of the past and the onslaught of a technological future. Chig Dunford, the product of private schools and the new black bourgeois propriety, finds himself the only black in a company of footloose expatriates who cluster together in a fictional European city. The group is catalyzed by private and public violence, and Dunford travels into himself to find there a bizarre reservoir of private language that evokes his Harlem antecedents. The linguistic explosion that follows is like a fusion of James Joyce and Dick Gregory:

> Now will ox you, Mr. Charlie? Be your satisfreed from the dimage of the Muffitoy? Heave you learned your caughtomkidsm? Can we send you out on your hownor? Passable. But proveably not yetso tokentinue the consolidation of the initiatory natsure of your helotionary sexperience, let we smiuve for illustration of cgiltural rackage on the cause of a Hardlim denteeth who had stopped loving his wife.[4]

Dunford then travels into the life of the Harlem dentist ("Hardlim denteeth") and from there, literally, everywhere, and always back to the same point, which Kelley calls the "Begending." Like Joyce's *Finnegan's Wake*, the novel inscribes a circle, and just as Joyce's hero, H.C.E., metamorphoses into "Here comes Everybody," so Dunford is a kind of "everybody" traveling everywhere – Harlem spade, Ivy League Negro, crook and cowboy and lover and artist and pilgrim.

133

Measured against the novels, Kelley's short stories must inevitably seem rather conventional in technique, although they have a formal integrity the novels lack; indeed, the longer fiction occasionally seems selfconsciously contrived. There are, however, interesting narrative links between the novels and the short stories. In *A Different Drummer* a minor character named Wallace Bedlow is seen waiting for a bus to take him to New York, where he plans to live with his brother Carlyle. Wallace appears again as a successful folk singer in the short story "Cry for Me." Carlyle Bedlow appears in "Brother Carlyle," "The Life You Save," "A Good Long Sidewalk," and "The Most Beautiful Legs in the World." In *dem* the white protagonists' guide to the Nighttown of Harlem is none other than Carlyle Bedlow, who surfaces yet again in *Dunfords Travels Everywheres* as the wrecker of marriages and saver of souls employed by the Harlem dentist to provide grounds for his divorce. In "The Servant Problem," Kelley portrays Carlyle's Aunt Opal, in an episode incorporated directly into the text of *dem*. Chig Dunford appears in "Saint Paul and the Monkey" and "What Shall We Do With the Drunken Sailor?" His mother is the central figure in "Aggie," and the entire Dunford family appears in "A Visit to Grandmother." Thus, many of the stories in *Dancers on the Shore* share narrative links with each other, as well as having associations with the longer fiction. In addition, several of the most distilled and memorable of the stories collected in this volume are concerned with a young boy's initiation into the adult world.

Kelley's earlier and least militant work clearly reveals his own intellectual background. He borrows the title of his first novel from Thoreau; the phrase *A Drop of Patience* is taken from Othello's first troubled accusation of Desdemona's fidelity;[5] and *Dancers on the Shore* is an allusion to Joseph Conrad's *Heart of Darkness*. In the long paragraph from Conrad with which Kelley prefaces his volume of stories, Marlowe watches figures that cavort on the river bank as the steamship moves farther and farther into the "heart of darkness." At first he finds them inhuman, but then he conceives his "remote kinship with this wild and passionate uproar," and knows that if he tries hard enough, he will comprehend their real meaning:

> The mind of man is capable of anything — because everything is in it, all the past as well as all the future. What was there after all? Joy, fear, sorrow, devotion, valor, rage — who can tell? but truth — truth stripped of its

cloak of time. Let the fool gape and shudder — the man knows, and can look on without a wink. But he must at least be as much of a man as these on the shore.[6]

Kelley's fictional characters are his "dancers," and the purpose of his stories is to explore those shared qualities — of joy and fear and sorrow and devotion, of valor and rage — which join them together in the ongoing dance of life.

"The Poker Party" is the third story in *Dancers on the Shore*; like the two preceding ones — "The Only Man on Liberty Street" and "Enemy Territory" — it is concerned with a child's first awareness of the unexpected perils that lurk in the adult world. Indeed, internal evidence suggests that the small boy who must make his way through "Enemy Territory" on an adult errand is the same who witnesses the violence of "The Poker Party." The threats revealed to this young, nameless protagonist have none of the viciousness or the brutality of those which await Richard Wright's *Black Boy* , and they have nothing to do with the color of his skin. The child is black, but his encounter with a bruising reality is part of a rite of passage which recognizes no color bar. Indeed, it remains one of the most persistent themes in American literature, so deeply ingrained as to seem almost a cultural reflex — a gesture memorably explored in such American classics as Cooper's *The Deerslayer*, Melville's *Moby Dick*, Twain's *Adventures of Huckleberry Finn*, Hemingway's Nick Adams stories, Faulkner's *The Bear*, and Salinger's *The Catcher in the Rye*. It is hardly surprising that a young country should often be concerned with young heroes, or that a nation insecure in her identity should create so many heroes who are precisely searching for an identity, often literally or figuratively for a "father" to give them a sense of self. The relationship of fathers and sons takes on a yet more dramatic significance in black literature — partly because of the historical circumstances which often separated fathers from their families, partly because a white America often sought to rob the black male of his manhood, to reduce him to a harmless "boy." Both aspects of that painful disinheritance are explored with particular authority in Alex Haley's family saga, *Roots*.

While Kelley's story contains none of the particular agony of the black search for identity, it clearly belongs within the broader tradition of initiation literature; it suggests, for instance, interesting parallels to Hemingway's celebrated short story, "Indian Camp."

135

The narrator of "The Poker Party" seems secure in the romance of childhood, which he thinks of in terms of "late summer Saturdays" perpetually tinted a deep green. Even the rain, which must occasionally have interfered with his play, becomes, with the help of his grandmother's imagination, princesses dancing in puddles. Throughout the opening paragraphs of the story, the images are bright-colored, and the mood is one of freedom: "I was not concerned with time,"[7] the narrator remarks. In contrast to these summery images of the natural world are those associated with the house to which the boy returns at the end of the day. The door is locked, and inside he must submit to the rituals of propriety — having his face swabbed, saying his prayers. But even in this more confining world of black bourgeois values, the boy can see childhood as a magical time: his homecomings are lovingly welcomed, there are occasional Sunday outings with his father, the radio nurtures his active fantasy life, and even the darkness does not threaten: "I listened until night pressed gently against the windows." (25)

As we soon realize, there is nothing extraordinary about the lives of Thomas Carey, his wife and son. The father has a job, there is an abundance of food on the table, the house in which they live is snug and comfortable, and no spectres of racial hatred loom in the shadows. What Kelley gives us here is the poetry of the commonplace, similar to the poetry John Updike often weaves in his short stories. The characters are ordinary, their experiences unexceptional, but the author forcefully denies that their emotional lives are therefore inconsequential, that there are no lessons to be learned here. Furthermore, into the idyllic landscape of the first section of the story, Kelley subtly intrudes images which anticipate the violence to come — the broken glass in a vacant lot, the sun setting behind the monuments in Woodlawn Cemetery, the war games the boy plays in his mind. His imaginary missions against the Japanese, like the war games in "Enemy Territory," locate the action of the story in the period of Kelley's own boyhood. References to the war are another means to underscore the lack of real racial stress in the narrator's life; Indian, Japanese, Cuban, Negro are all "darker" people, and while the boy can more readily identify with the Japanese than with their "white" antagonists, the choice is made within a context of fantasy. Interestingly, in "Enemy Territory" the same motif assumes a more aggressive dimension when the same young boy shouts at his youthful enemies, ' "I'll get you guys! I'll get you. I'm not really an American. I'm an African and Africans are friends of the Japs and I'll get them to *bomb your house!*' "[8] Similarly, while racial distinctions are muted in "The Poker Party," the boy is aware of the different skin tones of the adults who gather around the kitchen table, and feels a particular identification between the color of his skin and that of his father, "the same shade as my own."(25)

In marked contrast to the idyllic mood of the first section of the story, the second begins with images of threat. The darkness is no longer gentle: "I was afraid; each shape was a man in a long coat coming with a silver knife to slice my throat."(26) From this point, images of violence cease to be muted and fanciful; they become increasingly tangible and real. Similarly, the harmless games which dominate the first section give way to the accusations and frayed tempers of the adult "party." The boy gets out of bed to move along the hall between "walls straight on either side of me, moving into a blackness so thick I was not certain there was a ceiling to stop them,"(26) a counterpoint to the sun that soars overhead in the opening paragraphs. Kelley's technical virtuosity is amply displayed in the minute but always perfectly focused details which create the mood of this night sequence. The kitchen smells not so much of food as of "something burning," the "musty and ancient odor of dust in a cellar." (27) As so often in this section, images will suggest confinement and constriction. The boy sees his father "hunched" before the table, and his mother "clutching her cards desperately to her chest." (27) He instinctively knows that there is a significant difference between this game and the card games he has seen boys play in the schoolyard, and guesses that the poker chips are more valuable than money, without knowing they are associated with honor, pride, fair-play, propriety, cameraderie, and ultimately with his own identification with his father.

Kelley builds his effects meticulously. Constricted gestures like "hunched" and "clutching" give way to the more violent one: "My father clenched his fists." (29) In reply, Uncle Hernando places the cards in front of Carey "as forcefully as he might have squashed a scampering bug." (29) The implied violence becomes manifest when Carey seems to suggest that Uncle Hernando has cheated, and the men begin to shout. Seeing their anger, the boy

137

is reminded of "dogs fighting and snarling in the street" (34) – the same street where he had played harmless games earlier in the day. Even more traumatic for the boy than this display of vehemence is his sense that he himself has somehow committed an act of betrayal. He identifies so intensely with his father, respects so unquestioningly the "ritual of the game," the necessity of following the rules, that his brief comment on the card his father is dealt seems a horrible violation. "I knew then I had made a mistake," he says, "and that my father *would lose*. I wished I would never be able to talk again." (32) The reader sees and can properly evaluate Thomas Carey's unreasonableness, but the frightened child cannot. Identification with the father now takes on a new, fearsome dimension: "Everybody stopped and looked at my father, and it seemed they were looking at me too." (32)

In contrast to the light of the opening paragraphs, the story closes with darkness: "After that the house was silent and dark, except for the light in the kitchen which crept up the hall and under my door. I knew then my father was still sitting, alone now, at the kitchen table." (35) The light that burns in the kitchen illuminates only the father's loneliness and, perhaps, his shame; his son lies in mournful shadow. What the reader witnesses is no agonizing trauma, despite the momentary terror it strikes in the boy's heart; but it suffices to erode the perfect faith, the *intactness*, of the charmed circle of childhood. Like such adolescent predecessors as Huckleberry Finn and Holden Caulfield, the narrator has begun to *see*. His mother remarks, ' "You've seen enough," ' and he thinks that while he had heard adults arguing, "I had never *see* them argue ..." (34) The experience of "The Poker Party" thus involves the inevitable pain of growing up, of learning that the "games" adults play differ from those that children play; there are other rules, other stakes, other consequences. As a metaphor for adult communication and conflict, the socially ritualized poker game reveals the tenderness of the mother, the expansiveness of Mister Bixby and Uncle Hernando, the intransigence of the father. It also reveals – in the gleaming "business shirts" and "shining heavy shoes" of the men – the self-conscious respectability of the characters, an aura shattered by the allusion to "river boat" games, to card-sharps and hustlers and confidence men.

Kelley never strains to achieve his effects. It is precisely because

138

the tone of the story is so moderate, its themes sounded with such reserve, its commonplace setting evoked with such precise economy that the violence with which it climaxes seems so chilling. Indeed, we experience that moment as the boy experiences it, even though we may evaluate it differently. There is, throughout the story, that sense of craft to which Kelley dedicated himself at the beginning of his career, and which was uppermost in his mind when he made the decision to dedicate *Dancers on the Shore* to his grandmother, Jessie Garcia, who for seventy years had made her living as a seamstress. Reflecting on that dedication, he found it necessary to preface the collection by introducing her and describing an event that occured four years before the book was published:

> At that time, I had just decided I would try to write. Since most everyone I knew had expected me to choose a more secure and respectable occupation, and since the desire to write was really a vague undergraduate yearning, I felt called upon to give some explanation to someone. I also felt that if my grandmother, who was the only family I had, understood, I could stand up to the others when they asked me why I did not have a decent job.
> As I sat talking to her, I began to feel sure the sixty years separating us would be too much, that I would not be able to explain to her the feeling writing gave me.
> For a half hour, she sat sewing and listening. For a half hour I gave reasons, explanations and examples, and finally when I slumped back, exhausted and discouraged, it seemed to me I had made no sense at all.
> For a moment she looked at me, making certain I had finished. Then she smiled: "I know. I couldn't have made dresses for seventy years unless I loved it."[9]

That sense of vocation which he shared with an ancient grandmother informs all of Kelley's writings, even the later works in which his treatment of the racial situation in the United States becomes more conflicted and unsettling. In its wonderful economies, its technical precision, "The Poker Party" can stand as fitting tribute to the writer's craft. It sounds no monumental themes and issues no shout of protest or reform, but it plays a sensitive, memorable variation on one of the most enduring motifs in literature — a child's bruising confrontation with the vagaries and aggressions of the adult world.

139

NOTES

1. William Melvin Kelley, "Preface," *Dancers on the Shore* (New York, 1964).
2. Kelley's epigraph is taken from the "Conclusion" (Chapter18) of Thoreau's *Walden*.
3. William Melvin Kelley, *A Drop of Patience* (New York, 1965), p. 14.
4. William Melvin Kelley, *Dunfords Travels Everywheres* (New York, 1970), p. 61.
5. See William Shakespeare, *Othello*, IV, ii.
6. For the full context of Kelley's epigraph, see Joseph Conrad, *Heart of Darkness* (London, 1961), pp. 104-105.
7. Kelley, "The Poker Party," *Dancers on the Shore*, p. 23. Page numbers in parenthesis refer to the Doubleday edition of 1964. "The Poker Party" is widely anthologized. It was reprinted, among others, in William Adams, *et al.* edd., *Afro-American Literature: Fiction* (Boston, 1970); Woodie King, ed., *Black Short Story Anthology* (New York, 1972); Arnold Adoff, ed., *Brothers and Sisters: Modern Stories by Black Americans* (New York, 1975).
8. William Melvin Kelley, "Enemy Territory," *Dancers on the Shore*, p. 15.
9. William Melvin Kelley, "Dedication," *Dancers on the Shore*.

BIBLIOGRAPHY

Kelley is the author of the following novels:
  A Different Drummer. New York, 1963.
  A Drop of Patience. New York, 1965.
  dem. New York, 1967.
  Dunfords Travels Everywheres. New York, 1970.
Selected secondary sources:
  David Galloway, "Versions of Dissent: John A. Williams' *Sissie* and William Melvin Kelley's *A Different Drummer*," *Critique*, 6 (Winter, 1963), 150-156.
  Phylis R. Klotman, "An Examination of the Black Confidence Man in two Black Novels: *The Man Who Cried I Am* and *dem*," *American Literature*, 44 (1972-3), 596-611.
  Klotman, "The Passive Resistant in *A Different Drummer, Day of Absence*, and *Many Thousand Gone*," *Studies in Black Literature*, 3 (1971), 7-12.
  Robert L. Nadeau, "Black Jesus: A Study of Kelley's *A Different Drummer*," *Studies in Black Literature*, 2 (1970), 13-15.

Peter Freese

JOHN A. WILLIAMS
SON IN THE AFTERNOON
(1962)

> The most important thing is the message. I
> would like to feel that the better the craft, the
> smoother the message comes out. A clumsy
> vehicle delivers a clumsy message. A smooth
> vehicle delivers a clear message.

> John A. Williams in an interview.

John Alfred Williams, born in 1925 in Jackson, Mississippi, and at present Professor of English at the City University of New York, is one of the leading black writers in contemporary America. Eight novels, among which *The Man Who Cried I Am* (1967) is perhaps the most important, and six nonfiction books have helped him finally to gain the recognition which, during the early stages of his career, was so long denied to him. When, after three years in the Navy and his studies at Syracuse University which he finished in 1951 with a Bachelor's degree in Journalism and English, he embarked on his writing career, he had to earn his living by working at a number of odd jobs, and he could not find a publisher for his first novel, completed as *One for New York* in 1955, until it was finally published as *The Angry Ones* in 1960. During the summer of 1954 Williams and his wife separated and he went to California where he spent a very unhappy year in Los Angeles. He used the experience he gained there in some of his novels and, together with his continuing concern for the plight of the black family in a racist society, it certainly forms the background of one of the occasional short stories he wrote during this time. This story is entitled "Son in the Afternoon" ("SiA") and its publishing history provides a characteristic example of the many obstacles an unknown black writer had to face in those years. Williams sent this story to several magazines, among them *Playboy* and *The Atlantic Monthly*, but it was constantly rejected, not because it was considered a bad story but because, for reasons stemming from the very racial discrimination which the story attacked, the editors thought it inopportune to publish it. Phoebe Adams of *The Atlantic*, for example, wrote in a letter of January 30, 1958: "The Son story is no go unless run with a picture of the author who, believe me, had damn well better be black as the ace of spades. Since we can't manage that setup, there's no hope here ..."[1]

When, in 1962, Williams edited an anthology of texts meant to portray the black man's reality in America which was entitled *The Angry Black*, he stated in his introduction that "it is most imperative that the Negro be seen and seen as he is; the morality of the situation will then resolve itself, and truth, which is what we all presumably are after, will then be served,"[2] and he seized the long-awaited opportunity by putting "SiA" as his own contribution into this collection. Four years later, however, when Williams reissued his anthology, with new material and under the new title *Beyond the Angry Black*, he no longer retained "SiA" but replaced it by another story, described as a chapter from a novel in progress and entitled "Navy Black." The reason for such an exchange remains open to conjecture. Perhaps Williams, who had made use of some of the story's problems in his first three novels — several passages from the story reappear almost verbatim in *Sissie* (1963)[3] — thought that the story had nothing new to tell any more. Perhaps, having progressed as a writer by this time, he no longer deemed it good enough to be republished. If the latter was the case, he was certainly more severe in his judgement than the majority of present-day editors, for nowadays "SiA" is one of the stories most frequently anthologized in collections of black literature.[4]

*

"SiA" is a story about a black man's amorous encounter with a white woman and thus touches on the highly charged subject of interracial sex; it is a story about a black man's confrontation with the white woman for whom his mother works as a maid and thus conjures up the traditional topic of master-servant relations between whites and blacks; it is a story about the psychical consequences of a black youth's deficient socialization and thus has to do with the manifold problems of growing up black in America; it is a story about a young black's emancipation from the low status bequeathed to him at birth and thus refers to the social

142

obstacles and the price to be paid for black self-realization; and it is a story about a black man's sudden loss of self-control and his irresponsible attempt to revenge himself upon an innocent white child and thus deals with the havoc wrought upon the human mind by the poison of racism.

The small-scale action which, in a seemingly effortless way, combines all these aspects and fuses them into an exciting plot is easily retold. Wendell, a successful young writer who works for a Hollywood film company drives to Santa Monica to pick up his mother Nora who works as a maid for the well-to-do Couchman family. In their luxurious villa Wendell has to wait because Nora cannot leave little Ronnie, the Couchmans' spoiled nine-year-old son, before Kay, his mother, has come home. Wendell is deeply annoyed by Ronnie's brattish behaviour and by the thought that his mother, who had no time for him when he needed her as a child, lovingly pampers the white boy. When Kay, "a playgirl" (231),[5] appears in a rather intoxicated state and begins a condescending flirtation with her maid's son, Wendell cunningly seizes the opportunity in order to revenge himself upon Ronnie by making him see his mother in the arms of a black stranger:

> I had the scene laid right out. The kid breaks into the room, see, and sees his mother in this real wriggly clinch with this colored guy who's just shouted at him, see, and no matter how his mother explains it away, the kid has the image — the colored guy and his mother — for the rest of his life, see? (236)

Wendell succeeds and when he leaves with his mother he has the dubious satisfaction of seeing that Ronnie slaps his mother's hand away when she reaches for him.

Such a brief summary of the story's action must create the impression that "SiA" is a rather contrived story. It is, in a way, but the idea of the perfect revenge which it presents is so skilfully translated into believable and well-motivated individual behaviour that it is only on second thoughts that the reader detects the thoroughly planned and almost schematic arrangement of the story behind its seemingly spontaneous, fast-moving, and exciting action. This is mostly due to Williams' central artistic achievement, namely the choice and faultless realization of an appropriate narrative perspective. It is especially his masterly rendering of the point of view of the I as protagonist which turns "SiA" into a little gem of narrative art, and thus it would seem appropriate to start an analysis of the story with a consideration of its technique of presentation.

*

"SiA" is narrated by Wendell, the story's protagonist, who immediately introduces himself as "I." The effect of immediacy characteristic of this focus of narration is greatly enhanced by the strategy of direct address, for when Wendell follows his "*I* tend to be ..." with a "...*you* see" (230), he does not only create the illusion of turning the reader of the written word into a listener to the spoken word, but he also, right from the start, establishes rapport between narrator and reader, admits the reader into his confidence and thus creates a close and intimate contact with him. A plea like "Anyway ... hear me out now" (230), a question like "Can you imagine?" (234), and the frequent "see" (cf. "I'm a *Negro* writer, you see" [230]; "So you see ..." [231]; "The kid breaks into the room, see" [236]; or "... for the rest of his life, see?" [236]) call for the reader's attention and sympathy, whereas statements like "... you know what happened" (232) tacitly presume that narrator and reader understand each other and share common ways of behaviour. The reader who is thus deprived of his distance and almost turned into the narrator-protagonist's accomplice, is exposed to another, subliminal effect of this kind of narration, that is, its supposed veracity. Not content, however, with the effect of verification implicit in the basic formula 'as I'm telling you about what has happened to me personally, I must know what I'm talking about,' Wendell greatly intensifies it by means of his extreme outspokenness, his remarkable honesty, and the fact that he does not at all spare himself. A man who is not ashamed of confessing that he "tend[s] to be a bitch when it's hot" (230), who admits that he has "a nasty temper" (233), who comments upon somebody's sexual incontinence by saying that he has "been that way too, mostly in the spring" (232), and who acknowledges that he was "too angry to feel hatred for [him]self" (233), cannot but impress the reader as being absolutely honest and thus turns, in Wayne C. Booth's category, into a totally 'reliable' narrator. A third characteristic of this kind of narration, termed 'mediation' by Franz K. Stanzel, lies in the essential effect

144

that not the action as such is important but the effect of this action upon the narrator, and that the narrator-protagonist cannot mention a single detail without, at least by his choice of words, betraying its effect upon himself. Thus such seemingly insignificant details as Wendell's plan to "listen to some of the white boys play" (231) or his comment "I thought if I knew Couchman I'd like him" (232) gain importance because they show that Wendell is no fanatic, no indiscriminate hater of whites — a fact that makes his behaviour at the Couchmans' all the more telling. The narrative distance, that is, the distance in time between Wendell as protagonist and Wendell as narrator, is hinted at right at the beginning — "I was [at the time when this happened] — still am [now when I tell you about it] — a writer ..." (230) — but cannot be exactly defined. With the single exception of one statement which indicates that as narrator Wendell has gained an insight he was incapable of as participant and which will be discussed below, however, one gets the impression that Wendell has not yet gained sufficient distance from his experience and that he tells his story as if still under the immediate impression of what had happened.

The combined effects of directness and immediacy, reliability and 'mediation,' created by the brilliantly realized point of view are, of course, corroborated by Wendell's language. This unmistakable idiom, with its mixture of self-assertion, aggressiveness, and amused mockery, with its relaxed colloquial rhythms, and with its apt imagery, plays an important part for the overall effect of the story. Behind the consciously casual vocabulary and the pseudo-hardboiled speech of a young man, who expertly uses the insider slang of the contemporary jazz scene and who talks noncholantly about 'showcasing spades' or 'playing Uncle Tom,' about 'going into his sexy bastard routine' or 'real wriggly clinches' (cf. 230, 230, 235, 236), one senses the vulnerability of somebody who has been deeply hurt during his childhood and youth and who uses his tough speech to keep a hostile world at its distance and to cover up for his insecurity. At the same time one recognizes that Wendell's verbal irreverence with its implicit assertion of social criticism and individual freedom puts the story squarely in the genuine American tradition of the vernacular, which since its beginning in frontier tall talk and Southwestern humour has branched out into manifold contemporary mutations which reach from the prep-school jargon of Salinger's Holden Caulfield to the scatological effronteries of Mailer's D.J. Jethroe and which also include numerous convincing realizations in the field of the immensely creative black slang of today.

*

The length of the action time of "SiA" is extremely limited and can be measured in minutes rather than hours. Although the story, whose action cannot be precisely dated but must take place sometime in the mid-fifties,[6] makes use of both scenic and panoramic presentation, telling is greatly outweighed by showing because Wendell's reflections and reminiscences about the past are integrated into the present action and often generalized into timeless insights presented in a kind of gnomic present tense.[7] Thus the effect of immediacy created by the point of view and the language is further enhanced by the mode of presentation. While the treatment of time is relatively simple and the story unfolds in an almost straightforward chronological sequence, accompanied and briefly interrupted by the narrator-protagonist's memory fragments, the treatment of space is made to carry symbolic overtones. The story which takes place in "L. A." (230) – Los Angeles – mentions Watts as Wendell's place of residence, Hollywood as the place where he works, and Santa Monica as the place where the Couchmans live. In a very plain, perhaps even a little too obvious, way Watts, the black ghetto, is contrasted with Santa Monica, the exclusive residential area, whereas Hollywood, intent on gaining a new public by means of black movies (cf. 230), functions as the bohemian intermediate zone where, in the interracial field of arts, whites and blacks can, within limits, meet and cooperate. Such a symbolic geography, a western variation of the uptown-downtown-Greenwich Village cliché, as it were, is intensified by the fact that Kay, the rich white lady, drives around in a white Jaguar, whereas Wendell, the poor man from the ghetto, owns a little Ford. If one adds to these details that the Couchman villa looks to Wendell like "a transplanted New England Colonial" (231) – a comparison which conjures up all the associations of 'colonialism' – and that he is expected to enter this villa through the kitchen door, the setting is perfectly established. It would be quite wrong, however, to deduce from these details that "SiA" is mainly a sociocritical story about the confrontation of two classes, of white haves and

146

black have-nots. Such a contrast is obviously an important part of the story's atmosphere, but Wendell does not fit into these categories. His job in Hollywood, his elaborate and not inexpensive plans for the evening — having dinner at the Watkins, talking to some musicians, spending the night in a bar — his self-confident behaviour and, above all, his language clearly indicate that his world is no longer the black ghetto, and in the atmosphere of leisure and luxury that permeates the Couchmans' home he does not play the part of Bigger Thomas at the Daltons' but, on the contrary, is quite relaxed.

As the potential conflict already implied in the contrastive setting, is finally realized as the acting out of latent tensions, one should distinguish between cause and occasion. The cause of the climactic incident at the Couchmans' is not Wendell's confrontation with their world of luxury and affluence; and Ronnie's brattish behaviour and Kay's flirtatiousness provide only a long-awaited occasion. The climax is brought about by the psychic injuries sustained by Wendell during his childhood and youth. Thus the contrast sketched above only serves as an appropriate stage for the acting-out of old and pent-up frustrations. This climax, however, this sudden explosion of aggressions which have long been suppressed, is carefully and cumulatively prepared and motivated, and it is the gradual unfolding of the plot which lends the action of "SiA" its relentless and compelling logic. The story lacks an independent exposition but starts directly with the rising action, the necessary expository information being inserted piece by piece into the present action. The very first sentences — "It was hot. I tend to be a bitch when it's hot" (230) — have an ominous quality and serve as a kind of indirect foreshadowing, indicating that something unpleasant will happen. This first vague reference to some impending trouble is taken up and intensified by Wendell's explanation that he has had "a very lousy day at the studio" (230), and his irritation and anger are then heightened by the facts that he gets "stuck in the traffic" (230) and that his own plans for the evening are being crossed by his mother's request to pick her up. Thus instead of enjoying the "quiet evening" (230) he was looking forward to, Wendell must endure the long drive to Santa Monica, which is "a long haul for such a hot day" (230). When he finally reaches the Couchman villa he has to enter it through the kitchen door, and the host of unpleasant memories released by this infamous symbol of servitude do not at all improve his foul mood. The fact that his mother is not yet ready and that he is made to wait for Kay's return — "Just be patient ..." (233) — creates additional anger, and in his encounter with the spoiled and ill-behaved Ronnie Wendell finally loses his temper. Thus, when Kay arrives, Wendell, enraged by his tiring work, bothered by an unpleasant climate, annoyed by an exhausting drive and the crossing of his own plans, made impatient by his waiting, and irritated by several signs of discrimination and the unpleasant memories they evoked, has reached a state where his emotions get the better of his judgement, where he can no longer resist the temptations of an intoxicated playgirl and where, when an unforeseen situation suddenly offers a possibility to release his pent-up frustrations, he gives in to his longing for revenge. This situation, created by a particular and highly significant constellation of figures, stands at the centre of the story.

*

The title of "SiA" already indicates that this is a story about elementary human relationships, and there are really three mother-son relations, which are contrasted with each other, namely (1) Nora — Wendell, the poor black mother and her son, (2) Kay — Ronnie, the rich white mother and her son, and (3) Nora — Ronnie, the black maid and the white boy for whom she is a surrogate mother. And then there is (4) a short-lived sexual relationship, not taken seriously by either partner, namely Wendell — Kay, the black man and the white woman. Quite obviously, such a constellation of figures is not unique but, on the contrary, the fictional embodiment of a cluster of role-relations which have long become stereotypes and which represent some of the basic problems of black-white relations in America. The two role-stereotypes Williams makes use of can be labelled as that of the 'black mammy' and that of 'pinktoes.'

The black mammy, of course, is a recurring figure in American literature, and from Faulkner's Dilsey and Molly Beauchamp, both modelled on the real-life Caroline Barr to whom he dedicated *Go Down, Moses*, to Carson McCullers' Berenice Sadie Brown or Harper Lee's Calpurnia many examples come easily to mind. Tischler's summary:

The Negro mammy – in her role of nurse, witch doctor, priest, intercessor, wet nurse, comforter, permissive earth-mother – is still so intrinsic a part of the Southern memory that even the most vicious politicians, appealing to the basest emotions of their Negro-baiting audience, must yet tip their hats to "the memory of the humble black mammy of my childhood to whom I came for solace and comfort,"[8]

attests to the longevity of the cliché,while Lillian Smith's thoughtful analysis of the "dual relationship which so many white southerners have had with two mothers, one white and one colored and each of a different culture that centered in different human values,"[9] points out the complex psychological consequences of such an arrangement for the white child. Williams, however, is interested in the results of such a relationship on the black child, and Wendell's behaviour must be understood as the logical outcome of a vicious circle consisting of the following stages: Nora's life and that of her children was governed by poverty; because Nora loved her children she wanted to care for them; in order to do that she needed money; her only chance of earning money was to work as a maid for some well-to-do white family; working for this family meant that she had to be away from home; being away from home Nora had no time for her children. This destructive mechanism, which also lies at the centre of Williams' novel *Sissie*, hinges on the awful fact that in order to care for the physical wellbeing of her children the black maid has to take on work that forces her to neglect their psychical needs.[10] If one adds to this the fact that the black maid might well project her motherly instincts upon the white child or children with whom, contrary to her own, she is together during the whole day, one will begin to fathom the manifold implications of Wendell's laconic statement: "Nora's affection for us took the form of rushing out in the morning ..." (234) The black children, left to themselves, suffer from a lack of emotional warmth and therefore, being encouraged by nobody, cannot develop their innate abilities – a psychic mechanism which perpetuates their supposed 'inferiority' and which is a classic example of what sociologists call a 'self-fulfilling prophecy.' All of Nora's children, for example, were good at drawing, but "there's not a goddamn artist among us. We never had the physical affection, the pat on the head, the quick, smiling kiss, the 'gimme a hug' routine" (234). All of the encouragements which Wendell and his brothers and sisters were lacking – "all

149

of this Ronnie was getting" (234).

Such is the background which makes it all too understandable why Wendell, an independent and self-assertive adult, is nevertheless jealous of nine-year-old Ronnie and why, burdened with the heightened sensitivity developed by the victim of discrimination, he misinterprets the white boy's behaviour and thinks that Ronnie's 'roaring' (cf. 233) at Nora is caused by discriminatory motives, although it is obviously just an expression of the spoiled child's egotism and irascibility. When Wendell forbids the "little bastard" (233) to address his mother in a disrespectful way – note the revealing stress in "Don't talk to *my* mother like that..."(233) – he acts on a wrong assumption, and when he feels an overwhelming urge to beat the child, his pent-up anger is definitely vented on the wrong object. Significantly Wendell, who pretends to be controlled and 'cool,' is unable to admit to himself his mistaken estimation of the situation when Nora comes to Ronnie's aid. Only later on, from the distance he has gained as narrator, can he state: "I was too angry to feel hatred for myself" (233), and thus articulate the central insight which lends a developmental dimension to the story. As narrator, from the disinterested perspective of hindsight, he can even understand little Ronnie's miserable situation who, with his 'successful' father hardly at home and his selfish and pleasure-seeking mother not really caring for him, is as much a "son in the afternoon" as was Wendell, although the reasons, of course, are entirely different. But during the time of action Wendell's knowledge that "kids should have someone to love" (233) inevitably leads on to his unpleasant memories of his own childhood, and thus his anger at Ronnie has to deepen into jealousy. Therefore his insight that Ronnie "had only my mother" (233), which releases his reminiscences, brings him back to the present with the frustrating recognition that "all of this [i.e., the encouragements he was lacking as a child] Ronnie was getting" (234). Such an interweaving of the past with the present, which provides the motivation for Wendell's behaviour, is also a good example of the internal logic of the narration, which integrates digressions of this kind by means of associative links and thus demonstrates by its very structure how the present is defined by the past.

If one connects Wendell's foul mood, gradually intensified by his preceding experiences, with the anger and jealousy created by his encounter with Ronnie it is quite understandable that Wendell gives in to his desire for revenge. What he wants to do is at once simple and perfect: he plans to impose one of those shocks and humiliations which poisoned his own childhood upon the hated Ronnie, wants to create a kind of inverted 'colour shock' for the white child, and – what could be more appropriate – he plans to use the child's own mother as the instrument of his revenge.

While one can be quite certain about Wendell's motives, because with his characteristic honesty and bluntness he outlines them himself – "I had the scene laid right out ..." (236) – Kay's motives for her behaviour cannot be ascertained as easily, because the reader sees her only through Wendell's eyes and must thus depend on conjectures. What seems to be certain is her sexual curiosity regarding the black man she unexpectedly encounters in her own house, and it is here that a second role-stereotype comes into play. Since the very beginning of black-white relations in America the myth of the black man's exceptional sexual potency has played a prominent role, has been used to justify the Southerner's rape complex and the taboo of miscegenation or 'mongrelization,' and has led to such infamous products of morbid imagination as the sentencing of a black man in Mississippi for having attempted to rape a white woman by means of 'reckless eyeballing.' Calvin C. Hernton, Lillian Smith, Grace Halsell and many others have tried to analyse the complex hidden relations between racism and sexuality, Richard Wright and James Baldwin have time and again dealt with the pernicious stereotype of the black man as a 'walking phallic symbol,' and Eldridge Cleaver has invented the legend of the 'Omnipotent Administrator' and the 'Supermasculine Menial' to account for the genesis of this cliché.[11] This whole complex serves as the necessary background to "SiA," where, for want of a better term, the short relationship of Kay with Wendell could be labelled 'pinktoes.' This term, which in black usage denotes "a black man's white girl friend; a white girl,"[12] was given wider currency when, in 1961, Chester Himes published his novel *Pinktoes* and, in the motto, offered the following definition: "Pinktoes is a term of indulgent affection applied to white women by Negro men, and sometimes conversely by Negro women to white men, but never adversely by either.[13]

Ironically enough, in "SiA" it is the socially sanctioned relationship between white child and black mammy which calls forth, for

151

a brief period, the socially tabooed or at least frowned-upon relationship between white woman and black man. As the text, because of its point of view, offers no reliable clue to Kay's motive, one might argue that Kay, being drunk and thus freed of her inhibitions, is just a victim of her sexual curiosity aroused by the myth of the black man's potency and thus becomes the unwitting object of Wendell's cunning advances. The symmetry of the story, however, is so perfect in all other respects that a different reading seems worth considering.

Kay could well have a revenge motive of her own, and if so, she would not only be used by Wendell but would also be trying to use him as well. When she comes home, she goes to look for Ronnie, "the poor kid" (235). Obviously she does not feel like fulfilling a mother's duty — Wendell has to remind her that "Ronnie isn't feeling well" (235) — and is glad to have Nora. But when she comes back, she has to confess that "Nora was trying to put him to sleep and she made me stay out" (235f.), and her giggling could be a sign of her embarrassment about such a situation. Would it not be quite probable, then, that Kay is offended by the fact that Ronnie prefers his nursemaid to his mother and that she has been sent away like a stranger and therefore envies Nora her success with Ronnie? Nora has taken away her son Ronnie, and could not Kay, who is drunk and quite uninhibited, try to get her revenge by getting back at Nora and taking away Nora's son Wendell? Such a reading of "SiA," which would find some additional extrinsic support in the fact that the motive of mutual revenge as the basis of an interracial love affair is a recurring motif in Williams' early fiction,[14] would go well with the fact that both have a fair chance of winning their game. In the end Wendell proves victorious, for it is not Nora, as might well have been expected, who enters the living room to find her son in the embrace of her mistress, but Ronnie who sees the 'ignominy' of his mother in the arms of the aggressive black stranger. And Wendell's statement that Kay "was reaching for Ronnie's hand as we left, but the kid was slapping her hand away" (237), confirms that his calculation has proved right and that he has probably managed to subject Ronnie to a shock he will not forget. Wendell, however, cannot be happy about his ingeniously contrived victory, for one cannot undo one's own humiliations by humiliating somebody else. This final conciliatory — and perhaps most important — message of "SiA" is obliquely expressed in Wendell's statement, "I felt many things, but I made myself [!] think mostly, *There, you little bastard, there*" (237). And in the final, ambiguous sentence of the story in which Wendell says that he was "hating the long drive back to Watts" (237) one might legitimately detect the first dawning of that very "hatred for myself" (233) which, according to a previous statement by Wendell the narrator, Wendell the protagonist is still "too angry to feel" (233).

*

In spite of its sometimes rather slick quality and its almost too perfectly contrived contrasts and parallels "SiA," which compresses central aspects of racial relations in America into a small-scale every-day action, is a compelling and finally convincing story which bears testimony to Williams' belief that only "a smooth vehicle delivers a clear message."[15]

NOTES

1. Quoted in Earl A. Cash, *John A. Williams: The Evolution of a Black Writer* (New York, 1975), p. 93.
2. "Introduction to the First Edition," in John A. Williams, ed., *Beyond the Angry Black* (New York, 1971), p. xvii. (Mentor Book MY 1058)
3. Cf. especially Ralph's reflections in *Sissie* (New York, 1963), pp. 245f., with the respective reflections of Wendell in "SiA."
4. The story is included, for example, in: Langston Hughes, ed., *The Best Short Stories by Negro Writers: An Anthology from 1899 to the Present* (Boston, 1967); James A. Emanuel and Theodore L. Gross, edd., *Dark Symphony: Negro Literature in America* (New York, 1968); Penney Chapin Hills and L. Rust Hills, edd., *How We Live* (New York, 1968); Edward Margolies, *A Native Sons Reader* (Philadelphia and New York, 1970); in Germany it is available in Peter Freese, ed., *Growing Up Black in America: Stories and Studies of Socialization* (Paderborn, 1977).
5. All page numbers given in brackets in the text refer to the reprint of the story in Edward Margolies, ed., *A Native Sons Reader*.

6. Taking the date of Phoebe Adams' letter (1958) as *terminus ante quem* and taking into account that, according to Clarence Major, *Black Slang: A Dictionary of Afro-American Talk* (London, 1971), "spade," "hippie" in its particular, negative meaning, "on the scene," "roost" and "high" were used by black Americans in or up to the 1950's, one can date the story's action in the mid-fifties.

7. Cf. Williams' statement in John O'Brien, ed., *Interviews with Black Writers* (New York, 1973), p. 236, where, in regard to the relation between telling and showing, he says: "I find that too much narration becomes a pain in the ass. You get on a roller coaster and start breaking out the flags. Dialogue is always better."

8. Nancy M. Tischler, *Black Masks: Negro Characters in Modern Southern Fiction* (University Park and London, 1969), p. 32.

9. Lillian Smith, *Killers of the Dream* (New York, 1949), p. 127.

10. Here, too, some autobiographical influences can be detected. Cf. Williams' travel book *This Is My Country Too* (New York, 1966), p. 77, where he says that his own mother has spent "better than half her life in other people's kitchens and bedrooms and bathrooms. Like the mythical Aunt Bessie, she knows more about white people than they can ever know about her."

11. Cf. my interpretation of James Baldwin's "Going to Meet the Man" in this volume.

12. Cf. Clarence Major, *op. cit.*

13. Chester Himes, *Pinktoes* (Paris: Olympia Press, 1961), motto.

14. Cf., for example, *The Angry Ones*, where Steven Hill, the black protagonist, and Lois, the beautiful and neurotic Jewish girl with whom he has an affair, use each other: Steven to revenge himself upon the white world, Lois to shock her hated mother. Cf. esp. p. 173, where Steven bluntly says: "You used me as a tool against your parents – against your mother ... I used you too, baby ... Nearly every time I called you, it had been a bad day for me, and I had to get back, if not at them directly, at you, and that worked out fine. It kept me from going nuts." To use the novel as a point of comparison seems all the more legitimate as (1) the novel was written at approximately the same time as the story, (2) both texts have strong autobiographical traits (in the interview with John O'Brien, *op.cit.*, p. 232, Williams says that *The Angry Ones* "was in some ways a very autobiographical novel"), and (3) Steven is in many aspects a forerunner or successor of Wendell (he comes from Los Angeles, is an unpublished writer, and works in public relations; the motif of "suntanning" is taken up in the novel [cf. p. 153]; and Steven's insight, "I was a little disgusted with myself – I had a persecution complex, I figured" [p. 103], could serve to explain Wendell's heightened sensitivity to potential racial insults).

15. This statement, quoted in greater detail in the motto, is taken from an interview given to Earl A. Cash on October 25, 1971, and it is reprinted in

Cash, *op. cit.*, p. 147.

BIBLIOGRAPHY

Williams' eight novels are:

The Angry Ones (New York: Lancer, 1960).

Night Song (New York: Farrar, Straus & Cudahy, 1961).

Sissie (New York: Farrar, Straus & Cudahy, 1963).

The Man Who Cried I Am (Boston: Little, Brown, 1967).

Sons of Darkness, Sons of Light: A Novel of Some Probability (Boston: Little, Brown, 1969).

Captain Blackman: A Novel (Garden City: Doubleday, 1972).

Mothersill and the Foxes (Garden City: Doubleday, 1975).

The Junior Bachelor Society (Garden City: Doubleday, 1976).

Williams' nonfiction books include:

Africa: Her History, Lands and People Told With Pictures (New York: Lancer, 1963).

The Protectors (New York: Farrar, Straus & Cudahy, 1964); together with Harry T. Anslinger, under the pseudonym of J. Dennis Gregory).

This Is My Country Too (New York: New American Library, 1965).

The King God Didn't Save: Reflections on the Life and Death of Martin Luther King, Jr. (New York: Coward-McCann, 1970).

The Most Native of Sons: A Biography of Richard Wright (Garden City: Doubleday, 1970).

Flashbacks: A Twenty-Year Diary of Article Writing (Garden City: Doubleday, 1973).

Williams has edited *The Angry Black* (New York: Lancer, 1962) and *Beyond the Angry Black* (New York: Cooper Square, 1966) and, together with Charles F. Harris, the first two volumes of the now defunct magazine *Amistad* (New York: Random House, vol. I, 1970, and vol. II, 1971).

Barbara Puschmann-Nalenz

ERNEST J. GAINES
A LONG DAY IN NOVEMBER
(1963)

Ernest J. Gaines was born in 1933. He grew up on a plantation in the Louisiana "bayou country." At the age of sixteen he moved to San Francisco, where he still lives.

In 1963, *The Sewanee Review* published "Just like a Tree," one of his first stories. In the next year Dial Press brought out the first of his published novels, *Catherine Carmier*, which was followed by *Of Love and Dust*, in 1967. With the appearance of *The Autobiography of Miss Jane Pittman* he became known to a wider public. *Bloodline*, his only collection of short stories, appeared in 1968.

Ernest Gaines is the winner of several literary awards and fellowships.

*

The setting of Gaines' story "A Long Day in November," the first in his anthology,[1] is the rural South of the United States. In five sections it tells us the events of one day, seen through the eyes of a six-year-old negro boy, the only child of his parents Amy and Eddie who live and work on a white-owned plantation. At daybreak, while he is still in bed, his father and mother have a fight, because Eddie comes home late, having again spent most of his time on the old car he bought some time ago. In the morning, when his father has gone to work in the fields, the boy and his mother leave the house and go to live with his grandmother. Little "Sonny," as he is called most of the time, has a bad day in school, because he does not know his lesson: in his fear and agitation he wets himself, thus becoming the laughingstock of his classmates. After school he goes back to his grandmother's house. Sonny's father tries to talk to Amy, in order to make her return to their house — in vain. Eddie's strong-willed mother-in-law scares him away with a shotgun; he does not dare to go near the house but paces back and forth in front of the gate, looking up to the house, and crying. When Sonny goes outside for a moment his father calls to him and takes him along to the preacher's house where he first asks for advice. But the Reverend with his conventional attitude is not able to help; his only suggestion is for Eddie to be strong and pray. So the father and the son visit a fortune-teller, hoping that she can tell him what to do. The first time she sends them away because they do not have enough money to pay her. But Eddie, not yet discouraged, borrows three dollars and goes back. The hoodoo woman tells him that he must burn his car — then his wife will return to him. This is what he does, though reluctantly, and at the end of the day Amy, Eddie, and Sonny are reunited and back in their old home again.

*

The themes, events, and characters of the story are set in an environment typical of the author's novels and stories: the black worker's life on a white-owned plantation in the post-bellum South. The author deals with emotions and experiences of individuals, which at the same time are predetermined by traditional roles and accepted social standards.

In "A Long Day in November" Gaines concerns himself with the relationship between a man and a woman, its development and change. The change here is predominantly in the husband, Eddie, who from a childish, self-pitying man who seems to rely completely on his wife's strength and determination, develops into "a man," as his family calls it, accepting his responsibility as breadwinner and head of the family. It is his wife who makes him do what is required of him by forcing him to make a decision and to fulfill a given promise. It is all she wants. She is firm, but she certainly does not intend to reverse traditional roles by domineering over her husband. This becomes evident at the end, where she begs Eddie to beat her after they are reunited, since she is not able to bear the thought that her husband might become the aim of ridicule because he did what his wife demanded. It is she who insists on restoring the traditional family structure: on this point she is relentless.

The black male's search for identity and the problematic structure of the black family are, of course, main topics of the American novel and short story in the twentieth century. They have also been extensively explored in recent documentary studies.[2]

In Gaines' "A Long Day in November," however, the subject is dealt with in a surprising and refreshing manner. Its impact on the reader's mind is based on a mixture of pathos and humour which characterizes the narrative and has marked most of Gaines' fiction.

The story's effects of immediacy and sympathetic insight into the nature of its characters — people like those the author grew up with — are essentially the result of specific narrative methods, the most important of which is a limited point of view. The little boy is the first-person narrator and at the same time — as Amy's and Eddie's son — a main figure in this family drama, although he remains passive and is never in control of the events.

The main consequence of looking at adult experiences through the eyes of a child is a strong sense of remoteness and, at times, distortion. His parents' monetary, marital, and sexual problems are only partially accessible to Sonny's understanding, so that we get a detailed report of what he can observe, but little comment and no coherent interpretation. Instead we learn a lot about the efforts he has to make to control his bladder. The details we perceive through the narrator's consciousness, the exact meaning of which is often not clear to him, provide the material for the conclusions which the (adult) reader draws for himself. The narrative focus certainly is on Sonny's own problems, most of which are caused or intensified by his parents' quarrelling and separation. At first he only realizes that something is wrong, and not even this is very clear to him. He lets his father in when his mother does not open the door, not sure which of them will punish him more severely, trying to please them both. When Amy, angry and hurt, tries to ignore her husband, the only possibility Sonny can think of is, "Mama must be gone back to sleep, because she don't answer him." (9). Even his father's tears and complaints apparently do not move him — he does not know what they mean. He remains passive when his mother leaves the house, taking him with her. At this stage the boy is only an observer, a peripheral figure in the drama between his father and mother.

At the end of the first section the boy comes closer to the centre of the stage. On his way to school he seems to leave behind, — though very reluctantly, — the grown-ups with their conflicts and their incomprehensible behaviour. He enters a different world: that of his peers, the teacher, and his own tasks.

159

In the second rather short part the narrator's emphasis shifts to his own problems. But still he is deeply concerned with the recent rupture of his family. This part discloses his emotional reaction to what he (externally immovable and detached) has observed before. He feels confusion and distress at his parents' separation, and tries to anticipate what it will mean in his everyday life:

> I ain't go'n eat dinner at us house because me and Mama don't stay there no more. I'm go'n eat at Gran'mon's house. I don't know where Daddy go'n eat dinner. He must be go'n cook his own dinner. (23)

His failure in class is clearly the result of his parents' quarrel and their preoccupation with their own concerns:

> Everybody's studying their lesson, but I don't know mine. I wish I knowed it, but I don't. Mama didn't teach me my lesson last night, and she didn't teach it to me this morning, and I don't know it. (23)

Thus his misery forseeably takes its course. The only surprise for Sonny is his teacher's reaction when he does not know his lesson, wets himself, and starts crying with his eyes shut, paralysed with fear. What amazes him is the fact that he is neither beaten nor scolded. Again the adults' conduct seems unpredictable and impenetrable to his understanding. With mixed feelings he tries to cut off his relations to other people, feeling hurt and rejected by his classmates and a stranger in the sphere of adults. He decides not to come back to school after lunch.

But "home," now his grandmother's house, does not shelter him from the other children's cruel teasing and his own feelings of shame and loneliness. At the opening of chapter three the main emphasis is still on Sonny and his emotions, which now are more in the open:

> I go in the yard and I don't feel good any more. I know old Gran'mon go'n start her fussing. Lord in Heaven knows I get tired of all this fussing, day and night. (29)

Very soon, however, he is thrust into the background again and silently listens to his mother, grandmother, and Mrs. Freddie Jackson, the eternal competitor for Amy's affections, Grandmother's favorite, successful, eager to please and win Amy at last. It is true that Sonny feels he does not like him or his grandmother. But when Gran'mon gets the gun and shoots over his father's head

160

to make him go away from their door the boy shows no emotion.

He joins his father when he calls to him, but during their Odyssey — to the preacher's house, back to Eddie's mother-in-law, then to Madame Toussaint's, then through the fields to find somebody who might give him advice and lend him money, then back again to the hoodoo woman — Sonny hardly speaks a word, except to tell Daddy that he is terribly tired and cold.

The very short fourth section shows Sonny again detached and silent; the only thing he can think of and talk about is his fear of Madame Toussaint. But his father does not listen to him while he talks — he can only think of the advice he got: to burn his car — not to sell it, or to give it away, or to spend less time on it, but to destroy it completely.

It is only when they come back to his grandmother's house and meet his mother that the child starts taking part in the action. He tries to tell his mother about the advice his father was given at the fortune-teller's, and is interrupted by his parents again. But he is not to be discouraged now." " 'Come on, Daddy, (...). Let's go burn up the car.' " (67) At the beginning of chapter five, in which Eddie actually does what is required of him, Sonny urges his mother with similar words: " 'Mama, Daddy say come on if you want see the burning. (...) Come on, Mama.' " (69) He does not explain anything, but his perception is so attentive and clear that he observes the most subtle changes in his parents' behaviour:

'Give me a hand down here,' Daddy calls [setting fire to the car]. But that don't even sound like Daddy's voice. (71)

The child's mind operates as a filter, receptive and sensitive. While his parents are still struggling the narrator tells nothing explicit about his feelings. But they are unmistakably clear from what he does and says. From the moment when he knows the condition that will reunite his father and mother, he does everything in his power to make them meet it. We learn nothing about his emotional reaction when they are home again. But a new crisis seems to arise, because his father at first does not agree to beating his wife as she bids him do. She threatens to leave him again, telling Sonny to take his pot — for him a sure sign that she really means it and that they are going to be on the move again. Now he can no longer remain silent:

161

'Shucks,' I say. 'Now where we going? I'm getting tired walking in all that cold. 'Fore you know it 'm go'n have whooping cough.'
'Get your pot and stop answering me back, boy,' Mama says. I go to my bed and pick up the pot again.
'Shucks,' I say. (73)

But a new rupture is fortunately averted.

Significantly, Sonny (who from his parents' point of view has been in the background during the time of their separation) now becomes the centre of their concern and the touchstone of his father's newly assumed responsibility. He is going to take care of his son's problems in the same way his wife has done:

'One of us got to go to school with him tomorrow,' I hear Mama saying. I see her handing Daddy the note [his teacher gave him for his parents]. Daddy waves it back. 'Here,' she says.
'Honey, you know I don't know how to act in no place like that,' Daddy says.
'Time to learn,' Mama says. She gives Daddy the note.
(...)
'Your daddy 'll carry you over it [your lesson] tomorrow night,' Mama says. 'One night me, one night you.' (76)

The author's consistent application of the child's perspective results in a paradoxically mixed effect of immediacy on one hand and detachment on the other. The story's authentic tone is accounted for by the fact that it uses the first person singular, the present tense, and the vernacular of its narrator; but equally important is the ingenuousness with which the boy records what he observes, but is not supposed to hear and see, especially the adults' sexual behavior, the meaning of which he can only vaguely sense. Thus he intuitively feels that his parents are reconciled when he is in bed and listens to the familiar noises:

I hear the spring. I hear Mama and Daddy talking low, but I don't know what they saying. (...) I hear the spring on Mama and Daddy's bed. I hear it plenty now. It's some dark under here. It's warm. I feel good 'way under here. (78 f.)

Sonny's return to his womb-like shelter carries the emotional overtones of his new-found security and happiness. As far as he is concerned feelings are seldom and insufficiently explained or talked about; rarely are they perceived on the conscious level at all. The emotional climate is partly expressed by the boy's account of his physical condition. As in the passage quoted above the contrasts between warm and cold and between darkness and dazzling light generally imply a figurative meaning. The change in sensation corresponds to that in the boy's feeling: from stability to fear and loneliness, and back to safety.

That the reader gains an impression of directness and at the same time of remoteness is, however, not only the result of what we are told — and what we have to conclude for ourselves — but also of the manner in which it is told.

In this story dialogue, report, and interior monologue alternate. Gaines is sometimes criticized for imitating Hemingway too obviously, by giving a minute account of external details, marked by repetitions, curtness, and lack of causal connections. Here these characteristics fit in well with the child's perspective which renders things visible without explaining them. The preciseness of the descriptions, moreover, implies ironical overtones, since the adults seem to think that he will not realize what is going on.

Narrative immediacy is intensified by the language of the story, the vernacular of the region and the people Gaines spent most of his lifetime with. "Black English," the traditional Negro dialect of the Southern states, is the only language Sonny and his family and friends know. Everybody uses it, except Miss Hebert, the teacher. Even the preacher and the fortune-teller belong to the "common people" in that they think and talk the same language as the plantation workers.

*

On another level of the narrative texture the boy in his position as central character serves as a mirror, reflecting his father's image. He is named after his father,[3] thus becoming Eddie's younger version. Each of them identifies — though unconsciously — with the other or looks upon him as an extension of himself. The two worlds of father (adult) and son (child) are very closely connected and by no means as dissimilar as they seem to be at first sight. By making their attitudes and experiences cross and blend, the author produces ironic implications, and offers new insights to the reader.

Right from the beginning "Sonny" becomes his father's ally. Whereas Amy answers her son's questions with a "You won't understand, honey, (...). You too young still," (6) and then almost excludes him from her thoughts and feelings during this day, his father completely turns to his six-year-old son for support when he is rejected by his wife. It is Sonny who opens the door for him. Seeking comfort, Eddie tries to find it in him, whereas Amy wants to keep Sonny out of their conflict.

Eddie's effort to win his son as an ally and a friend when his wife turns away from him is mainly based on the fact that he is a male child: the father looks upon him as a second self, anticipating a similar fate for the boy:

> 'A man needs somebody to love him,' he says. (...) 'The suffering a man got to go through in this world,' he says. 'Sonny, I hope you never have to go through all this.' (13)

But this scene, pathetic as it is showing Eddie in his helpless appeal for love and comfort, also discloses the simple-minded and childish elements in his character. He imagines that Sonny can be his friend and partner, hoping that he will give him what he cannot get from his wife:

> 'You love your daddy, Sonny?' (...) 'Please love me' (...) 'A man needs somebody to love him.' (13)

> 'You love your daddy?' he says.
> 'Uh-huh,' I say.
> 'That's a good boy,' he says. 'Always love your daddy.'
> 'I love Mama, too. I love her more than I love you.' (15)

His complaints and demands not only seem inadequate compared to Sonny's capacity; they also exhibit Eddie's sentimentality and self-pity. Unable to take his fate in his own hands, although he frequently refers to himself as "a man," Eddie happily regresses to a childlike behaviour, whining and making demands on other people for unconditional love, or trying to win it back by gestures of self-abasement, which are, however, ignored and despised by his wife: " 'You got a right to be mad,' Daddy says. 'I ain't nothing but a' old rotten dog.'" (15) Paradoxically, this is exactly the kind of conduct denied to the child. He is not allowed to stay in bed, or away from school, he is expected to act responsibly, and not to be a whiner. Besides, he is left alone with his own fear and insecurity by everybody, except for the compassion and care he receives from his Uncle Al.

The effect produced by the overlapping of two spheres — the adult's and the child's — is chiefly one of comic irony. It is reinforced by the fact that the father and the son have similar relationships to other people. Both dislike Amy's mother and are disliked by her. Both rely on Amy to take care of their problems.

Eddie's behaviour during the course of the story increases the impression of naïveté and simple-mindedness. He wrings his hands and cries, standing in the road in front of Gran'mon's house until she gets the shotgun and threatens him. He seeks advice from various people — but not from himself — about how he might get his wife back. Especially his superstition, which he obviously shares with other men on the plantation, seems grotesque. Several men have been seeking advice at Madame Toussaint's, and all the advice she gave them for their good money is exactly what they might have easily found out for themselves. Instead, everybody considers her down-to-earth suggestions, which invariably turn out to be helpful, the result of occult powers. On this point Eddie is equally deluded.

Unable to think about his problems, he wants to rely blindly on other people's experiences with similar — though different — marital conflicts: "'Maybe if I try the same thing, maybe I'll be able to get her back, too,'" he says (53). He is grotesquely mistaken and has to realize that what could help other people solve their problems is no cure for his.

The solution at first sight seems to be a kind of magic trick. That it is not can be seen from Eddie's reaction. He has to make a personal sacrifice in order to get his wife back, and he suffers, since he has never before had this experience. Through this act he undergoes a change which bears the marks of a true initiation. Those who watch him are aware of this change in him:

'I just do declare,' Gran'mon says. 'I must be dreaming. He is a man after all.' (71)

'Never thought that was in Eddie,' somebody says real low.
'You not the only one,' somebody else says. (72)

If the father is presented as a person who is emotionally still a child and then through the events of the story achieves a new kind of manhood, his son resembles him in many respects, the basic difference being, of course, that he *is* a child whereas his father acts like one. Sonny literally shuts his eyes in front of a painful and humiliating situation;[4] his father does this in a metaphorical sense. Also the end of the story shows a parallel development in both. The boy, too, has "grown up" and found a new strength to master his problems, and a new self-confidence through his father:

> ... I know my lesson. I ain't go'n wee-wee on myself no more. Daddy's going to school with me tomorrow. I'm go'n show him I can beat Billy Joe Martin .... (79)

Still, Sonny has to await *his* initiation. In his dreams he experiences this new confidence, but reality might still prove painful. The scenes that show him with his peers exemplify how vulnerable he is. He tries to win the attention and sympathy of his little girl-friend Lucy, and is deeply hurt when she despises him for his failure in class. He is so fascinated by the youthful lovers Bill and Juanita that he includes them in his prayer that night. Their happiness is what he himself looks forward to — a romatic lover, still lacking his father's experience with love and its ordeals.

*

"A Long Day in November" exemplifies several characteristics, thematic and stylistic, of Gaines' fiction. Like Faulkner a native Southerner, his novels and stories all deal with Southerners, the environment in which they live and the changes they undergo. The familiar clipped, journalistic style he derives from Hemingway is most obvious and at times less functional in the author's earlier novels than in his later work, including *Bloodline*. Gaines himself looks upon the anthology as his personal and public breakthrough:

> I always knew my stories were better than anything else I had written. (...) And they have been successful.[5]

His five long stories in *Bloodline* appear in an order which signalizes a chronological and thematic development: the narrator of "A Long Day" is six years old; the second story is told by the time the central character is eight, and in the following stories he is a young man. The process of growing up is illustrated by an expansion both of the area in which the characters move and of the range of topics they are concerned with.

166

The only book that Gaines published after *Bloodline*, so far, his novel *The Autobiography of Miss Jane Pittman*, has been enthu- siastically received by American critics because in it the author displays a maturity in selecting his themes and techniques which makes it superior to the other novels. In this book the central figure, Jane Pittman, a 110-year-old negro woman, tells the story of her life. As in all of Gaines' fiction, the clash between different generations is an important theme. The narrator here is a simple old woman. But she has lived through the fate of black people in the post-bellum South for more than one generation, and she bears witness of what this historical change meant for people like her. She tells about events and feelings without caring too much about motivation or causality. In this respect Jane Pittman resembles the youthful narrator of "A Long Day in November."

Unlike "A Long Day," the author's novels as well as some of his stories (for example, the anthology's title story "Bloodline") are more directly concerned with the collective fate of the black people in the United States, with interracial antagonisms of the past and the present, and with rebellion. But political topics in Gaines' fiction are always interlaced with the account of everyday life and individual experience. In "A Long Day" he dispenses completely with the clash of different racial and historical patterns, restricting the narrative to the black community. He displays a microcosm of private life and personal relationships. Nevertheless, the characters of the novella are implicitly shown as products of a people's history and social traditions.

The author feels free to deal with aspects of the black condition that have seldom been pointed out by black writers in this manner. Eddie, who is exclusively presented in his role as a "family man" is certainly not a hero in the traditional sense; we have seen that weakness and confusion are clear marks of his nature. Neverteless, without eliminating comic and even grotesque features or apolo- gizing for them, Gaines does not in the least expose his characters to ridicule. Rather he makes Eddie achieve a kind of pride and dignity which is the result of the author's humour and his human understanding of "common folks." By interweaving the content and the narrative technique of this story so that they become mutually reinforcing and complementary, Gaines succeeds in rendering his characters, their environment, and their emotions al- most palpable. His ability and the ease with which he presents the world of average black people "from within," as it were, seem to be the main reason why he is hailed as one of a new generation of black writers.

NOTES

1. Ernest J. Gaines, *Bloodline* (New York, 1968). "A Long Day in November," pp. 3-79; all page numbers in parenthesis refer to this Dial edition. The story has also been anthologized in Langston Hughes, ed., *The Best Short stories by Negro Writers: An Anthology from 1899 to the Present* (Boston, 1967).

2. The most well-known and noteworthy among them are the so-called Moynihan Report (Daniel Patrick Moynihan, *Perspectives on Poverty*. 2 vols. New York, London, 1966-67), which was used as an official document in the political endeavours of the late sixties, and Herbert G. Gutman's new book *The Black Family in Slavery and Freedom*. 1750-1925 (1976).

Moynihan argued that slavery destroyed black family structure, as a result of which the black family is characterized by "high rates of marital instability (desertion, divorce, separation), high incidence of household headed by females, high rates of illegitimacy."

Gutmann maintains that the family ideal and strong family solidarity remained basically unbroken, in spite of the disruptive and demoralizing effects of slavery. He looks upon the economic problems caused by the Depression, especially the post-1925 migration of blacks to the North and their urbanization, as the main reason for the difficulties of the lower-class black family today.

3. His real name is mentioned only once. Significantly this is in class, where his teacher calls him Eddie instead of his familiar pet name (p. 24 f.).

4. Again this takes place at school, where Sonny's ordeal occurs (p. 24 f.). Miss Hebert, the teacher, recognizes the boy's agony and, to his surprise, treats him as what he is: a child in distress.

5. Ruth Laney, "A Conversation with Ernest Gaines," *Southern Review* N.S. 10 (1974), pp. 6-7.

BIBLIOGRAPHY

Gaines' novels are:

Catherine Carmier. New York, 1964.

Of Love and Dust. New York, 1967.

The Autobiography of Miss Jane Pittman. New York, 1971.

Major secondary sources:

Jerry, H. Bryant, "From Death to Life: The Fiction of Ernest J. Gaines," *Iowa Review*, 3 (1973), 106-120.

Bryant, "Ernest J. Gaines: Change, Growth, and History," *Southern Review* N.S., 10 (1974), 1-14.

Winfried L. Stoelting, "Human Dignity and Pride in the Novels of Ernest Gaines," *CLA Journal*, 14 (1971), 340-358.

Peter Freese

JAMES BALDWIN
GOING TO MEET THE MAN
(1965)

> *Whoever debases others is debasing himself.*
> That is not a mystical statement but a most
> realistic one, which is proved by the eyes
> of any Alabama sheriff.
>
> James Baldwin, *The Fire Next Time*.

James Arthur Baldwin, born in Harlem in 1924, grew up as the
eldest of nine children in a world of poverty, racial discrimination,
and store-front-church fanaticism. In 1948 he ran away from the
pressures of the ghetto and, like many American writers before
him, went to Paris. During the thirteen years of his European exile
he made the "The Discovery of What It Means to Be an American,"[1] finished two novels, and wrote his first collection of essays.
The central concerns of these early works were the search for a
usable past and an acceptable identity on the basis of a reconciliation with the black man's collective and individual history, the
hidden connexions between sexuality and racism, the liberation
from internalized role-stereotypes, and the painful accommodation
in a culture and language which for centuries had barred the Afro-
American from participation on equal terms, but which proved the
only one at his disposal. When Baldwin came back to America in
1957 as a successful young author, he found his autobiographical
sources exhausted and his initial theme of reconciliation with self
and world grown stale.[2] Moreover, his strict distinction between
literature and sociology, art and propaganda, a result of the literary
parricide which was meant to free him from the disturbing shadow
of his great predecessor and former benefactor Richard Wright,
had lost its persuasive power in the face of American reality. Thus
the death of Wright in 1960 was like a signal, for now Baldwin
could give in to his growing urge to protest without being accused
of imitating Wright. Promptly his new novel, *Another Country*
(1962), which instantly became a bestseller mostly for the wrong
reasons, turned out, in many respects, to be the very kind of protest

171

novel he had formerly denounced. And his third volume of essays, probably his most influential book to date, replaced the promise of salvation with the threat of retribution, and the announcement of the birth of Christ — *Go Tell It on the Mountain* — which had served as a title for Baldwin's first novel, turned into God's warning after the deluge that there would be no more water, but *The Fire Next Time*. During the following years Baldwin enjoyed an immense popularity and became a leading figure in the Civil Rights Movement. But he was forced to realize that he could not be an artist and a public spokesman at the same time, and while still being pampered by white liberal America he had to face a growing antagonism in his own camp, where the adherents of a black aesthetic denounced his claims for universality as assimilationism or, like Cleaver, reviled him as a literary Uncle Tom because of his idealistic love ethics. Baldwin fled again and, in 1970, retired for a second time into his European exile in the south of France. His more recent publications have been decidedly less successful than his earlier work, and his latest novel, *If Beale Street Could Talk* (1974), was almost unanimously rejected as a complete failure. The question of whether Baldwin's exceptional talent will be able to survive that "war between his [i.e. the black artist's] social and artistic responsibilities"[3] which Baldwin had once detected in the works of Langston Hughes, can only be answered by his future development.

In 1965, at the height of his fame, Baldwin published his only volume of short stories to date. Of ten stories which had been printed between 1948 and 1962 in magazines as diverse as *Mademoiselle* and *Partisan Review* he selected five for this collection. Four of the other five had been prepublications of parts of novels in progress and thus were no longer available, while the fifth, "The Death of the Prophet" (*Commentary*, March 1950), may have been too openly autobiographical for another publication. To these five reprints, one of which was written as far back as 1948, Baldwin added, with "The Rockpile," "The Man Child," and the title story, three hitherto unpublished pieces. This collection, *Going to Meet the Man*, became a great success with the general reading public, but it got rather mixed reviews, and, with the possible exception of "Sonny's Blues,"[4] so far Baldwin's stories have scarcely attracted any sustained critical commentary. This is regrettable because an early story like "Previous Condition" contains nearly all the themes and techniques Baldwin was to unfold in his *oeuvre* and thus serves as a useful introduction to an understanding of his work,[5] an ambiguous parable like "The Man Child" merits the closest scrutiny, and the highly controversial "Going to Meet the Man" is one of the most brilliant among the rich crop of contemporary Afro-American stories.

It was only in the fall of 1957 that Baldwin, the urban Northerner, visited the South for the first time, and he went there, as he states in his "Nobody Knows My Name: A Letter from the South," with his mind "filled with the image of a black man, ..., hanging from a tree, while white men watched him and cut his sex from him with a knife."[6] It is this nightmarish image of the 'strange fruit' of the sexless black man hanging from a tree that lies at the core of "Going to Meet the Man" ("GMM") and that puts the story in a group with other narratives about the 'lynching bee' like Faulkner's "Dry September," Caldwell's "Saturday Afternoon," or Wright's "Big Boy Leaves Home."[7] But the story has also a topical significance, as it alludes directly to the events of the sixties in Alabama. In October 1963 Baldwin went South again to help James Forman, the executive secretary of SNCC, to launch a Negro-voter registration drive in Selma, Alabama. There he encountered James Clark, the Dallas County sheriff known as Big Jim Clark and notorious for his violent measures against black demonstrators. It seems quite obvious that this man served as the model for the "Big Jim C." (201)[8] of the story who is also engaged in dispersing a line of demonstrators claiming the right "to register" (201). Even the recurring motif of the lonely car whose lights hit the shutters of a room and frighten the people inside (cf. 199, 209, 218) seems to come directly from Baldwin's own experience: telling Fern Marja Eckman about his secret nightly meeting with Forman, he said:

> We were sitting around talking ... And then you'd realize that a car was coming. And that everyone was listening ... And the car would – you'd see the lights of the car pass the window. In this total silence. And you'd be aware that everyone, including you, was waiting for bullets. Or a *bomb*. And the car would pass and you'd go to the blinds and look out ...[9]

Thus the story, which must have been written between 1963 and 1965, combines Baldwin's personal experiences in the South with his almost obsessive concern with the hidden connexions between racism and sexuality, and it might be read as a fictional variation upon his earlier statement that the inexorable law that "whoever debases others is debasing himself" could be "proved by the eyes of any Alabama sheriff."[10]

*

The action of "GMM" covers about three hours in the life of a deputy sheriff named Jesse in some nameless Southern town torn out of its tranquillity by protesting Blacks who no longer accept 'their place.' But Baldwin, as in all his work, cannot renounce his conviction "that the past is all that makes the present coherent,"[11] and, in order to convey this central message, he makes use of his favoured technique, the flashback. Thus the story unfolds in an intricate sequence of flashbacks within flashbacks within a frame, and the three hours of the present action are gradually extended through diverse memory fragments until almost the whole of Jesse's life is compressed into the limited scope of the story.

The present action, which hardly contains any action, shows Jesse in bed with his wife Grace, and it reaches from "two in the morning" (199) to the time of "the first cock crow" (218). Sleepless, bewildered by the violent events of the preceding day, and deeply disturbed by his sudden sexual impotence, he tosses around beside his sleeping wife, and while he hovers on the edge between wakefulness and sleep his thoughts start wandering back into the past. From the incidents of the day they move back to a long forgotten encounter several years ago, and then the "forty-two" (199) -year-old man suddenly recalls the day when, as a boy of "eight" (208), he was taken by his parents to participate in the gory ritual of a lynching. Inbetween Jesse's thoughts always return to the present, so that the time-structure of the story looks like this:

```
two o'clock at night (198 - 200/3)  ◄─────────────────────┐
    the preceding day (200/3 - 202)  ◄──────────────────┐  │
        several years ago (203 - 204/3)                 │  │
    the preceding day (204/4 - 204/19)  ◄───────────────┘  │
two o'clock — the first cock crow (204/20 - 208/12)  ◄──────┤
    the evening of the lynching day (208/13 - 210/4)        │
    the lynching day (210/5 - 217/31)                       │
the time of the first cock crow (217/32 - 218/12)  ◄────────┘
```

174

A look at the spatial structure shows a similar pattern:

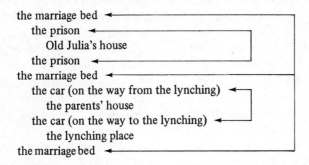

These surveys show that the seemingly arbitrary and aimless chain of Jesse's thoughts is arranged in a symmetrical pattern, both halves of which begin and end on the level of the present action. The first part starts the exploration of the past with a return to the immediately preceding day, into which is inserted the memory of an event of several years ago. The second part moves back thirty-four years to the day of the lynching, which, in accordance with the overall direction of the narration, is remembered backwards, beginning with the evening. Such a reconstruction of the story's movement in time might give the impression that "GMM" is a rather artless thesis story in which the rigid patterning of an author intent upon his message becomes visible behind the supposedly random thoughts of his protagonist. This, however, is not at all the case, for, on the contrary, the reader never gets the feeling of a manipulating authorial presence, but accepts the flow of Jesse's thoughts as the reminiscences of a deeply disturbed man which only follow the relentless logic of an obsessed mind. To create such an effect Baldwin makes use of the technique of association, and a closer look at the 'seams' between the different sections will show how naturally Jesse's mind moves from one level to the next and thus finally and compulsively reaches the traumatic experience which has determined his future development and formed his racial and sexual attitudes alike.

When Jesse gives up his fruitless attempts to have sex with his passive wife, his thoughts run back to the events of the day, and his wish that he might "never have to enter that jail house again" (200) triggers off memories of his violent confrontation with the black leader of the registration drive. His next step further back

175

into the past is convincingly prompted by his sudden recognition that, several years ago, he had encountered that very person and that even then the still boyish Black had dared demand equal treatment. While thus a place of action and a person figure as associative signals linking different time levels, the next switch seems to be entirely arbitrary and therefore inexplicable, for the transition is marked by a melody, the first line of a spiritual, that comes "flying up at" Jesse "out of nowhere" (207). But whereas the sheriff cannot see the connexion, the attentive reader knows full well that it was the constant and defiant singing of the black demonstrators that unnerved Jesse the most. When the sheriff asks himself, "Where had he heard that song?" (208), it is clear that some hidden and hitherto suppressed nexus will soon come to light, and it is of an additional, ironic significance that it is a song from the black man's past of slavery and oppression and a song about the hoped-for rebirth in Christ that serves as the catalyst of Jesse's self-recognition and the revelation of his buried past. The final movement back to the present is brought off by a phrase which Jesse has taken over from his father, for it is his father's "I reckon" (217) that is repeated thirty-four years later by the son and that serves as an indication of the fact that Jesse has inherited his whole view of life from his father, that the son, as the pitiable heir of an inhumane tradition, has to pay for the sins of the father, that the present is nothing but a logical extension of the past.

It is the very "psychoanalytische Untersuchungsmethode"[12] that Wüstenhagen, from his Marxist point of view, criticized as one of Baldwin's central shortcomings, that lends a relentless logic and a compelling drive to "GMM." The evident parallels between the unfolding of this story and the standard procedures of the psychoanalytical session that turn Jesse's marriage bed into the analyst's couch and link his chain of memories with a patient's process of free association make the story all the more convincing and add a new level of significance. The obvious temptation, however, to understand Jesse's finally regained potency as the result of a successful act of autotherapy should not be accepted too quickly.

The ominous atmosphere of the story's frame is determined by recurring details, among which three are of special importance: the light of the "full ... moon" (198), which has "grown cold as ice" (218) at the end of the story; the two dogs "barking at each other"

(198) in the silent night, which "begin to bark" (218) again when Jesse comes back out of his reverie; and the sound of a car "hit-[ting] gravel" (199), which is repeated as "the sound of tires on the gravel road" (218) in the very last sentence. These details, which link beginning and end and create an effect of threat — Jesse is "reaching for his holster" (199) when the car appears —, of lone-liness, and of sterility, have another, more important function, for they are also meaningfully connected with the decisive incidents in Jesse's past. The light of the passing car hitting the shutters of the sheriff's bedroom is reminiscent of the return from the lynching when "the car lights picked up their wooden house" (209), and the barking of the dogs in the silence of the night may subcon-sciously remind Jesse of the night of the lynching when their dog "began to bark" and was "yawning and moaning outside" (209). The icy light of the moon, on the other hand, is contrasted with the burning light of the sun (cf. 212, 213, 214, 216) during the lynching; and the singing of the demonstrators which so inex-plicably angered and unsettled the sheriff, reminds him, although he does not yet realize it, of "the singing [that] came from far away, across the dark fields" (208) as a dirge for the murdered man on the evening of the lynching.

Thirty-four years have elapsed between the night in which an eight-year-old boy, who had just witnessed the abominable tortur-ing and killing of a black man, was lying sleeplessly in his bed and listening fearfully to the sounds of his parents copulating, and the night in which a forty-two-year-old man, who has cruelly torment-ed a black prisoner, is tossing sleeplessly in his bed and worrying about his newly discovered impotence. All the carefully but un-obtrusively rendered details of the story conspire to create an eerie effect of *deja-vu* and contribute to the brilliant illumination of hitherto hidden connexions between a boy's traumatic experience and a man's pathological behaviour. The missing link between past and present is suddenly brought to light, the behaviour of the brutal racist is exposed as the inevitable result of his socialization, the victimizer revealed as the victim of his diseased mind.

It is obvious that for Jesse racial and sexual attitudes are inextri-cably linked, and a closer look at the sexual aspects of his behaviour should help to clarify his particular syndrome. When he cannot reach an orgasm, excitement fills him "just like a toothache" (198), and the indistinct image of some black girl whom, in contrast

177

to his wife, he might have asked "to do just a little thing for him" (198) fills him with new excitement, which is, again, "more like pain" (198). When his wife has gone to sleep, Jesse — "one hand between his legs" (198) — is frightened by the sound of a passing car, and fervently wishes — an ironic ambiguity — "to let whatever was in him come out, but it wouldn't come out" (199). Again he reflects that unfortunately he cannot ask Grace to act "the way he would ask a nigger girl to do it" (198), and his recollection that "sometimes ... he would ... pick up a black piece or arrest her, it came to the same thing" (199), reveals that he is used to finding his sexual gratification with black women and that he does not mind misusing his official authority in order to make them comply with his wishes. For the Jesse of the present action sexual excitement is closely linked with pain, fear, some indistinct memories, and a belief in the sexual superiority of black people.

When during the first flashback Jesse tortures his black prisoner he suddenly feels "that peculiar excitement which refused to be released" (201) and begins "to hurt all over" (201). When he hits his victim in the testicles he feels "very close to a very peculiar, particular joy" (202), and "something deep in him and deep in his memory was stirred, but whatever was in his memory eluded him" (202). Torturing his prisoner gives Jesse an erection, but he also feels "an icy fear rise in him" (204), and when he beats the black man who appears to him as "a goddamn bull" (202), "for some reason, he grabbed his privates" (202), an instinctive gesture of defense reminiscent of that in the preceding scene. Here, again, the same syndrome can be observed: for Jesse, the sadist, sexual excitement is linked with the notion of black skin, accompanied by fear, released by violence, and related to some indistinct memory.

It is the lynching scene that provides an account of the genesis of this syndrome. Jesse, the eight-year-old boy, is "full of excitement" (208) like all the other spectators. He is "at once very happy and a little afraid" (212), and when he looks at the body of the victim, which for him is "the most beautiful and terrible object" (216), he feels "a joy he had never felt before" (216). When watching the castration "in terror" (215) he feels "his scrotum tighten" (216). Thus the first sexual awakening of the white boy is connected with the violent emasculation of a black man, and the idea of the black man's dangerous and enviable potency is unforget-

178

tably implanted in the child's mind. All the grown-up participants in the gruesome ritual are sexually aroused – the radiant eyes and open mouth of Jesse's mother (cf. 216) prove this as well as his father's tongue and the light in his eyes (cf. 213) – and when Jesse's parents come home, they engage in a lovemaking for which the lynching serves as a kind of stimulating foreplay, while the child in the adjoining room is "terribly afraid," "frightened" (209), and full of "fear" (210) because of what he has seen and is now listening to.

Jesse, the impotent husband in the marriage bed, pays the price for Jesse, the sadistic tormentor in the prison cell, and both act out the pathologically disturbed attitudes once acquired by Jesse, the terrified child at the lynching. The vague and indistinct memories which puzzled the sheriff in the first and second scene can now be located, and the child's feeling "that his father [by taking him to the lynching] had carried him through a mighty test, had revealed to him a great secret which would be the key to his life forever" (217) has come true with a vengeance. What Jesse has acquired in his shocking initiation is an utterly diseased attitude toward sexuality linked with a peculiar mixture of contempt for and envy of black people. For him Negroes are "no better than animals" (200), are "black stinking coons" (198) stigmatized by racial characteristics like strong body odour, "kinky, greasy hair" (200) and "fat lips" (200). But they are also "pretty good at that [i.e. sex]" (199), have testicles that are "the largest thing" (216), and seem to be "goddamn bull[s]" (202). Thus they are objects of scorn and contempt as well as of envy and secret admiration. But one cannot envy and despise the same people at the same time, and so Jesse has to sort out his feelings by destroying the threatening potency of black men and enjoying the sexual prowess of black women, by accepting old and sexually no longer active Blacks as 'good niggers' – of "some of the old women" and "a few of the old men" he knows "that they were singing for mercy for his soul, too" (204) – and by rejecting young and sexually dangerous Blacks as 'bad niggers' – it is the "young people" (204) who have changed the words of the songs and are "singing white people into hell" (205). Such a double standard, however, cannot be emotionally sustained; the peculiar mixture of aggression and suffering, violence and fear, envy and contempt corrupts the mind, and thus finally the victimizer turns out to be the victim of his own obsession,

179

the man who debases others is found to debase himself.

Jesse's contradictory sexual attitudes are paralleled by other, even more obvious contradictions. The man who bears the ironically inappropriate name of the father of King David and ancestor of Jesus, who takes himself to be "a good man, a God-fearing man" (199), and who seriously believes that "God was the same for everyone" (204), daily sins against the basic tenets of Christianity, does not love his neighbour if he is black, rejects the idea of a common brotherhood of man, and jeers at the notion of equality. The man who believes that he is doing nothing but "his duty" (199) in his devoted fight for "law and order" (205) and who feels that he is "fighting to save the civilized world" (207) against the onslaught of black animals — and at the same time being undeservedly criticized by "the bastards from the North" (206) — misuses his official authority in order to act out his sadistic urges upon defenseless prisoners and to degrade black women into the objects of his lust. Jesse has inherited all these contradictions, together with his perverted sexual mores, from "his models" (205), the men of his father's generation, who have taught him "what it meant to be a man" (205). From them, too, he has learned how to treat a white woman, and it fits the overall pattern of the story only too well that his passionless wife, who is so aptly named Grace, appears to him like a "frail sanctuary" (198) covered by the moonlight "like glory" (217). Her he does not dare importune with his sexual desires; she, who talks "gently" (198) to her labouring husband, must not be asked to "help him out" (198), and whenever he wants "a little more spice than Grace could give him" (199) he has to visit some black girl. Grace becomes the embodiment of 'Southern womanhood,' the pure, sexless lady raised upon a pedestal to serve as an object of glorification for Southern chivalric gyneolatry.

It should be obvious by now that Jesse, although convincingly portrayed as an individual, is not so much the single man, but the "Man," the representative of a whole social system, the embodiment of the old order of the South, and that Jesse's plight and his psychically induced impotence stand for the downfall of a social system that has lost its power because of its innate contradictions, its inhumanity, and its moral corruption. Thus, as it were, the ontogenetic process gains a phylogenetic dimension, the story of an individual aberration becomes the paradigm of the pathology of a whole society.

The aspects of this failure are sufficiently familiar from count-less sociological studies: Calvin C. Hernton's analysis of the "myth of Negro sexual virility" is as relevant to an understanding of "GMM" as his interpretation of the ritual of castration, which according to him does not only represent

> ... the destruction of a mythical monster, but also the *partaking* of that monster ... In taking the black man's genitals, the hooded men in white are amputating that portion of themselves which they secretly consider vile, filthy, and most of all inadequate. At the same time, castration is the acting out of the white man's guilt for having sex with Negro women, and of the white man's hate and envy of the Negro male's supposed relations with and appeal to the white woman. And finally, through the castration rite, white men hope to acquire the grotesque powers they have assigned to the Negro phallus, which they symbolically extol by the act of destroy-ing it.[13]

Also appropriate as a comment on Jesse's behaviour is Lillian Smith's observation that "the lynched Negro becomes *not an ob-ject that must die* but a receptacle for every man's damned-up hate, and a receptacle for every man's forbidden sex feelings;"[14] equally illuminating with regard to Baldwin's story in general is her ominous image of the *Strange Fruit*. W.C. Cash's discussion of the Southerner's rape complex is as pertinent to an understanding of the disturbed deputy sheriff as his exposition of Southern gyneolatry is to the portraiture of Grace. Thornton Stringfellow's notorious pamphlet "A Scriptural View of Slavery" illustrates why Jesse can take himself to be a God-fearing man and a good Christian and provides the necessary background for a figure like Big Jim C., whose initials, ironically enough, remind the reader of Jesus Christ as well as of Jim Crow. And Eldridge Cleaver's parable about the Omnipotent Administrator who after his pact with the Supermas-culine Menial suddenly "discovered that in the fury of his scheming he had blundered and clipped himself of his penis"[15] reads like a commentary upon Jesse's syndrome. These few references must suffice, for want of space, to prove that the connexion between a perverted sexuality and racism is by no means Baldwin's private invention. Admittedly, Baldwin seems to be obsessed by the discovery "that white men who invented the nigger's big black prick, are still at the mercy of this nightmare, and are still, for the most part, doomed, in one way or another, to attempt to make this prick their own,"[16] but whereas the reduction of the complex 'American dilemma' to this aspect only makes his *Blues for Mister Charlie* a heavily biased and only partly convincing play,[17] it should be evident by now that it does not detract from the power of his story.

When, at the end of "GMM," Jesse's uncovering of his suppressed past makes him regain his potency, he can satisfy his wife only by throwing off his deepest inhibitions, giving in to his hitherto repressed fantasies and assuming the role of the over-potent "nigger": "Come on, sugar, I'm going to do you like a nigger, just like a nigger, come on, sugar, and love me just like you'd love a nigger" (218). A reading of this development as a successful act of auto-therapy would certainly be wrong. One might argue, however, that self-recognition is a first step towards improvement and that the acting out of one's hidden dreams has a cathartic effect. A prejudiced white racist who indulges in his fantasies in the privacy of his marriage bed might be a lesser risk to society; a man who is "going to meet the man," that is, on the way to discovering himself and confronting his own perversions, might be cured of his disease; a correct diagnosis could lead to a succesful therapy.

If seen in this light, Baldwin's story neither "reduce[s] complexity to caricature,"[18] as Stern would have it, nor can it be summed up in the flippant statement of Featherstone, "that what all this racial fuss stems from is the white man's inability to get it up."[19] Quite the contrary, "GMM" probes deeply into the hidden connexions between distorted sexuality, mindless bigotry, and violent racism; and the very fact that Baldwin, through the choice of his narrative perspective, remains sufficiently detached to stand back completely and to let his protagonist reveal himself as both victimizer and victim makes it a compelling and deeply moving story about the havoc worked by racial prejudice among the oppressed and the oppressors alike.

NOTES

1. Cf. the essay with the same title in James Baldwin, *Nobody Knows My Name: More Notes of a Native Son* (New York, 1967), pp. 17-23. (Dell Book 6435)

2. Cf. the statements in Baldwin's essay "The Black Boy Looks at the White Boy," in *Nobody Knows My Name*, pp. 175 and 177. There Baldwin says, in 1961: "... the things I had written were behind me, could not be written again, could not be repeated. I was also realizing that all that the world could give me as an artist, it had, in effect, already given ... I think it is the most dangerous point in the life of any artist, his longest, most hideous turning ..."

3. James Baldwin, "Sermons and Blues," *The New York Times Book Review*, (March 29, 1959), p. 6.

4. Cf. John M. Reilly, " 'Sonny's Blues': James Baldwin's Image of Black Community," *Negro American Literature Forum*, 4 (1970), 56-60; Elaine R. Ognibene, "Black Literature Revisited: 'Sonny's Blues,' " *English Journal*, 60 (1971), 36-37; M. Thomas Inge, "James Baldwin's Blues," *Notes on Contemporary Literature*, 2, No. 4 (1972), pp. 8-11; Peter Freese, *Die amerikanische Kurzgeschichte nach 1945: Salinger, Malamud, Baldwin, Purdy, Barth* (Frankfurt, 1974), pp. 303-308; Bernhard Ostendorf, "James Baldwin, 'Sonny's Blues,' " in Peter Freese, ed., *Die amerikanische Short Story der Gegenwart: Interpretationen* (Berlin, 1976), pp. 194-204; Peter Freese, "Eine Jugend in Harlem: James Baldwins 'Sonny's Blues' als Ausgangstext eines Kurses zur amerikanischen Rassenfrage," *Der fremdsprachliche Unterricht*, 11, 2 (1977), 16-26.

5. Cf. Sam Bluefarb, "James Baldwin's 'Previous Condition': A Problem of Identification," *Negro American Literature Forum*, 3 (1969), 26-29; Peter Freese, "James Baldwin und das Syndrom des Identitätsverlustes: 'Previous Condition' im Lichte des Gesamtwerkes," *Literatur in Wissenschaft und Unterricht*, 4 (1972), 73-98; reprinted, in a revised and enlarged version, in *Die amerikanische Kurzgeschichte nach 1945*, pp. 264-301.

6. James Baldwin, "Nobody Knows My Name: A Letter from the South," in *Nobody Knows My Name*, p. 87.

7. Cf., e.g., the chapter "The Black Christ," in Nancy M. Tischler, *Black Masks: Negro Characters in Modern Southern Fiction* (University Park and London, 1969), pp. 103-118.

8. The page numbers given in brackets in the text refer to James Baldwin, *Going to Meet the Man* (New York, 1967). (Dell Book 2931)

9. Fern Marja Eckman, *The Furious Passage of James Baldwin* (London, 1968), pp. 16f.

10. James Baldwin, *The Fire Next Time* (New York, 1969), p. 113. (Dell Book 2542)

11. James Baldwin, "Autobiographical Notes," in *Notes of a Native Son*

(London, 1969), p. 4. (Corgi Book 08138)

12. Heinz Wüstenhagen, "James Baldwins Essays und Romane: Versuch einer ersten Einschätzung," *Zeitschrift für Anglistik und Amerikanistik*, 13 (1965), 128.

13. Calvin C. Hernton, *Sex and Racism* (London, 1970), pp. 103 and 102. (Paladin Book 08032)

14. Lillian Smith, *Killers of the Dream* (New York, 1949), p. 158.

15. Eldridge Cleaver, *Soul on Ice* (New York, without date), p. 153. (Dell Book 8163)

16. James Baldwin, *No Name in the Street* (London, 1973), p. 47. (Corgi Book 09249)

17. Cf., for a more detailed analysis and evaluation, Peter Freese, "James Baldwin, *Blues for Mister Charlie*," in Rudolf Haas, ed., *Theater und Drama in Amerika: Von den Anfängen bis zur Gegenwart* (Berlin, to be published 1977).

18. Daniel Stern, "A Special Corner on Truth," *Saturday Review*, 48, No. 45 (November 6, 1965), p. 32. (review article).

19. Joseph Featherstone, "Blues for Mister Baldwin," *The New Republic*, 153 (November 27, 1965), p. 37. (review article)

BIBLIOGRAPHY

Baldwin's novels are:
  Go Tell It on the Mountain. New York, 1953.
  Giovanni's Room. New York, 1956.
  Another Country. New York, 1962.
  Tell Me How Long the Train's Been Gone. New York, 1968.
  If Beale Street Could Talk. New York, 1974.
Short Stories:
  Going to Meet the Man. New York, 1965.
Plays:
  Blues for Mister Charlie. New York, 1964.
  The Amen Corner. New York, 1965.
Baldwin's nonfiction books include:
  Notes of a Native Son. Boston, 1955.
  Nobody Knows My Name: More Notes of a Native Son. New York, 1961.
  The Fire Next Time. New York, 1963.
  Nothing Personal (with Richard Avedon). New York, 1964.
  A Rap on Race (with Margaret Mead). New York, 1971.
  No Name in the Street. New York, 1972.

One Day When I Was Lost. New York, 1972.
A Dialogue (with Nikki Giovanni). Philadelphia and New York, 1973.
The Devil Finds Work. London, 1976.

John Wakefield

AMIRI BARAKA (LeROI JONES)
THE ALTERNATIVE
(1965)

Early in his career Baraka faced the question of whether the black writer was "to exhibit his familiarity with the social graces" of white literature, or to find a genuine mode of black expression.[1] Baraka's disapproval of the course of black literature was based on his conviction that the black middle-class had approached writing in the wrong way. The black writer strived simply to prove himself the cultural equal of the white, and in so doing had failed to create a means of expressing his own cultural and racial identity. As Baraka complained in his essay, "The Myth of a Negro Literature," the history of black writing had only expressed the social aspirations of the black middle-class. It was an inauthentic performance of "almost amazing mediocrity."[2]

Baraka's fiction tells the story of his struggle to disengage himself from the lure of white culture's "social grace" — by which Baraka means, basically, the attractions of wealth and position which a supposedly superior white culture holds for the ambitious black.[3] Baraka's own life and education was beset by the moral ambiguities of growing up in a divided culture: at home and at school, he met the values of middle-class black culture, while on the streets of Newark he encountered the values of jazz musicians, junkies and whores. Out of these conflicting and contradictory materials, Baraka sought for a new mode of black expression. It is a difficult story, but one more easily followed, I believe, in his stories than in his better known essays and plays. Such a study involves not only looking at the origins of Baraka's expressive theories themselves, but a study of the social forces in his life against which he had to fight to realize them.

Although we can assume that Baraka's hostility to the world of black-middle class values did not emerge at birth, his short stories in *Tales* (1967) do trace his growing alienation from the kind of social role for which his education seemed to be preparing him. Amiri Baraka was born Everett LeRoi Jones in Newark, New

187

Jersey, the son of a postal employer and a social worker. As Baraka views his life in retrospect he seemed destined to a fate against which, as he grew older, he more and more consciously rebelled. More specifically, as the titles of his stories indicate, "The Death of Horatio Alger" and "Uncle Tom's Cabin: Alternate Ending," Baraka's fate early threatened to make him another conventional member of the black middle-class.[4] As his education continued, life seemed to hold few meaningful alternatives:

> Willing for any experience, any image, any further separation from where my good grades were sure to lead. Frightened of post offices, lawyer's offices, doctor's cars, the death of clean politicians.[5]

Fortunately, life on the streets away from the schoolbooks, his membership of gangs, his excursions into the 3rd. Ward slums of Newark, opened up to Baraka other possibilities. Street fights with local Italians taught the aspiring black of the story "The Death of Horatio Alger" to re-evaluate his dreams of white culture:

> So that even sprawled there in the snow, with my blood and pompous isolation, I vaguely knew of a glamorous world and was mistaken into thinking it could be gotten from books. Negroes and Italians beat and shaped me, and my allegiance is there. (p. 45)

As the irony shows, Baraka's education was not immediate.

Finding a language able to express the moral ambiguities of growing up in the 1940's lends a complexity to Baraka's life-story, which is often reflected in his style: "we are named by all the things we will never understand." (p. 46) School in the forties involved Baraka and other blacks in the dream of progress in the form of wealth and possible social preferment; the kind he would later reject in his essay "Tokenism: 300 Years for Five Cents."[6] Education meant for the intelligent black the opportunity of joining the growing ranks of the black middle-class, it also represented, in Baraka's view, a temporary alienation from traditional black values:

> And in this class sat 30 dreary sons and daughters of such circumstance. Specifically, the thriving children of the thriving urban lower middle classes. Postmen's sons and factory-worker debutantes. Making a great run for America, now prosperity and the war had silenced for a time the intelligent cackle of tradition. (p. 6)

Although Baraka was proud to note such tradition as there was still

188

to be found in his family — he recalls a class photograph of his mother whom he imagines surrounded by angels, "carrying life from our ancestors" — he had to look elsewhere for signs of a living black tradition.[7] Even the local Baptist church Baraka attended as a boy had to import spiritual groups from outside, while at Graham's the "histories and rhythms" (p. 73) of jazz spoke to but a few, and then only to the poor, not the future middle-class black:

> And these carefully scrubbed children of my parent's friends fattened on their rhythms until they could join the Urban League or Household Finance and hound the poor for their honesty. (p. 74)

The moral ambivalence experienced by an aspiring black would meet Baraka at every stage of his early career. Each step forward on the social scale might become a step further away from his racial identity.

A fuller realization of this came naturally enough later in Baraka's educational career. According to Baraka, it was his stay at Howard University that really "shocked me into realizing how desperately sick the Negro could be."[8] Perhaps it would be pointless to give any precise date to Baraka's perception of the moral ambiguities surrounding the black college student, but his story "The Alternative" from *Tales* reveals the narrator as endangered by the loss of his black culture, and at the same time alienated by the white. Once more it is to jazz that Baraka returns to express the divorce of the black middle-class from their culture. In "The Alternative," a certain Professor Gorsun sits brooding over jazz in the fine-arts building: "Goddamit none of that nigger music in my new building. Culture. Goddamit, ladies and gentlemen, line up and be baptized." (p. 23)

The readiness of the black establishment to sacrifice their culture, as if it were artistically inferior to western culture, was the specific malaise Baraka was at pains to identify and exorcise. Since jazz is regarded by Baraka as "one of the few areas of human expression" still available to the black, and since its cultural integrity was untainted by a desire to compete with white literature which has corrupted black fiction, jazz has been treated by Baraka as *the* measure of the black tradition.[9]

It is for this reason that the rituals of baptism, initiation, and sacrifice or death form the structure of plays like *The Dutchman*

(1964), or *Black Mass* (1965). Baraka has a quite different form of baptism in his head than Professor Gorsun, the guardian of white values. And yet the kind of clarity that the dramas display was not so apparent to the graduate of Howard, who started life as a writer in the Greenwich Village of the late fifties. On the one hand were the liberal white poets, in particular the Black Mountain group, Olson, Creeley, and Dorn; on the other hand, Ornette Colemand and Don Cherry.[10] Baraka found himself editing the works of the white literary avant-garde and promoting the new jazz at the same time.[11] The Greenwich Village years, that would last until he left for Harlem in the summer of 1965, were an invaluable apprenticeship for Baraka, but the attempt to free himself from their moral ambiguities is partly reflected in the first collection of stories Baraka was to publish in New York, *"A System of Dante's Inferno"* (1959).

It is guilt, moral evasion, the sin of failing to identify with the language and values of black culture that characterizes Baraka's first important contribution to black fiction. *A System of Dante's Inferno* is an early effort by Baraka to find a means of expressing his black identity using the biographical materials of his progress from Newark to Greenwich Village. Baraka's own early vacillation between the worlds of black and white culture is projected in terms of "The Neutrals" which is set in Newark and deals with the Methodist church he attended with his parents:

> Natives down the street. All dead. All walking slowly towards their lives. Already, each Sunday forever.[12]

Baraka will repeat these lines years later in the conclusion to "The Alternative." The significance of this fact lies surely in Baraka's seeing in his fiction the right medium for exploring the theme of moral ambiguity and the related problem of black expression.

In terms of Baraka's publishing career it was the plays, not the poetry and short stories, that were to make him famous. After the production of *Dutchman* (1964), Baraka reached a national audience. Just over a year later he broke with the Greenwich Village group to all intents and purposes, and left for Harlem. As a writer, his career was also to move from poet and short story writer to playwright, and finally to essayist and spokesman for black culture. Unfortunately, the neglect of his fiction on account of its reliance on private experience and the difficulty of its prose style still leaves a considerable critical gap. The study of the stories, while it does not entirely alter our picture of Baraka, does help us to understand better the development of his prose. It reminds us that the assertive style of his essays on black expression, *Home* (1965) and *Raise, Race, Raze* (1969), are but the final product of much doubt and soul-searching.

For us, the year 1959 is important to an understanding of Baraka's beginnings as a fiction writer. In this year Baraka publishes two essays by Olson, "Projective Verse," and the "Letter to Elaine Feinstein;" it is to be the start of a long and fruitful relationship. Baraka's first response to Olson's ideas on expression "How You Sound??" appeared that same year.[13] At first, as Baraka's essay makes clear, it was Olson's theories on "Projective Verse" that attracted him, but as Olson expanded on these themes in his cryptic and difficult "Letter to Elaine Feinstein," the ex-philosopher minor from Howard kept pace. Baraka made good sense of Olson's ideas and turned them to his own purposes.

In the years that followed Baraka became increasingly articulate on the subject of Olson and expressive language. So much so, that he is far easier to read and his ideas have a far greater circulation now than Olson's. Undoubtedly, Baraka's early interest in the relationship of phenomenology to literature gave him unqiue insights into Olson. For example, the three key ideas on the writer's ability to *name* correctly, to *place* himself in the real world and to create a means of expression more authentic than that of *social reality* Olson derived ultimately from Heidegger and phenomenology.[14] Baraka began his essays on expression with "How You Sound??" (1959), quoting both the "Heideggerian *Umwelt*," and Olson's, "Projective Verse."[15] Later he would simply list his influences as "Olson, Heidegger" and declare himself "secured to phenomenology and religion."[16] But the main bond between the two friends was their attack on the false values expressed by the "People the poet Charles Olson called 'the pimps of progress.'"[17]

We can begin discussing "The Alternative" in more simple terms, without reference to either Olson or phenomenology. Right away we notice that it is a difficult story to read. Such plot as we find is interrupted by the narrator's private sensations, his memories, his desires. Broken conversations and quotations distract the reader away from the narrative. What is being said is clearly less important

191

than how it is being said. The clash between language and experience is deliberate. Baraka wants to involve us in the conflict of the different perceptual worlds of the narrator and his friends. Ray's rejection of the language of social reality determines the plot. Thus the social, the clear logic of normal prose is felt inadequate by Baraka. How explain the complex confusion that attends the babble of tongues on this particular night in a dormitory of Howard University?

This becomes in many respects the task of the narrator-hero or "leader" as Baraka calls him. The narrator, though he talks and acts, exists for the reader more as a state of mind. He is peculiarly isolated from his fellows, considering that he is supposed to be their leader. In fact his fall is felt to be imminent: "Man, we do not need cats like that in the frat. '(Agreed)'." (p. 9) In terms of plot, this is important as we shall see, but in this story perception is prior to plot. The main difference between the hero and his peers is that they inhabit different perceptual worlds. These different worlds require different modes of expression.

It is the leader after all, who broods on the meaning Camus' lines have in terms of his life, not the other students. If an alternative way of looking at one's experience has to be found, then this is the leader's job alone. Camus had written:

This may not seem like much, but it makes a difference. And there are those who prefer to look their fate in the eyes. (p. 5)

Baraka uses this as the ironic motto of his story which so lacks the "lucidity" that Camus had hoped to achieve. The familiar existential theme is there: a man must choose, and he must choose an authentic existence.[18] The idea of authentic identity does have relevance for black literature, but surely Baraka is more interested in the problems that looking your face in the eyes might pose for a black. Quite apart from the individual meaning of Camus' words, how does a black look at his "fate," and more important, how would he choose to express it? It is my belief that "The Alternative" as a whole explores an alternative way.

Returning to the plot we see the leader unhappy and isolated, facing the prospect of a palace revolt. He entertains the pleasing paradox that, although he may be thought to lose, it is in fact his friends who will be portrayed as losers. The narrator's revenge, if so we might call it, lies in the writing of the story itself. Thus when the plot develops into a conflict between an ex-rival Rick and Ray, the leader, over whether the students should go and eavesdrop on a homosexual affair a certain Bobby Hutchens is having in his room, it is Rick who wins the others over to go and have a look. Ray's attempt to stop Rick is answered by violence, there is a fight, and the story ends with the leader on the floor.

If the key to the story lay in the plot, no more would need to be said. However, we must take an alternative view. Most of the students are interpreting their social roles. They are regarded with frank irony by the hero-narrator as the heirs apparent of middle-class mediocrity. As they stand outside the homosexual student's room, shouting their facile abuse, Ray sees them in their future roles:

> Doctors, judges, first negro director of welfare chain, morticians, chemists, ad man, fighters for civil rights, all admirable, useful men. "BREAK THE FUCKIN' DOOR OPEN, RICK! YEH!" (p. 28)

The supposed moral superiority of these blacks over their fellow student is belied by their irrational and violent language. The fraudulent "authority of the social grace" (p. 15) that motivates all their actions is characteristic of Rick (p. 10) and the dictatorial floor proctor Mr. Bush. But in the case of Bush, this kind of moral stance derives from white western culture, not from black. Thus Mr. Bush reminds Ray of "Gregory at Canossa, raging softly in his dignity and power." (p. 15)

Significantly, Ray's only overt victory is in a duel of words with this same Mr. Bush. The students who have been cooking and drinking in their room against dormitory regulations are interrupted by Bush. The strange smell made by the pork chops that are now burning the waste paper in the basket where they have been hidden, is plausibly explained away by the leader. Bush begins his rebuke to the students as follows:

> "What are you running here, a boy's club?" (That's it.) He could narrow his eyes even in that affluence. Put his hands on his hips. Shove that stomach at you as proof he was an authority of the social grace ... a western man, no matter the color of his skin. (pp. 15-16)

Ray quickly analyses both the import of Bush's words and the gestures that accompany his performance. Ray understands to

193

which world this language belongs. Bush's words derive from what Baraka had called in "Expressive Language" "the semantic rituals of power," by which white society projects its image and enforces its will.[19] Bush's success at Howard is a measure of how well he can appropriate the white code. Bush, unlike Ray, is busily translating himself into this other world where black values get turned upside down. Ray's own vision of the moral conflict that orders the action of this evening is expressed early on in the story. The leader's allegiance is to the streets of New York, and in particular to the memory of his friend, the struggling jazz saxophonist, Jimmy Lassiter. Ray's memory of Lassiter keeps alive in his mind a region of experience, the other students never knew or have chosen to forget:

> Those blue and empty afternoons I saw him walking at my side. Criminals in that world. Complete heroes of our time. (add Allen to complete an early splinter group. Muslim heroes with flapping pants. Raincoats. Trolley car romances.) (p. 8)

The moral ambiguities that result from Baraka's ironic application of Camus' words from "Between Yes and No," reflect the antagonism of the colonized towards the language of the master race. When Baraka observes later in *Tales* in his essay "Words" that, as a writer, he is forced to speak "in the language of an alien Tribe," (p. 90) he is but echoing the cries of many black African writers before him. Baraka is aware, as perhaps we are not, that Camus was a bourgeois-liberal interpreting his fate in terms of the superiority of European culture.[20]

Whether or not Baraka was this unsympathetic to Camus would perhaps be difficult to prove, that he could identify with Charles Olson's attack on the language and values of "the pimps of progress" in the American establishment is more openly demonstrable. As late as 1964 in his essay "LeRoi Jones Talking," Baraka is still impressed by Olson's theories as to how the establishment controls society through language: in presenting his argument Baraka admits that he is "again paraphrasing Olson."[21] Baraka looks, naturally enough, toward the creation of a specifically black mode of expression, a kind of "American Dada," Ornette Coleman style: but in 1964, Olson and Ginsberg's assault on the contemporary consciousness was something Baraka could still readily identify with.

Something of what Baraka meant was achieved in "The Screamers" (1963) where a certain Lynn Hope leads a march of blacks on
Belmont Avenue. Although Lynn Hope realizes for Baraka the
kind of Black expression that might rout the lies of the white
establishment of Newark, "The Screamers" is placed toward the
end of *Tales*. "The Screamers" represents the victory of black
culture, whereas "The Alternative" explores the ambiguities that
proceed and make such a victory finally possible. As regards
jazz, Baraka clearly did not need Olson, but for the exploration of
the possibilities of oral culture he did. And it is language in "The
Alternative" that is important, as indeed elsewhere in *Tales*. It was
Olson's defence of the vernacular as the carrier of a race's accumulated wisdom in the essays on "Projective Verse" and the
"Letter to Elaine Feinstein" that helped, in great measure, to
shape Baraka's own views.[22]

Olson's own picture of language was that it was specific. The
spoken word, unlike the written, had reference to a particular
context and a particular time. The method of applying this idea
could lead to the appearance of confusion; in being true to the
local conditions, the writer's language would tend to keep "all
accompanying circumstance."[23] Still, the inclusive character of
such writing was preferable to the exclusive character of rational-
ism and its logic, which falsified the nature of our sense experience
in a way which orality did not. For Olson, the truth of sense-
perception was prior to the false lucidity of a logical narrative; a
characteristic which, as we have seen, plays its part in *Tales*. In
short, apparent ambiguity should not frighten us off, since ambiguity and confusion are only tiresome to the rationalist.

In this sense, the character of Ray becomes easier to understand.
Baraka's use of language here tries to follow the sense-perceptions
and intuitions of Ray rather than his thought. The cold logic that
distorts the order of the human world is of secondary importance.
The language of logic is what organizes the white man's world for
him. And yet, language based on sense-experience names accurately
both persons and places. Ray, for example, sees it as his duty to
name people, to examine the here and now, to watch. All those
things that the "Higher learning" tends to shut us off from, (consider the "wall" imagery that runs throughout the story, p. 7,
p. 19, p. 26, p. 28), are summed up in Ray's responsibility: "The
leader's job ... to make attention for the place." (p. 7) The other

students neither know the ambiguity of their condition (place) as aspirants to white society, nor do they share his ability to name. The two abilities of placing and naming are reciprocal. As Olson says in his "Letter to Elaine Feinstein," the writer's business is "landscape" or the accuracy with which he relates to a given environment; only when his sense-perceptions are working properly can he proceed to the next step, naming.[24]

Ray, we will note, also finds it a part of his duty to assign names. Indeed, his friends exist for him as somewhat unsubstantial, "floating empty nouns." (p. 11) Their speech is similarly devoid of meaning, "their talk (these nouns) is bitter vegetable." (p. 7) His friends do not share his ironic perception of what assigning a name entails. Thus Ray's observation – "they give, what he has given them. Names." (p. 6) – which, despite its somewhat cryptic tone, suggests that real identity is not so easily come by. And so Ray lives among his ambiguities in preference to the lies that invisibly entangle his mates.

The loss of black identity is related to a man's inability to find the words to say where he happens to be. Hence for Ray the meaning of his fate depends on his being able to solve the problem of place. Throughout *Tales* the problem of place and its definition recurs. The agony of Ray in "The Alternative" is repeated throughout the book: on the streets of Newark ("A Chase Alighieri's Dream"), in its schools ("The Death of Horatio Alger"), and finally in the unhappy realization in "No Body No Place" that the white world denies black identity by not providing a cultural context within which the black could begin to exist.

Ray's alienation from the middle-class is best put in his own words about his college friends: "They don't dig completely where I'm at." (p. 8) That the vernacular can supply a clue to the ambiguities of black identity comes out in the narrator's account of Rick's return from his victory over his "D.C. Babes." When Rick has finished parading his bogus manhood, the leader's friend Tom teases Rick about his sexual prowess:

> Tom knew immediately where that bit was at. And he pulled Rick into virtual madness ... lies at least. "Yeh, Rick Yeh? You mean you got a little Jones, huh? Was it good?" (Tom pulls on Rick's sleeve like Laurel and Rick swings.) (p. 10)

Here the oral mode reveals the truth. The narrator records not only what was said and how, but also the dynamics of the scene — the accompanying gestures. Rick stands now revealed and another friend, Dick Smith, delivers the last blow with the ironic compliment of "O.K. you're bad." (p. 10) Baraka's confidence that hip jargon can morally "place" or evaluate Rick's performance recalls the jaunty conclusion to Olson's "Letter to Elaine Feinstein," where he wrote: "To animate the scene today: wow: You say 'orientate me.' Yessir. Place it.!"[25]

If, as we saw, Baraka subordinates his hero and narrative to the interests of place, he does so in accord with a new theory of composition that derives also from the same "Letter to Elaine Feinstein." Olson had suggested the re-arrangement of the conventional structure of prose or verse in which things like narrative, plot and hero would be less important than the physical context in which the action took place.[26] Baraka's narrator, Ray, follows this advice only to find out that a black is "without cause of place." (p. 18) Ray's discovery is not without interest. When he finally reaches the third floor of Park Hall, Ray can convert the meaning that higher education has for him into historical terms. The message of the nineteenth century benevolent tradition which led to the founding of Howard University expresses the white ethic: "Be clean, thrifty, and responsible." (p. 22)

Ray's defeat at the hands of Rick should be read in the light of this. Ray has been portrayed as dirty, "each foot in need of washing," (p. 5) and opposed to the "authority of the social grace" (p. 15) on which white power rests. Ray even sits masturbating on his bed before going upstairs to face Rick. (p. 25) Education in white America for such a black creates the same moral confusions that Herman Melville had explored in his account of growing up under the nineteenth century ethic of benevolence in his book *Pierre: Or the Ambiguities*. It is not for nothing that Baraka will use a quotation from this book as an introduction to a later study of a black man's moral dilemmas in his story from *Tales* called "Going Down Slow" (p. 49)

Why *Pierre: Or the Ambiguities* appealed so strongly to Baraka and to Olson is fairly obvious.[27] For them, Melville had shown how the moral hypocrisy of America could be revealed through the conflict between his young hero's perception of life and the moral code of the day. Again, it was Charles Olson who was the Melville expert, it was he who had explored the crippling effects of

Christianity on Melville's creative powers in his book *Call me Ishmael* (1948). What Olson may have said to Baraka about this book, we cannot as yet know. We can see how the perceptions of Melville's *Pierre* in penetrating the ambiguities of 19th century benevolism relate to Ray in "The Alternative." We can find in *Pierre* the same use of Dante's technique of a moral landscape adapted to a world in which moral values can no longer be established with Dante's kind of authority.[28]

In the character of Ray, Baraka seeks to embody his hostility to the value of the rational abstractions of the white ethic. Black expression, as he has insisted in so many of his essays, demands a live, emotional response to experience. The puritan fear of sex inherited by white Protestant America is symptomatic of its preference for thought over sensation, the mind over the body.[29] Ray remains at all times aware of his body, he tries to give expression to a different form of experience in which "all move, from flesh to love. From love to flesh." (p. 20) Ray's immediate environment reflects only asceticism. Jazz is discarded so that the students may remain "white and featureless under this roof." (p. 23) Ray's fellow students wander aimlessly to his mind like "dead souls" (p. 22) in an ascetic purgatory, whose walls Ray dreams of scaling to enter a different land.

And yet escape, even for Ray, would be difficult. The leader's mind still remains filled by the idealized virgin of white poetry, who embodies for Baraka the abstract cast of western values. Ray quotes from Richard Lovelace's poem, "To Lucasta going to the Warres," and finds it has a little relevance to his situation as Robert Herrick's, "To Anthea, Who May Command Him Anything." These desexualized ladies seem to exist outside of any real physical context. Ray's derisive attitude to them reflects Baraka's own, such images from the ideal world of whites create only images of effete weakness in his eyes: "even white homosexual poets speak of The Lady, who is generally *never* supposed to be popped, by nobody."[30] Ray reflects on white literature as follows:

As, "Tell me not, Sweet, I am unkind,/That from the nunnery/Of thy chaste breast and quiet mind/To war arms I fly."
"You talking about a lightweight mammy-tapper, boy, you really king."
"Oh, Lucasta, find me here on the bed with hard pecker and dirty feet. Oh, I suffer, in my green glasses, under the canopy of my loves. (p. 18)

In a similar way, Charles Olson looked to another culture, the Mayan, for evidence of a true physical response toward experience: "The marked thing about them is, that it is only love and flesh which seems to carry their antecedence."[31] Olson's discussion includes the point that physical contact between men in America is shunned, the fear of being called homosexual reflects their deeper fear of the body itself.

Ray's respect for the body, then, leads him to defend the homosexual act of Bobby Hutchens from the gaze of his friends. It is not a defence of homosexuality but a realization that the black middle-class students see their own weakness and crime in this act. Bobby Hutchens serves merely as the scapegoat of their private fears at being emasculated by their entry into the black middle-class world.

Only one writer seems to survive Ray's contempt for the western literary tradition, his old favourite Federico Garcia Lorca.[32] The refrain from Lorca's well-known poem, "Romance sonambulo," "Verde que te quiero verde," is constantly on Ray's lips. The quality of this Spaniard's richly sensuous appreciation of life, his love of the body and acceptance of death, form the literary stimulus of Ray's dreams of expressing his perceptual world. Part of Ray's revolt is his habit of wearing green glasses as a kind of ironically sad tribute to Lorca's own effort to create a green and living world. Throughout the story the quality of the light seen by the students and seen by Ray is contrasted: "They sit around, in real light. The leader in his green glasses, fidgeting with his joint." (p. 11) The literal darkness of the night with which the story begins leads Ray to questions as to his own "flesh," to his cultural allegiance to the memory of black tradition:

> The leader sits straddling the bed, and the night, though innocent, blinds him. (Who is our flesh. Our lover, marched from where we sit now sweating and remembering. Old man, find me, who am your only blood. (p. 5)

Years earlier Olson's own quest for a more accurate tradition of sense-perception had led him to much the same source "the Mediterranean/man." It was not Lorca but Columbus to whom Olson turned. Columbus' description of the Carribean is used by Olson in *The Maximus Poems* in the same way as Baraka draws on Lorca's vision in "The Alternative." These men note the greeness of the landscape, their loving attention to the colour, sound, and

199

smell measures the fullness of their response. The failure of abstract thought to relate man to Nature is implicit in the following:

"Always the land
was of the same beauty,
and the fields
very green"
    The Isles
of the Very Green.[33]

The islands of the Carribean remind Olson of the Cyclades, or as the French call them, "Les Isles de la Tres Verte." In short, the attention paid to green by these various writers is used by Baraka and Olson alike as an admirable alternative to the cold language of rational expression. Baraka's Ray seeks to find his way in Lorca's poetry out of his dark walled cell, but is barred by the words of Lovelace, "A wall. O Lucasta." (p. 20)

Ray' struggle to give expression to the black experience is not easy, and yet it is central to an understanding of Baraka's later prose. These are Baraka's stylistic beginnings set in fictional form. As he points out in his essay-tale entitled "New Sense," the name Ray was one Baraka had reserved for himself. (p. 96) Although Ray-Baraka is no noble Odysseus-Columbus persona — "sailing around the stupid seas" (p. 96) — his indebtedness to the literary theories available in the post-Pound era of the fifties and to Charles Olson in particular needs recognizing.[34] Ray may very well be connected by a "vector" (p. 8) to such an exponent of the black tradition as he takes his friend, the jazz-man Jimmy Lassiter, to be. But Ray-Baraka's "vector" is itself borrowed from the "Letter to Elaine Feinstein." Olson's examination of the nature of the American vernacular as a medium for writing was, in part, addressed to the Baraka group and its "friends from the American Underground;" by vector Olson meant the line of emotional force between man and his environment, while Baraka interprets it as the link between a black man and his culture.[35] Baraka saw, better than any other writer at this time, what could be done with Olson's language theories in terms of the black writer.

In the beginning of their relationship, Baraka and Olson were united by their common interest in language. They had a common objective in trying to rescue speech from the moral abstractions imposed on it by society. Ray despises the way in which his "gang" can only relate its experiences socially: "Sociologists, artistic arbiters of our times." (p. 9) The black, however, cannot attain dignity or identity simply by earning more. An improved standard of living does not amount to much for someone like Baraka or Olson, who do not wish to join the stampede to the supermarket.[36] Baraka and Olson seek a language that will once more express the values of the human world as revealed by our sense but beyond this point the two friends parted company.

Although the differences between the cultural expression of one race as opposed to another were clear to Olson, I do not believe that was his principle interest. Olson, too, finally speaks a different language than Baraka. He put the contest between self-expression and society in a broad context worthy of a student of Herman Melville. Olson and Melville are fascinated by *Truth* (which both writers are in the habit of capitalizing). If language is again to have the energy to connect man to the real world, then man freed from the social lies will reenter the cosmos and find his lost identity there. This is the final message of the "Letter to Elaine Feinstein:"

Wahrheit: I find the contemporary substitution of society for the cosmos, captive and deathly. Image, therefore, is vector.[37]

Olson, despite the similarities, is finally different. Baraka's need to find an expressive language for black literature was, if anything, far more urgent to him than Olson's concerns. In Baraka's eyes, black fiction had been written in America from almost the beginning in the white man's code. Baraka borrowed hastily, but intelligently from Olson, but the result was not the same. Olson might talk hip, but finally his vernacular with its borrowings from the speech of blacks belonged by right to Baraka. It would be an advantage that Baraka would make use of.

NOTES

1. In Baraka's, "The Myth of a Negro Literature," *Home: Social Essays* (New York, 1966), pp. 107-108.

2. *Home*, p. 105.

3. These problems of the black middle-class had been discussed in much the same terms by E. Franklin Frazier, *Black Bourgeoisie* (New York, 1957). Baraka clearly knew this book well, and my assumptions here on the black middle-class are based on Frazier.

4. By placing his life under titles derived from the white man's literature, Baraka focuses the problem of interpreting black experience in terms drawn from white society values. Again Frazier's account of the middle-class rush to acquire wealth, the strange alliance of philanthropy and capitalism, illuminate the structural principles of Baraka's work. *Black Bourgeoisie*, pp. 30-59, pp. 65-78.

5. This quotation comes from Baraka's story, "The Screamers," in *Tales* (New York, 1967), p. 75. All subsequent references to these stories in the text will be taken from this edition. An able discussion of this writing and the social irrelevanve of "middle-brow" writing is to be found in Werner Sollors, "Amiri Baraka (LeRoi Jones), "The Screamers," in *Die Amerikanische Short Story der Gegenwart*, ed. by Peter Freese (Berlin, 1976), pp. 270-279.

6. *Home*, pp. 68-81.

7. Theodore R. Hudson, *From LeRoi Jones to Amiri Baraka: The Literary Works* (Durham, North Carolina, 1973), p. 5.

8. *Ibid.*, p. 10.

9. *Black Music* (New York, 1968), p. 12.

10. *From LeRoi Jones to Amiri Baraka*, pp. 14-15.

11. The first jazz reviews Baraka wrote appear to date from 1959. For a detailed account of Baraka's published work see, Letitia Dace, *LeRoi Jones (Imamu Amiri Baraka): A Checklist of Works By and About Him* (London, 1971).

12. *A System of Dante's Inferno* was later retitled *The System of Dante's Hell* (1965). My quotation comes from a later edition, *Three Books by Imamu Amiri Baraka (LeRoi Jones)* (New York, 1975), p. 11.

13. "How You Sound??" *The New American Poetry*, ed. by Donald M. Allen (New York, 1960), pp. 424-425. Olson's essays were also reprinted here, "Projective Verse," pp. 386-397 and *"Letter to Elaine Feinstein,"* pp. 397-400. An alternative edition with a useful introduction to Olson's work can be found in *Selected Writings of Charles Olson*, ed. by Robert Creeley (New York, 1966).

14. See my forthcoming article, "'The Maximus Poems': a Phenomenological Approach" in *The Dutch Quarterly Review*.

15. *New American Poetry*, p. 424, 425.

16. *New American Story*, ed. by Donald M. Allen and Robert Creely (New York, 1965), pp. 267-268.

17. *Home*, p. 182.

18. Albert Camus, *L'Envers et L'Endroit* (Algiers, 1937; reprint ed. 1958). This book which contains the essay, "Entre Qui et Non," was to my knowledge not translated in America until 1968.

19. *Home*, p. 169.

20. Donald Jazez, *The Unique Creation of Albert Camus* (New Haven, Conn., 1973), p. 149. Jazez points out that Sartre, whom Baraka respects, called Camus an intellectual bourgeois rebel on this account.

21. *Home*, p. 182.

22. Olson is carrying the Pound-Williams defence of American vernacular a stage further here. Olson remarks of oral language as follows in the "Letter to Elaine Feinstein":

> The only advantage of speech rhythms (to take your 2nd question 1st) is illiterary: the non-literary, exactly in Dante's sense of the value of the vernacular over grammar — that speech as a communicator prior to the individual and picked up as soon as and with ma's milk ... he said nurse's tit.

Selected Writings of Charles Olson, p. 27.

23. *Ibid.*, p. 29.

24. Thus Baraka looks for a language prior to logic. He seeks a naming that will retain force. The danger of naming as we find it in western culture is that language has lost this ability: "The *naming*, nominalization, of that force is finally a step at making it artificial." *Home*, p. 173. Compare Olson's "You would know already I'm buggy on say the Proper Noun," from the Feinstein letter, *Selected Writings*, p. 29. If Baraka sounds more articulate, that is because he is writing down what Olson was saying as I know from attending Olson's classes at the State University of New York, Buffalo, 1963-1965. Baraka's essay, quoted above, was entitled "Hunting is Not Those Heads on the Wall," and was published in 1964.

25. *Selected Writings*, p. 30. Olson's joking manner may conceal his meaning which is essentially that the vernacular is a language that both spiritualizes and makes alive the world we live in.

26. Olson, *loc. cit.*

27. Melville's *Pierre* was also admired by Allen Ginsberg and other members of the former Greenwich Village Group.

28. *Pierre: or the Ambiguities* (1852). Pierre's first moral conventions in which he was brought up. When Pierre reads in his Dante, this false clarity disappears.

29. The *Tales*, too, contain a long attack on the Puritan inheritance of the whites: "No one would think of them as beautiful but these mysterious scions of the puritans." (pp. 44-45)

30. *Home*, p. 222.

31. *Selected Writings*, p. 56.

32. "For me, Lorca, Williams, Pound and Charles Olson have had the greatest influence." *New American Poetry*, p. 425.

33. *The Maximus Poems* (London, 1968), p. 56. The best guide to the poems and the one I used here is George F. Butterick's, *An Annotated Guide to the Maximus Poems of Charles Olson* (Ph.D. dissertation, State University of New York at Buffalo, 1971), pp. 52-53.

34. I am assuming that Baraka's reference here is to Pound. By post-Pound era I simply mean that Olson and Baraka acknowledge their debt to Pound and try to develop his ideas.

35. *Selected Writings*, p. 29. Olson himself has borrowed the term from Whitehead who used it to describe the kind of energy transferred by feelings: "The experience has a vector character, a common measure of intensity, and specific forms of feelings conveying that intensity," Alfred North Whitehead, *Process and Reality: An Essay in Cosmology* (New York, 1929; reprint ed., New York, 1960), p. 177.

36. My paraphrase of Olson's way of referring to the values expressed in "social" language. Baraka, of course, often echoes the jibe. See, *Selected Writings*, p. 47.

37. *Selected Writings*, p. 29.

Peter Bruck

SELECTED BIBLIOGRAPHY

I. BLACK AMERICAN SHORT STORY COLLECTIONS 1898-1977

1898: Paul Laurence Dunbar, *Folks From Dixie.*
1899: Charles W. Chesnutt, *The Conjure Woman.*
      Charles W. Chesnutt, *The Wife of His Youth and Other Stories of the Color Line.*
1900: Paul Laurence Dunbar, *The Strength of Gideon.*
1903: Paul Laurence Dunbar, *In Old Plantation Days.*
1904: Paul Laurence Dunbar, *The Heart of Happy Hollow.*
1906: George M. McClellan, *Old Greenbottom Inn and Other Stories.*
1907: James E. McGirt, *The Triumphs of Ephraim.*
1912: Joseph Cotter, *Negro Tales.*
1920: Fenton Johnson, *Tales of Darkest America.*
1922: William Pickens, *The Vengeance of the Gods.*
1923: Jean Toomer, *Cane.*
1926: Eric Walrond, *Tropic Death.*
1932: Claude McKay, *Gingertown.*
1934: Langston Hughes, *The Ways of White Folk.*
1937: Lew Patton, *Did Adam Sin and Other Stories.*
1938: Richard Wright, *Uncle's Tom's Children.*
1952: Langston Hughes, *Laughing to Keep From Crying.*
1953: John Wesley Groves, *Phyrrhic Victory.*
1959: Alston Anderson, *Lover Man.*
      Harold Fenderson, *The Phony and Other Stories.*
      Roy L. Hill, *Two Ways and Other Stories.*
1961: Will A. Madden, *Two and One.*
      Paule Marshall, *Soul Clap Hands and Sing.*
      Richard Wright, *Eight Men.*
1962: Theodosia B. Skinner, *Ice Cream from Heaven.*
1963: Langston Hughes, *Something in Common and Other Stories.*
      Will A. Madden, *Five More Short Stories.*
      Sadie L. Roberson, *Killer of the Dream.*
1964: William Melvin Kelley, *Dancers on the Shore.*
1965: James Baldwin, *Going to Meet the Man.*
      Georgia McKinley, *The Mighty Distance.*
1967: LeRoi Jones, *Tales.*
1968: Ernest J. Gaines, *Bloodline.*

1969: James Alan McPherson, *Hue and Cry*.
1970: Cyrus Colter, *The Beach Umbrella*.
Henry Dumas, *Ark of Bones and Other Stories*.
1971: Ed Bullins, *The Hungered Ones*.
Horace Mungin, *How Many Niggers Make Half a Dozen*.
Ann Petry, *Miss Muriel and Other Stories*
1972: Toni Cade Bambera, *Gorilla, My Love*.
1973: Arna Bontemps, *The Old South. 'A Summer Tragedy' and Other Stories of the Thirties*.
Chester Himes, *Black on Black: Baby Sister and Selected Writings*.
Alice Walker, *Love and Trouble: Stories of Black Women*.
1974: Sylvia Lyons Render, ed., *The Short Fiction of Charles W. Chesnutt*.
1975: Clifton Bullock, *Baby Chocolate and Other Short Stories*.
1977: Hal Bennett, *Insanity Runs In Our Family*.

II. MAJOR ANTHOLOGIES

Adams, William *et al.*, edd. *Afro-American Literature: Fiction*. Boston, 1970.

Adoff, Arnold, ed. *Brothers and Sisters: Modern Stories by Black Americans*. New York, 1970

Brown, Sterling A. *et al.*, edd. *The Negro Caravan*. New York, rpt., 1969.

Chapman, Abraham, ed. *Black Voices: An Anthology of Afro-American Literature*. New York, 1968.

—— *New Black Voices: An Anthology of Contemporary Afro-American Literature*. New York, 1972.

Clarke, John Henrik, ed. *American Negro Short Stories*. New York, 1966.

—— *Harlem: Voices from the Soul of Black America*. New York, 1970.

Coombs, Orde, ed. *What We Must See: Young Black Storytellers*. New York, 1971.

Davis, Arthur P., and Saunders Redding, edd. *Calvacade: Negro American Writing from 1760 to the Present*. Boston, 1971.

Emanuel, James A., and Theodore Gross, edd. *Dark Symphony: Negro Literature in America*. New York, 1968.

Ford, Nick Aaron, ed. *Best Short Stories by Afro-American Writers 1925-1950*. Boston, 1950.

Gibson, Donald B., and Carol Anselment, edd. *Black and White: Stories of American Life*. New York, 1971.

Hughes, Langston, ed. *The Best Stories by Negro Writers: An Anthology from 1899 to the Present*. Boston, 1971.

James, Charles L., ed. *From the Roots: Short Stories by Black Americans*. New York, 1970.

Kearns, Francis E., ed. *The Black Experience*. New York, 1970.

King, Woodie, ed. *Black Short Story Anthology*. New York, 1972.

Kissin, Eva, ed. *Stories in Black and White*. New York, 1970.

Locke, Alain, ed. *The New Negro*. New York, rpt. 1974.

Margolies, Edward, ed. *A Native Sons Reader*. Philadelphia, 1970.

Mayfield, Julian, ed. *Ten Times Black: Stories from the Black Experience*. New York, 1972.

Mirer, Martin, ed. *Modern Black Stories*. Woodbury, N.Y., 1971.

Sanchez, Sonia, ed. *We Be Word Sorcerers: 25 Stories by Black Americans*. New York, 1973.

Turner, Darwin T., ed. *Black American Literature: Fiction*. Columbus, 1969.

Washington, Mary Helen, ed. *Black-Eyed Susans: Classic Stories By and About Black Women*. Garden City, 1975.

III. MAJOR SECONDARY SOURCES ON THE BLACK SHORT STORY

Bone, Robert. *Down Home: A History of Afro-American Short Fiction from Its Beginning to the End of the Harlem Renaissance*. New York, 1975. (discusses among others Dunbar, Chesnutt, Toomer, Hughes, and Walrond)

Freese, Peter, ed. *Die amerikanische Short Story der Gegenwart*. Berlin, 1976. (contains articles on short stories by Wright, Ellison, Baldwin, and LeRoi Jones)

Peden, William. *The American Short Story: Continuity and Change 1940-1975*. Boston, 1975.

(contains a survey chapter on the black short story since 1940)

Perry, Margaret. *Silence to the Drums: A Survey of the Literature of the Harlem Renaissance*. Westport, Ct., 1976.

(contains a chapter on the short fiction of the Harlem Renaissance)

CONTRIBUTORS

Dr. Peter Bruck, Englisches Seminar, Pädagogische Hochschule, Scharnhorststrasse 100, D-4400 Münster.

Prof. Dr. Peter Freese, Englisches Seminar, Pädagogische Hochschule, Scharnhorststrasse 100, D-4400 Münster.

Prof. Dr. David Galloway, Englisches Seminar, Ruhr-Universität, Universitätsstrasse 150, D-4630 Bochum.

Dr. Udo Jung, Englisches Seminar, Christian-Albrechts-Universität, Olshausenstrasse 40-60, D-2300 Kiel.

Prof. Dr. Wolfgang Karrer, Fachbereich VII, Anglistik, Universität Osnabrück, Neuer Graben/Schloss, D-4500 Osnabrück.

Maureen Liston, Englisches Seminar, Ruhr-Universität, Universitätsstrasse 150, D-4630 Bochum.

Dr. Barbara Puschmann-Nalenz, Englisches Seminar, Ruhr-Universität, Universitätsstrasse 150, D-4630 Bochum.

Dr. Willi Real, Englisches Seminar, Pädagogische Hochschule, Scharnhorststrasse 100, D-4400 Münster.

Dr. Hartmut K. Selke, Feldstrasse 131, D-2300 Kiel.

Dr. John Wakefield, Englisches Seminar, Ruhr-Universität, Universitätsstrasse 150, D-4630 Bochum.